I've travelled the world twice over,
Met the famous: saints and sinners,
Poets and artists, kings and queens,
Old stars and hopeful beginners,
I've been where no-one's been before,
Learned secrets from writers and cooks
All with one library ticket
To the wonderful world of books.

© Janice James.

The wisdom of the ages
Is there for you and me,
The wisdom of the ages,
In your local library

There's large print books
And talking books,
For those who cannot see,
The wisdom of the ages,
It's fantastic, and it's free.

Written by Sam Wood, aged 92

DOUBLE INDEMNITY

This is a collection of extraordinary true cases of murderers who insured their victims then killed them — or attempted to. Each tense, compelling account tells a story of cold-blooded plotting and elaborate deception: the successful insurance killer has to fool not only the victim but also doctors, police and the insurance companies. The nineteen stories will both shock and fascinate. They are tales of callous crimes, frequently committed by people who were already well off and did not even need the money.

JAD ADAMS

DOUBLE INDEMNITY

Murder for Insurance

Complete and Unabridged

ULVERSCROFT
Leicester

First published in Great Britain in 1994 by
Headline Book Publishing Limited
London

First Large Print Edition
published 1997
by arrangement with
Headline Book Publishing
a division of Hodder Headline Plc
London

British Library CIP Data

Adams, Jad
   Double indemnity:
   murder for insurance.—Large print ed.—
   Ulverscroft large print series: non-fiction
   1. Insurance crimes
   2. Murderers—Great Britain
   3. Large type books
   I. Title
   364.1′523′0922

   ISBN 0–7089–3677–6

Published by
F. A. Thorpe (Publishing) Ltd.
Anstey, Leicestershire

Set by Words & Graphics Ltd.
Anstey, Leicestershire
Printed and bound in Great Britain by
T. J. Press (Padstow) Ltd., Padstow, Cornwall

This book is printed on acid-free paper

for JULIE PEAKMAN
the beneficiary of all my policies

Contents

Introduction

A Civilised Crime

PEOPLE see death in the same way they see life, and the cases that follow are no exception to this: the flashy bar owner uses cars to kill; the doctor uses poison; the businessman uses an aeroplane.

It is droll how even in murder people remain within the boundaries of their class and profession. These stories show how physicians kill and use their professional qualifications to quell suspicions; solicitors kill and use their knowledge of the legal system to evade detection; teachers talk their pupils into covering up murder for them; and insurance company officials kill with expert knowledge of how to maximise profits. People whose lives are surrounded by the minutiae of business, by mortgages, deeds and policies, commit crimes related to that world, just as kids who inhabit the streets commit muggings.

The middle-class atmosphere in which these crimes were committed somehow makes them more disgusting than the crimes of the poor. Only one of the people whose crimes are recorded here really needed the money, and he was a con-man who had always lived as if he were upper middle class. Apart from him, none of these murderers were poor, some were even very well off by ordinary standards. They did not kill to escape poverty so much as to be richer, or to hang on to what they had already got with minimal effort.

As Pauline Leyshon said of her attempted murderer Sheila Stroud, whom she knew from childhood, 'She's always been a spoilt brat.' This is a remark that could easily be made about almost all these insurance murderers, from Paul Perveler in Los Angeles to Warren Green in Wigan.

So many of them were infected with a putrid morality which took the place of any human decency. Child murderer Bill Bradfield had a fixation about virginity and lectured his students about staying chaste until they were married. Paul

Perveler was disgusted to hear a woman utter the mildest swear word. Alfred Rouse was a teetotaller, a church-going member of the local tennis club, and the torturer Henry Holmes was sanctimonious about drinking. Frederick Seddon thought his minute attention to the details of money transactions was such a virtue that a jury would let him off the murder charge out of blind respect. He really believed that giving a Freemason's sign to the judge would help him. Yet these were people who, by any standards of decency pertaining in any human society, were despicable.

'You doing it to her isn't fair to Mommie,' Joseph Kallinger's son said when his father prepared to rape a victim. Murder and rape could not stimulate his indignation: it was adultery that did.

Their respectability lent a surreal quality to their crimes. They had to kill in a manner which would not be suspected, so everything had to be exactly as it should be, with the one difference that at the end of the day some well-insured person would end up dead. So young Deana Wild had to be killed on a sightseeing holiday with smiling pictures being taken of her up to the point at which she was thrown over the edge. Dr Edmond de la Pommerais had to smile and make small talk throughout the dinner he was having served to his mother-in-law and which he had poisoned. He then had to tend her through her illness.

Some characteristics are shared by a number of insurance murderers. They crop up again and again in the lives studied here, to such an extent that they can be recognised like old friends in trial reports. Some characteristics, such as a grossly dysfunctional family, and a tendency to arson, are common only in cases of the most extreme repeat insurance murderers. These are also characteristics of other serial killers and can hardly be considered diagnostic of insurance murderers.

Others, however, recur with more frequency, so it is possible to say that a typical insurance murderer:

Is male, aged between twenty-five and thirty-five;

Has had further education and may even have a professional qualification;

Has ambitions in excess of his abilities: he works in a white-collar job at a fairly lowly level and feels undervalued at work or is an undistinguished professional;

Is acquisitive and will take excessive pride in the ownership of such things as motor cars and houses;

Shows an unnatural interest in crime and often speaks of different crimes;

Likes to be thought of as tough and boasts of military or even criminal exploits;

Lies for self-aggrandisement and self-enrichment but also for no obvious purpose, when the truth would serve as well;

Is selfish and heedless, if not openly contemptuous, of the feelings of others;

Is emotionally immature himself and expresses extreme emotion badly because he is not feeling it but imitating what he has seen in other people;

Is of questionable sexual potency;

Tends to surround himself with friends who are younger than himself, more vulnerable, or who are not his intellectual equals, or all three.

The writer Vladimir Nabokov in his novel *Despair*, about an insurance murderer, depicts his first-person anti-hero in exactly the mould of these killers, down to the comfortable background, the intellectually weak friends, the contempt for the feelings of others and exaggerated feelings of superiority. Such men are always prolific liars, and Nabokov depicts this trait, too, with his character taking a pride in 'my light hearted, inspired lying'.

Another feature which distinguishes insurance murders from most other murders is the cold-blooded planning which goes into them, particularly because the killers and victims are often members of the same family and are usually living together.

The killer has to be cool all the way through. Unlike most murder cases, where concealment of the body is a problem, in these cases the body has to be on display so that death by natural causes or accident can be certified. Preferably, too, the body should be found by another person. The killer has to be prepared to go through a callous charade of grief for his or her victim.

The successful murderer for insurance has to fool the victim; the doctor who certifies death and the insurance company. Often the police and coroner also have to be tricked, though that is more difficult, as these cases show.

Though the most important aspect of this type of crime is the murder itself, insurance companies are victims too, and in some cases the victims of accomplished criminals who could have fooled anyone. After all, a professional criminal with twenty years of experience, who may be at the top of his chosen profession, is going to win in a battle of wits with a middle-ranking or inexperienced insurance sales clerk. But this book is not only about accomplished criminals.

Many of the policies made out on victims referred to here screamed out 'Fraud' and any fool should have noticed it.

Clear warning signs flashed up in a number of these cases, including one where an insurance salesman regularly dealt with a suspicious character and flagged all her insurance applications to be specifically checked and certified by head office. Yet the application on a twenty-year-old woman who died the day after the policy came into force was accepted routinely.

Over and over again in these cases the killers made one application after another to different insurance companies until they found one where staff were stupid or careless enough to accept a dubious proposal.

It is too much to hope that criminals will stop plotting to murder people. The least we can expect is that employees working in areas where fraud is rife should stay alert to its possibilities. In these cases many people died who would otherwise have lived because insurance companies took no notice of obvious frauds.

It is notable — and worth pointing out to enthusiasts for capital punishment — that the presence or otherwise of the death sentence had no effect whatsoever on the behaviour of the criminals in this most premeditated of murders. No one reading these cases could guess from the behaviour of the villain whether the crimes were committed in states where murder carried a death sentence. There is no difference in the level of brutality or callousness of murderers who were likely to face death if caught, and those who were not. These cases cover several countries over a long period of time. In not one was there any reference by the criminal to the punishment they might receive. When planning their crimes, all believed they were going to get away with them (and were often accurate, over a long period) and the form of punishment which they might receive was immaterial.

The term 'double indemnity' has a specific meaning. It is where an insurance company offers a double insurance payout if death occurs in an improbable manner, an unusual accident for example. The

11

1944 film *Double Indemnity*, based on a novel of the same name by James M. Cain, brought the expression into common use. In the film, directed by Billy Wilder, an insurance agent played by Fred MacMurray schemes with the glamorous wife of a client (Barbara Stanwyck), to kill her husband and collect the money. Since this film, 'double indemnity' has popularly come to be a term for all insurance murders, and that is the sense in which it is being used in the title of this book.

All the details reported here are as accurate as the research would permit and no names have been changed. In cases where writers on cases have changed names in already published works, I have used the correct names, but I cannot be sure to have picked up every alteration, as they are not always indicated.

There is one case involving a number of sexual assaults and an attempted rape. As the victims would have had the legal right to have their identity concealed in the case of actual rape, it seems proper to omit their names in the case of these assaults.

Often the murderers had small children which they used as props, to give themselves an air of innocence and gentleness. Where these children are likely to be still alive, their names have been omitted unless they played some part in the crimes. To be the child of a murderer seems to be enough of a burden, without being constantly reminded of it.

Jad Adams, June 1993

Elaborate Deceptions

The Bunch of Keys

GIDLOW LANE is not at the up-market end of Wigan, but it is very far from being the poorest street in the northern town. It is the sort of road where young couples who have the good fortune to be fully employed would buy their first homes.

In the store-room at the back of one of these neat red houses with latticework windows, at 10.45 on the morning of Thursday, 31 October 1991, a middle-aged woman and a young man leaned over a body lying in a pool of blood.

The corpse was that of 24-year-old student nurse Julie Green, still in her nurse's uniform, battered and covered in blood. Her head was a mass of injuries, and blood surrounded her in a pool on the concrete floor. She had sustained at least sixteen fierce blows to the skull with a heavy instrument, causing fractures and brain damage from which she quickly died. She had also been punched at least four times in the face before her skull had been fractured. A hammer, which was obviously the murder weapon, was lying beside her. When the first policeman arrived, he found Warren Green, a 26–year-old solicitor, convulsed with sobs at the death of his wife.

The relationship between Julie Sillitoe and Warren Green had been what friends described as a storybook romance. They were teenage sweethearts who met at Deanery High School in 1982, when she was fourteen and he was sixteen. They could often be seen cuddling in corners during lunchtime and breaks. Everyone imagined that one day they would marry.

Warren Green was the elder of two brothers from a comfortable middle-class home. His father had been a solicitor but Warren's early life had been disrupted by his parents' difficult marriage and divorce. Julie Sillitoe was the only child of a headmaster who died when she was still at school and she was then brought up by her mother.

The two young people shared an enthusiasm for the Scouting and Guide movement and Julie gained the Queen's Guide award. Warren left school with good examination results in science subjects and went to Lancaster University where he studied law, then went on to law college. Julie went to Salford Technical College to do a medical secretary's course.

As a student, Warren joined the Territorial Army which did not please Julie. They became engaged on Julie's eighteenth birthday in 1985 but two years later the engagement was broken off after an argument about the Territorials. It seemed that their adolescent relationship was over, but when Julie started going out with another man, Warren Green showered her with flowers and chocolates in a bid to get her back.

They made up their differences and became re-engaged in 1988. He even bought her a second engagement ring. They continued their commitment to Scouting in adult life, he eventually becoming a Scout leader and she a Guide leader.

At the end of 1988 they bought the house at 179 Gidlow Lane and worked hard making a home of it. They were married in St Andrew's Church, Springfield, in June 1989, at a ceremony attended by crowds of uniformed Guides and Scouts. By the autumn of 1990 Julie had stopped working as a medical secretary and started training to be a nurse. Warren Green had qualified as a solicitor and joined the Crown Prosecution Service at nearby Salford.

They bought the next-door property, at 177 Gidlow Lane, and set about improving both houses. Warren and Julie were described as a lovely couple, industrious and home-loving. Warren worked on the house and Julie made her own clothes and baked cakes. He gave her an eternity ring for their first wedding anniversary. Julie was described by friends as a girl with 'old fashioned values', 'the sort of girl any mother would want as her daughter'.

Warren was described as polite and pleasant, always ready to lend a hand if anyone needed it. He was well-dressed, intelligent and restrained. A Scouting friend described him as 'a great organiser, always making lists, very meticulous', and added, 'He never showed many feelings, he never seemed to get angry or lose his temper.' Warren was the quiet one of the marriage; Julie was much more cheerful and vivacious.

Confronted with the body of the dark-haired nurse, officers from Wigan CID established there was no obvious motive for her murder: she had not been sexually attacked, nothing was missing from the house, and there were no signs of a break-in. They quickly began piecing together her last hours.

Julie had left the house for her night shift at Wigan Infirmary at 9.15 p.m. on Wednesday. Warren was still working on the store-room, which he was converting to a garage, so their friend Stuwart Skett had given her a lift to the hospital, then returned to the house in Gidlow Lane and went out drinking with Warren Green.

After work at 8 a.m., Julie had been given a lift home by a colleague, Staff Nurse Jeanette Moseley, and was dropped off at shops in Park Road near her home — the local butcher saw her as he was opening up his shop. She left the house at about 9.10 a.m., and was seen by Jane Hardy, an old schoolmate with whom she exchanged greetings. Green said he had got up around 10 a.m. and, finding no sign of her in the house, telephoned the hospital to see if she had left.

He then looked for Jeanette Moseley's number to call her, and telephoned Stuwart Skett's mother, asking if Stuwart had seen Julie. Skett's mother rang her son at work then called back to say he had not. Green then called their doctor, as Julie had complained of feeling ill. It was possible she had gone to the surgery. Green said it was only then that he noticed her coat and bag and realised she must be in the house, but the only place she could be was the store-room. This room had a door on either side, one which led to the Greens' kitchen, and an outside door which led to an alley beside the house.

Green said he could not find his keys for the outside door. The door leading to his kitchen was locked with the key on the inside of the store-room. He said he had tried to recover the key using a

22

technique he had seen in a television programme, where a piece of paper was slipped under the door, and the key was pushed through the lock so that it fell on the paper, which could then be withdrawn from under the door.

He had managed to push the key in, he explained, but could not retrieve it, so he approached Cecilia McGuire, the wife of the undertaker who rented part of the house next door from him, and who had access to the store-room from the outside door. He asked Mrs McGuire if she had seen Julie and explained in some detail how he had looked for her and telephoned people who might know where she was. He asked to use Mrs McGuire's key, as he said he could not remember where he had put his own.

He went off with the key and Mrs McGuire heard him shout, 'Oh, no!' and she ran over to the store-room to find Green crouching over Julie's body with the hammer nearby. The body was lying in a thick pool of blood.

'Warren, who could have done this?' said Mrs McGuire. 'Things like this don't happen in Wigan.'

She told Green to come away, and pulled him back, saying, 'Don't touch her or they will blame you.' He went to her office to call for the police, dialling 999 and saying, 'I think my wife has been murdered.'

Detectives already had a number of questions: where was Julie between 8 a.m. when she finished her shift and the discovery of her body at 10.45 a.m.? Where were the keys which must have been used to gain access to the store-room? Who had access to the keys? What motive could there be for killing her?

The murder weapon was undoubtedly the two-and-a-half pound lump hammer which was lying near the body and was always previously to be found in the store-room. In Julie's hand was a screwed-up piece of paper and near her body was an empty bottle of the sleeping drug temazepam. The police searched the house and made house-to-house inquiries to see if the neighbours had seen anything suspicious.

The investigation came time and again to the missing keys. It was a bunch of five keys with a black leather fob carrying a Jaguar car motif. Green said they had vanished from a kitchen work surface where he had left them the night before the murder. He had last seen them around 9 p.m. One of those keys opened the outside door to the store-room with a mortice lock — and closed it. The killer had to have used the keys to lock the door after the murder. The only other key to the door was in the possession of the McGuires.

The keys were to feature strongly in a press conference six days after the murder, at which Warren Green held up a replica of them as part of an appeal for anyone seeing them to hand them in. Green called for witnesses to come forward if they had seen anyone 'loitering' around the house in Gidlow Lane before the murder. About Julie he said, 'She was full of life . . . I loved her, I still love her. I cannot say anything more than that . . . she was a lovely person.'

He had already been arrested and had been interviewed by the police over a period of four days, until

25

3 November, but was then released. It was not surprising that he should be questioned — most murder victims have been killed by a close relative and the husband who found the body would be an obvious suspect.

As to motive, Green said there were a number of people who were in prison as a result of prosecutions brought by him. Perhaps they bore a grudge. However, as he dealt with minor road traffic offences and public order offences at the Crown Prosecution Service, it is unlikely any of those convicted would have been moved to commit murder in revenge.

During questioning, Green suggested that his wife had been taking medicines from the hospital where she worked. 'She never talked about dealing in drugs,' he said, with the obvious implication that she had been selling drugs and that a purchaser had turned savage and had killed her.

Because Julie had been punched in the face as well as beaten with the hammer, Warren Green's hands were examined by a police surgeon but no bruising was found.

Police were certain that Julie knew her killer and they interviewed up to fifty of her friends and acquaintances. A very short time into their inquiries the idyllic life this young couple were supposed to have led started to look much more shabby. Love letters to Julie were found in a cabinet by the bed. They were from Stuwart Skett. Skett, a 22-year-old apprentice engineer, was also a keen Scout and a Cub Scout leader — which was how he had met Julie and Warren Green in early 1991. At first he and Julie were simply close friends, calling each other Bro and Sis, but they became lovers in July or August 1991. Skett would park his car in a nearby road, to avoid gossip from the neighbours, when he visited her during Warren Green's absences. They exchanged love letters and she had written him a love poem. They had sex in the Greens' bed and often did so when Warren was at work or out Scouting. He was frequently away for whole weekends at a time and Skett was a constant presence in the house even when Warren was there. Stuwart and Julie had discussed both breaking the affair off, and her leaving Warren and setting up house with Stuwart.

Stuwart and Julie last had sex less than a week before Julie's death. When the police first asked Skett when they had last had sex, however, he had said it was two months previously. Why lie about such a thing? the police wondered. He said they had wanted to end the affair but he had found it impossible to give her up. Here was a possible motive: perhaps Skett had killed her because she wanted to end their relationship and he could not bear the thought of her being with anyone but him.

When Skett's mother telephoned her son's place of work, after Warren Green had called her, asking if she had seen Julie, Skett had said, 'If they've harmed her, I'll kill them.' During questioning, he was never able to explain who 'they' were, and said it was just a figure of speech.

At first he said he did not know anything about Julie's taking drugs from the hospital, but later said she did have some, but only tablets to help her sleep, which he had discouraged, saying that such drugs were addictive.

Skett had taken Julie to work on the night before she died, and they had kissed and cuddled in the car before she started her shift. She was looking forward to the end of an eight-week stint of night work which was due to finish at the end of that week. Skett then returned to her house and went out drinking with Warren Green and another man.

Most dangerously for Skett, he admitted using the lump hammer with which Julie was killed, when he was knocking down a wall while helping in the Greens' house renovations. He told police, 'If there are prints on the hammer, they will be mine.' He later explained this by saying he knew from police the hammer was the murder weapon, and he knew he had used the hammer without gloves.

Skett had access to the house. He had used the set of keys with the Jaguar fob before and had also used a spare front door key to enter the house. He said the last time he had used it was the Friday before the murder and he had returned it to the kitchen drawer where it was kept. He said the reason for his anger when he heard she was missing was that she had told him that if she were going to leave Warren, he would be the first to know.

Skett had a perfect alibi, however. He was at work at an engineering firm all morning and was seen by senior personnel as well as by men working with him. His car had gone through security clearance when he went in to work and he was not able to take it out without going through the same security check when the exact time would be noted. He had not left work. He could not possibly have killed Julie.

Police found the financial side of Julie and Warren Green's life together was no more secure than the emotional. His salary was £18,700 a year and hers was £6500. They had an £80,000 mortgage on their two properties: in December 1990 they bought the house next door, letting part of it to an undertaker, Joe McGuire, and part of it as a flat. In addition to the mortgages, Green had taken out more loans for renovations on the house.

The mortgages were insured so they would be paid off in the event of the death of either partner, so Julie's death would mean the £80,000 would be paid. She was also heavily personally insured, for £120,000. Green had actually received professional advice from the area manager of the Teachers Assurance Company that they were over-insured. Alive, the couple were in trouble financially. If one of them were dead, their money problems would be over.

Eight days after Julie's death, Green visited her cousin Jacqueline Forshaw, and surprised her by his emotional detachment. He said they had been well covered by insurance, and that he would be using the money to buy himself a Jaguar. Presumably he wanted it to go with the Jaguar fob for the key ring which he had bought at a Bank Holiday car show.

Another complication, the police discovered, was Green's relationship with a law student at King's College, London who was working for the Salford Crown Prosecution Service on a work experience placement. The elegant, attractive Julie Warburton, aged twenty, was staying with her grandmother in Atherton, near

Wigan. One day, another worker from the office, Warren Green, started chatting to her on Salford railway station. He acted as if he had just bumped into her but in fact the meeting was planned — he had been watching her in the office and engineered an opportunity to meet her alone.

Julie Warburton said, 'He was perfectly friendly. He told me he was a Scout leader and I told him I loved dancing. He was like anyone else in the office.' Later, when the train times were changed, Green obtained permission for Warburton to leave work early so that they would be alone on the train together every evening. Soon Green began to drive to work and to drive Julie Warburton home. He explained how he found his wife too domineering and thought she was having an affair.

Warburton said, 'Then one evening his attitude changed towards me. We were stopped at traffic lights when he took my hand and said he was becoming more attached to me and asked me out to dinner. I said I wasn't sure . . . I didn't ever go out with him. I tried to fob him off. I said I'd let him know. I was scared to turn him down. I didn't want him saying things about me in the office.'

On one occasion, at a social evening for young solicitors, Green kissed and fondled Julie Warburton but she pulled away. She said, 'Before he went on holiday he said he thought he was falling in love with me and kissed me before I got out of the car.'

While his wife was on the beach, on their holiday in Corfu in July 1991, Green would go back to the hotel under some pretext to write love letters to Warburton. The letters were full of a fantasy life of intimacy which Warburton insists they did not share. One began:

Dear Pumpkin [crossed out and her name inserted] I miss you. How did your weekend go? I was thinking about you on Saturday night. It amazes me how much you love and care for somebody and yet neither of us can do anything about it . . . I wish I'd got a photograph of you to hold at moments like this. I cannot say 'all my love' because we both know that wouldn't quite ring true but I am in love with you Julie, so I can say, I love you.

It was signed with seven kisses.

Another letter read, 'Darling Julie, I miss you even more now. I can see a tan developing and I long for you to inspect it closely. Talking of dreaming, I'm finding it very hard to think of little other than you. Look after yourself and be ready for me when I return.' He gave Warburton small gifts: a golden coloured owl, and a gold bracelet.

After the holiday he resumed seeing her to drive her home. 'He seemed to be more and more attached to me,' she said, 'saying he was not happily married and wanted a divorce.' Julie Warburton may have been flattered by his attentions, for though she did not welcome Green, she did not discourage him either. She felt under great emotional pressure and said she was 'sick with worry' about his advances. She confessed the pressure once led her to say she loved him. 'In fact,' she later said, 'I didn't have strong feelings for him. I just didn't want to hurt him.'

She finished her placement and returned to London, deliberately not giving him her address and asking him not to try to contact her.

In fact his feelings for her were more to do with infatuation than love. She was the fifth young woman working at the Crown Prosecution Service to whom he had made advances. This seems more like avarice than lust: looking at women as if he were looking at models in a car showroom.

★ ★ ★

On a bitterly cold November day, hundreds of mourners watched Julie Green's coffin being carried in the funeral procession at the service in the church where she had been married. Guides and nurses, all in uniform, came to the service, which was conducted by the same vicar who had married her. A distraught Stuwart Skett was also present, for he really had loved her.

By the time of the funeral, Warren Green had been rearrested and charged with the murder. He had behaved suspiciously from the start, not in the nervous, furtive way of a guilty person, but in the calm and rehearsed manner of a cold-blooded killer who intended to get away with it.

Suspicions about Green had been aroused in the first professional emergency service worker he spoke to. He had made the 999 call calmly, beginning with these words: 'I think my wife's been murdered.' In the four-and-a-half-minute call he said she was not in bed when he woke up, and that he had telephoned the hospital and friends and so on, going out of his way to explain what his movements had been that morning. It was only towards the end of the call that the operator discovered that Green himself had found his wife's body. The telephonist was suspicious about the call and summoned over other staff to listen as Green went into detail as to how he had tried to unlock the store-room door from the kitchen side and so on.

He was sobbing when police arrived, but soon began detailing his movements again, without having been asked. This made it the third time he had made an unrequested announcement of his movements that morning: to Cecilia McGuire, to the emergency operator and to the police.

Martin Cunliffe, the police officer who went to the Gidlow Lane house immediately the 999 call was received, said that Green composed himself and started telling his story 'in a cool, clear voice ... I began to feel embarrassed because I had been told about a woman being found covered in blood but he did not tell me about it . . . I asked him where his wife was but he carried on with the story in a cool, composed way showing no signs of distress.' He said Mrs McGuire was in a much worse state emotionally than Green, and it was she who eventually showed him Julie's body.

Green was clearly trying to put on record his deceptive version of events — most of which he had actually acted out so that they could be corroborated and the trail of deception would lead away from him. He never departed from this story.

To the eye of experienced detectives, however, the scene in the kitchen was just too neat. There were the bradawl and screwdriver which Green had used to try and push out the key from the kitchen door to the store-room, then retrieve it from under the door, just as he said. There was the telephone book, open at the page where he had tried to contact Jeanette Moseley, whom he knew was giving Julie a lift home; there was the list of other calls he had made.

Detectives took Green away for questioning and first did a basic search of the house, then a more thorough, fingertip search. Traces of blood were found in the bathroom, but too little to be tested to ascertain whether it was Julie's. No traces of blood were found on newly washed items in the washing machine. A pair of damp slip-on shoes was found in an airing cupboard, however. There were numerous spots of blood on them, which were found by DNA testing to be Julie's.

Exactly a week after the killing, police flooded the area, and questioned everyone who was living there or was out and about in the streets. No one had seen the mystery assailant, but neither had they seen Warren Green coming out of the house. Everything connected with the murder had to be still in that house at 179 Gidlow Lane.

Thirteen days after Julie's murder, the police had still not found the keys which the murderer had almost certainly used to gain access to the store-room. They decided to do a third, more thorough search of the house, this time concentrating on the structure. On 12 November, they searched under the floorboards. When the hall carpet was lifted, it exposed six boards which formed a kind of trap door that had been constructed to give access to wiring below. A police constable, Ian McAuley, went into the cold, wet, narrow space under the floorboards, lying on his stomach and pushing himself along with his elbows. After half an hour he was about to come out for a rest when his torch beam glinted on a pipe, four or five inches in diameter and set back into the wall.

The pipe, which looked like an old sewer pipe, did not lead anywhere, and was filled with bits of glass and a lump of brick. When McAuley took out some of the rubble he could make out a bunch of keys. When they were pulled out, it could be seen they were a bunch of five keys with a Jaguar fob. They were Warren Green's personal set of keys, and the blood on them was Julie Green's.

The area near the trap door was tested for fingerprints and the architrave near the removed floorboards was found to have four different clear thumbprints of Green's on it, all pointing downwards, as if he had lowered himself down the hatch to hide the keys.

When police interviewing Green told him that the keys had been found he looked shocked, swallowed hard, and carried on as normal. Detective Superintendent Frank Smout, leading the inquiry, said that this was a rare slackening of Green's control. He said, 'Green was very cold and calculating and never showed any emotion — not even when we showed him Stuwart Skett's love letters to his wife. He was very skilful in the interview, very confident, and even took over the interrogation on several occasions . . . All his answers were long

40

and detailed and he stuck to the same story, never wavering throughout.'

When police put it to Green that he had killed Julie because of her affair with Stuwart Skett, he denied knowing about it until the police told him. He said, 'I had my suspicions but Julie said I was being silly and after I had expressed my concerns she was very passionate and affectionate,' and they had ended up in bed.

When Green was re-arrested on 14 November and the police presented the full extent of their evidence against him, he said quietly, 'It looks like you have enough evidence to charge me now.'

At his first appearance before the magistrates, Green represented himself and was refused bail for seven weeks. He then appointed a solicitor and was eventually given bail on condition that he stayed with an old university friend in Birmingham and did not visit Wigan or make contact with any witnesses.

The trial opened on Tuesday, 23 February 1993 at Liverpool Crown Court. The prosecution counsel, Michael Kallisher QC, described how Green had arranged to take the three days off work, from 30 October to 1 November, so that he could install garage doors in the store-room and fit electricity to it.

Green claimed he had been woken by his alarm clock at 10 a.m. and expected to find Julie at home but did not, and so started his telephone inquiries as to her whereabouts. In fact, the police had found Julie's handbag, knitting bag and coat in the dining-room, so it was obvious that she had come home.

Green had told Julie's cousin, Jacqueline Forshaw, that drugs were a likely motive for her death because of the drug bottle and the torn-off fragment of a £10 note found with the body. But even the police did not know that the piece of paper was a banknote until 4 November, it was so stained with blood. When they found out, Detective Superintendent Smout gave instructions for the information not to be released. They deliberately did not tell Green it was a banknote, but he knew. He knew because he had put it there.

The idea of temazepam being a drug

of abuse came from an edition of the television series *Casualty*, which Green had taped for his wife a few weeks before the murder. In the programme a pensioner had obtained temazepam (often used for sleeplessness in the elderly) to give to a young relative who was an addict.

In fact, Julie was given a small amount of these capsules by a colleague to help her sleep. No drugs had been stolen from Wigan Infirmary. If the murder had been committed by a drug user for a modest quantity of temazepam (a rather improbable proposition anyway), why had he not taken the bottle as well as the capsules? The most probable explanation was that Green had flushed away the capsules and planted the bottle by his dead wife.

Mr Kallisher described the slip-on shoes, found in Green's airing cupboard, as 'powerful evidence'. When police were questioning Green, they took him to his home to collect clothing and personal items and he collected several pairs of shoes. He pointed out that one pair of trainers there was not his but was owned by Stuwart Skett. When asked if he was happy he had all the shoes he wanted, he did not reply. Police officers who were present thought his attitude was suspicious.

Green always slept naked and sometimes walked around the house naked. It was thus that he confronted Julie on the morning of Thursday, 31 October when she came home. He probably started a row as soon as she came in, and she walked out to cool off, and this was when she was seen by her old school-fellow in the street. She returned and Green attacked her, hitting her in the face and manoeuvring her into the storeroom through the door which led to the kitchen. He had already placed the lump hammer in a place where he could easily find it and he now delivered one hard blow, which was the lethal blow, then stood astride her and hit her on the skull another fifteen times. The blows were cold and calculated, hitting the victim's head, not her shoulders or anything else in the room as would be expected in a frenzied attack. He had set up a utility light for the purpose of carrying out the murder as the store-room did not yet have electricity and it would be impossible to strike the killing blows accurately in the dim conditions.

The prosecution suggested that Green had killed Julie naked but for the pair of slip-on shoes, because he knew that the evidence of blood on clothes was the most incriminating of all. As he stood astride her, blood had splashed only on his shoes. He had then gone upstairs with the slip-on shoes in his hands to wash off the blood, had wiped the shoes and hidden them in an airing cupboard, under a box of dried flowers. He had then planted the fragment of a £10 note and the bottle of temazepam by the body.

The outside door to the store-room had remained locked throughout, of course, so he did not need to lock it, but he had to get back into the kitchen with both store-room doors locked, so he took the key and locked the door from the kitchen side. He then pushed the key through the gap under the door so that it was inside the locked store-room with the body. He could now claim that the kitchen door key had fallen into the locked store-room when he had pushed it out with the bradawl and screwdriver in his Boy Scout's imitation of something he had seen in the plot of a *Dr Who* television programme.

Green had unscrewed the trap door in the hallway and got down under the floorboards to hide his set of keys in the pipe, then he sat down by the telephone and calmly began ringing people in his deception of looking for Julie. Mr Kallisher said Green had been 'cool and cunning in his attempt to escape his guilt for this murder'.

In his defence, Green recounted the same story of having got up and not found Julie at home, then telephoning people, asking for her, looking for her outside — including in the storeroom — and eventually asking Mrs McGuire for her key to it. When he saw the body lying face down with the large pool of blood he said, 'I knelt at Julie's head and touched her with my right hand. She was ice cold. That was the first moment I realised she was dead. I just wanted to pick her up.' He was pulled away by

46

Mrs McGuire and then dialled 999 and asked for the police. He said he had not asked for an ambulance because he knew she was dead. He said he had no idea why his wife had been killed or who had killed her.

Green's barrister, Anthony Morris QC, did his best with unpromising material. He was critical of the Crown's submission that the crime was committed by Warren Green naked except for his shoes and said that this had only been postulated because of the lack of evidence. 'Somehow he lured his wife into the garage clad like that . . . Pause and you realise the scenario is a ridiculous one because it is one into which the prosecution found themselves forced. There are no blood stained clothes in the house . . . not even in the washing machine. Because they cannot find blood stained clothing in the house then they say Warren Green must have carried out the murder in the nude.' He criticised the police for their lack of objectivity, saying that they had decided at an early stage that Green was their man and allowed this to influence the fairness of their investigation.

On 16 March 1993, after almost four hours of deliberations following the three-week trial, the jury of seven women and five men was unanimous in finding Green guilty. Mr Justice Ognall said, 'This was murder of a grave kind, probably prompted by sex and money. You killed her with a chilling degree of control and concentration. You then took determined and sophisticated steps to mislead the police and these steps included maligning your dead wife as a criminal and a drugs dealer . . . You did not shrink either from pointing the finger at Stuwart Skett.'

As he was jailed for life, Green put his head in his hands, then mouthed, 'It's alright' to his family as he was led away. Behind him were the shattered lives of his own family and that of Julie, and the damage done to Stuwart Skett.

Detective Superintendent Smout felt that Skett had a central role to play in the crime. 'He was the sacrificial lamb,' he later said in reflection about the case. 'Skett was drawn into the situation and left alone with Warren's wife for lengthy time spells, Warren knowing full well what would happen. He still went away for weekends even after he was suspicious of the affair.'

It may be that putting Stuwart and Julie together so that they would have an affair was part of Warren Green's plan. Then suspicion would fall on Stuwart who was not, as Green knew, a very meticulous thinker, and who did in the event make some extremely compromising statements to the police. Smout said, 'It's just as well that he was heavily alibied. There was no way he could have been near the place when the murder happened. His vehicle was secured on the car park and could not be released until he asked permission.'

Smout thought that marriage between Stuwart and Julie had never been part of Green's plan; it was always murder, 'Being the proud man he was, he couldn't see her leaving him for his best friend. He couldn't face the embarrassment of that.' He described Green as 'a very polite young man but with a total greed for cash. He was a very precise individual who wanted to know where every ha'penny went, he was full of his own self importance, he did not like to lose anything.' It may be that his affections for Julie were running out even before they were married, when they had a parting of over a year, and he tried so hard to get her back when she was going out with other people: she was his property and he was not going to give her up.

One mystery remains: why did Warren Green even take the Jaguar fob key ring with its five keys home the night before the murder? Why did he not just throw it away somewhere, perhaps keeping a key or two which he would need to get back in the house? He was planning to commit the murder from the kitchen side of the store-room and did not need the keys, which locked and unlocked the outside door. Why waste precious minutes after the murder in opening up the trap door in the hallway to secrete the keys then closing it again?

The reason Green did not hide or lose the keys before the murder is probably that he thought things might go wrong — Julie might invite Jeanette in for a cup of tea, say, or Julie might fight back with sufficient vigour to prevent his getting her in the store-room. Then he would have lost a set of essential keys for nothing. There was probably also an element of sheer meanness in this business of the keys: he did not like losing things, especially things which had a value. It would just hurt him too much to throw away his keys and his Jaguar fob.

Green's greed was probably the motivating factor in the murder: not only to gain the insurance money and the paid-up mortgages, but to ensure that he did not lose money on the houses he had bought. He could not go through a divorce. That would mean the property would be sold and the money divided. Warren Green would receive half, and anyway they would realise only as much or less than he had paid for them. It was an offence to his deepest feelings: those of avarice.

The McGuires took over the house where Warren and Julie Green lived, and converted it into a funeral parlour.

Fire in the Night

ON 14 November 1991, at the dead of night, a motorist saw what he thought was an Unidentified Flying Object on a Cotswold hill top. It was an orange glow which plunged downward from the high Barrow Wake beauty spot near Gloucester.

He watched the UFO in astonishment then, when he was able to make out the apparition more clearly, he saw it had the outlines of a burning car, and telephoned the police to report it.

Two police cars were quickly on the scene at Birdlip, an attractive spot, popular with families having picnics during the day and with lovers at night. The constables jumped out of their car and looked around. Two hundred and fifty feet below them, over the cliff edge, an overturned Vauxhall Viva was burning. Cries and groans were coming from the end of the car park.

A moaning figure staggered up the

52

slope out of the darkness, a figure from a nightmare. One officer described it as 'zombified'. His face was covered in soot and smoke arose from his blackened clothing. Ropes were tied under his arms, around his torso and his neck. 'Please help me,' he cried to Policewoman Susan Lowry. 'My girlfriend's been murdered — burned alive.'

He slumped down against the side door of the police car. He had been badly burned and there was fluid oozing from his left ear, indicating that he had a fractured skull.

Constable David Spencer went towards the edge of the cliff and aimed his torch towards more human sounds coming from the slope. He saw a second blackened figure staggering out of the darkness. It was so burned and its clothes so charred that he could not even tell it was a woman until it collapsed into his arms. He said, 'I saw a shape coming towards me. I was aware that it was a human figure. My impression was that of something out of a horror film. Her clothes were melted and burned. Her face had the appearance of a golliwog with burned hair, and she was shaking uncontrollably.'

The two were rushed to Cheltenham General Hospital, still very distressed and crying out in pain, where they were examined and found to have 30 – 40 per cent burns. They were transferred to the Burns Unit at Frenchay Hospital, where they were to be in-patients for two months. Detectives interviewed them as soon as possible. They were Ivor Stockle, who was thirty-three, and Pauline Leyshon, forty-two and a mother of four children.

The bizarre events of the night of 14 – 15 November 1991 had their origins ten years earlier, in Ivor Stockle's relationship with Sheila Stroud. He met the fiery, dark-haired woman at the Walls ice cream factory social club in Barnwood, Gloucester, when they were both in their early twenties. They went out together and in 1986 jointly bought a house in Gloucester. Ivor remarked that 'horses and land were an obsession of hers,' and said she was always working towards obtaining a place where she could ride and train horses. They moved out of

Gloucester, to Rudford, in 1988. Sheila Stroud was dealing in horses and Ivor Stockle became a director of her horse feed company, T. & J. Grain.

Stockle remarked that Stroud had a quick temper and liked to get her own way. One argument between them had left Stockle needing twenty-eight stitches for a head wound caused by a coffee mug, and Stroud with a broken arm. The fight was over Stockle's refusal to tell her why he was late home from work. He said, 'She even made a fuss when I went to see a rugby game. She didn't like it either when I started racing her father's horses in trotting races and training her brother's horses . . . I was more successful than her and she resented it. She lived for horses and she wanted to be the most successful.'

The relationship was breaking down at the same time that the economic recession meant business was bad, and Stroud had the added strain of her father's death and her mother's suffering two strokes. In 1990 she began to see an old boyfriend, the virtually illiterate 28–year-old Mark Evans, who had lived on the same caravan site as her as a child. Evans had served many prison sentences, having been in court sixteen times for offences ranging from deception to handling stolen property. He was good with horses and she had him look after her six, which were said to be worth £40,000.

Evans had stayed with Ivor Stockle and Sheila Stroud several times, and when he came out of prison in 1990 Sheila asked Ivor if Mark Evans could live with them as a lodger. Ivor said, 'Like an idiot I agreed because Sheila was a very volatile woman with a violent temper and I like the quiet life. I couldn't really leave her at that stage because I had nowhere to go and I had been made redundant in the summer of 1990 so I decided to weather the storm.' Soon after Mark Evans arrived, he and Sheila Stroud became lovers.

The sexual relationship between Stroud and Ivor Stockle was finished, though they still had a business relationship and they still lived together. In November 1990, Ivor suggested they should go their separate ways, but Stroud was insistent that they should buy 'Lynallen', a bungalow at Staunton, which they could improve then sell at a profit which they could divide between them. Ivor did not want to proceed with this but, he said, 'She threw a tantrum. I was badgered into agreeing and we bought the Staunton place.'

As part of the deal in purchasing the bungalow, they both signed £108,900 life insurance policies, with each being a beneficiary on the death of the other.

The three of them moved in to the £141,500 bungalow, and Ivor Stockle began sleeping alone, Mark Evans sharing a bed with Sheila Stroud. Ivor found new work, at a Lucas factory in Stonehouse, and there met Pauline Leyshon who was nearing the end of a divorce. They fell in love, and in July 1991, Ivor moved out of the bungalow in Staunton and into a flat in Gloucester with Pauline. Sheila was furious but Ivor promised he would still pay the endowment insurance to the end of the year and would be responsible for his half of the mortgage. Sheila maintained a keen interest in Ivor's financial state, and discovered that, in addition to the endowment, he now had a £30,000 life insurance policy taken out by his new employer.

Sheila Stroud wanted it both ways. She wanted the solid, hard-working Ivor Stockle to keep the roof over her head, while she kept the criminal Mark Evans as her lover. When this collapsed, and trading difficulties threatened her business, she was raging to the point of destruction. She wrote to Ivor, 'My life is hell, I don't want you any more. You make me sick, you think you're it. Just stay out of my way or I'll see you buried.' To her family she wrote, 'I hate everything about him. He was the worst thing I ever met in my life, but I will make sure he will never have any rest.'

She considered suicide the month Ivor left her and wrote a note saying her life was 'just torture' and that she hated everything about him. She wrote, 'I was not going to have my home, land and horses taken away from me, which I knew was happening . . . So instead I went in peace and took myself. This is what Mr Stockle had in mind — to see me down and out. It was either his life or mine.'

Obviously she must have thought better of it, as no suicide attempt is recorded.

Now Ivor had a flourishing relationship with Pauline Leyshon, they were both keen to buy a house together, preferably close to the Lucas factory where they worked. They found a place and needed money. Ivor put pressure on Sheila Stroud to give him the £20,000 he had put into the Staunton bungalow, or sell it and divide the proceeds.

On 14 September 1991, he telephoned Sheila Stroud and left a message on her answering machine to say he had an appointment to meet a solicitor on 15 November so that a legal document could be put together stating that she would pay him £20,000 on 1 January 1992 or sell the property.

Sheila Stroud arranged a meeting with Ivor Stockle and Pauline Leyshon at the Air Balloon pub near Birdlip, saying she wanted to resolve the situation. At the meeting, Stroud said she had forgotten the papers they needed to refer to; they were back at the bungalow.

They went back with her to 'Lynallen', where Mark Evans was, to continue the discussion. As they approached the bungalow, Ivor sensed there was something wrong but only later realised it was that the cottage was in darkness (normally it would be a blaze of light). He dismissed his forebodings, however, when the dogs came out to greet him. The four of them sat in the lounge drinking tea with the television on, then Evans left, saying he was going to get a battery charger, which Ivor wanted, from the garage.

A few minutes later, a large, hooded man wearing a wet weather suit and carrying a carving knife burst into the room. He ordered them to get on the floor. Ivor got down. Pauline panicked and ran, crying and shouting, into the bedroom, from where Mark Evans retrieved her. Her jersey was pulled tightly over her head and she was dragged into the kitchen where her hands and feet were tied. The masked man kicked her in the ribs. Ivor's hands were tied behind his back, and his ankles were tied to his wrists with rope and leather horse reins. The hooded man pressed his knife between Ivor's shoulders and

Stroud shouted, 'This will teach you to shit on me.'

They were both dumped in the back of Sheila Stroud's pickup truck which had been waiting outside and tarpaulin was thrown over them. Stroud drove the truck. They had taken the keys to Ivor's Vauxhall Viva and Mark Evans drove it behind the truck. On the way, Evans stopped to fill a can with petrol.

They drove the fourteen miles on the A417 to Barrow Wake, a familiar place to Ivor Stockle and to Sheila Stroud as they used to go there when they were courting. The beauty spot was deserted at that late hour on a Thursday night in November.

The truck was placed behind the Viva and the big man let down the tailgate and pulled Ivor out. He put him near the Viva, went back to the truck and returned with a car jack which he smashed into Ivor's head, fracturing his skull. Ivor later said, 'I had already decided the best way to get out of this was to play dead, so I pretended to be semi-conscious . . . I was moaning on the ground because I thought if I had another blow I probably would be unconscious.' The man picked him up and put him in the passenger seat, and he slumped over with his eyes closed.

Pauline was put in the driver's seat. Evans said, 'Blade her,' to the hooded man but he did not.

'Mark, why are you doing this to us, we don't deserve this,' Pauline pleaded but he did not reply.

When the door closed, Ivor whispered urgently, 'Don't worry love, they aren't going to kill us.' Realising they were going to be plunged over the edge of the cliff, Ivor assessed their chances of escaping before the big drop began. There was an increasingly steep slope after the top of the hill, then a sheer drop. If he could get his legs up, between the time the car went over the top and the drop began, he might be able to kick out the door on Pauline's side.

Outside, the truck was driven right up to the car, on the edge of the precipice. Evans poured petrol over the car and the truck began shunting it forward.

One of the conspirators set fire to the car and Evans shouted, 'Flame ho and away we go,' as the vehicle exploded in flames. The front of the car tipped over the cliff and in a second the truck had shoved it over and it started on a 250-foot drop.

Inside the car, the lovers heard a roaring *whoosh* as the petrol ignited. 'The car is on fire,' shouted Pauline. Ivor smelled the strong chemical odour of burning plastic. The whole car was engulfed in flames. Ivor managed to free his hands and put them to his face, screaming. He could feel himself burning. They were burning alive. They were both shouting and struggling to protect themselves from the fire all around them. The car was rolling with its own momentum down the hillside. Ivor turned and leaned against his door with his legs over Pauline's lap and kicked at the driver's door. He kicked once with his still tied feet, then again, and the glass of the window gave way. He kicked a third time and the door opened. Now Pauline could get out but he could not see whether she did, he was so blinded by the flames and smoke.

The car was trundling along the slope,

gathering speed as Ivor struggled to open his door, fighting for breath with his hands in the fire. He knew the slope was coming to an end and he must get out before it went over the edge. He tried to breathe but the fire had taken the air, he was suffocating and would soon black out. He put his hand into the flames and gripped the molten plastic of the handle. With a supreme effort he managed to open his door. As the car approached the edge he flung it open, dived out and rolled over, and the car crashed down the cliff.

He could hear the car roll on to its destruction, then there was silence in the night. He could not see Pauline and thought she must have died in the car. He pulled the ropes from his legs and staggered up the hill, then hid behind a wall in case his assailants returned. Soon the police arrived.

Pauline was stunned and numb with pain when she fell out of the car. She stood up and saw the car bouncing along with Ivor still inside and tried to follow it but it went too far. She said, 'I was burning. I rolled over on the grass. I thought if I rolled around in the damp, it would put me out.' She tried to peel her clothes away from her, tearing off the charred remnants. Her nylon bra had melted to her body. She said, 'I was burned from my waist up to my left breast, around my left shoulder blade and all along my left arm. The pain was so fierce, I was numb.' She hid in a gully, thinking Stroud and Evans might return, then staggered out and into the arms of a police officer when she saw the police car.

The three conspirators were convinced they had killed Ivor and Pauline and drove off happily, though they were concerned about the amount of damage done to the pick-up truck. The hooded man was particularly adamant that all evidence connecting him to the truck and the scene should be destroyed. Stroud and Evans dropped him off near Matson, where he lived on a housing estate, and drove on.

Stroud and Evans were identified by their victims, though they could not identify the hooded man. The police arrived at the fateful bungalow at 4 a.m.

on 15 November and arrested Evans, taking him to Cheltenham police station.

Accounts of these few hours, between committing the crime and the first arrest, are confused. Something made the conspirators worried. It was not hearing that their victims were still alive on the radio, as the first reports were only of a car going over a cliff and anyway were not broadcast until 4 a.m. It may have been that the big man started threatening Stroud and Evans, and this was certainly their version, but there is no good reason for him to have done so. It is most likely that, in the wake of the excitement of the attack they became anxious and frightened of detection. They might have been seen driving in the two vehicles to Barrow Wake, there might be evidence still in the bungalow or in the truck. Sometimes fear just takes over for no good reason. Whatever their reasons, Stroud now dropped off Evans, not at the bungalow but near to it and he ran home over the fields. She took the pick-up truck away, and may have slept in it.

At 7 a.m. on the morning of the attack, Stroud turned up at a garage driving the pick-up truck. The garage owner said she was 'very, very agitated' when she asked him to repair the nudge bar, indicators and respray the damaged front of the truck.

She spoke to her father by telephone and he said the police had already called, looking for her. That afternoon Stroud walked into Cheltenham police station with her father.

In early interviews Stroud and Evans denied being at the scene of the crime or knowing anything about it. As soon as the police had the evidence to charge them, they were both charged with attempted murder and kidnap.

Under the rules of criminal evidence, police were not now allowed to question them, but could simply take down statements which they made. Their story now was that they had been involved in the attack on Pauline Leyshon and Ivor Stockle, but had been unwilling partners. They had engaged the services of a man called Norman White who would frighten Ivor into staying in the deal with Stroud over the bungalow. When White had started being violent, they claimed, they were powerless to stop him.

This gave the police a lead, but they did not automatically assume that Stroud and Evans were now telling the truth, or that White was definitely the third man. He certainly could be, he was not unknown to the police.

Norman White was a man Evans had met in prison at first and later met up with again in Gloucester. Thirty years old at the time of the attack, he was a drug dealer with a penchant for beating up women. He was imprisoned three times for attacking former girlfriend Joy Foster. In one incident, he attacked her with a knife, leaving her needing eighteen stitches. His last sentence for attacks on this woman was two years. While serving this sentence he was visited in prison by a woman called Rae Smith whom he had met when they were both working at the Bird's Eye Walls factory near Gloucester. Quite what Rae Smith expected out of this relationship is uncertain, but soon after his release when he went to live with her in Tuffley, Gloucester, he started attacking her too. She said, 'It was like living in hell. Norman started drinking a lot and was violent towards me. I lived in fear of him.' He was finally imprisoned for a year for kicking down a door, grabbing her by the throat and hitting her.

White was interviewed on 3 December 1991 and released. He had been in all evening on the night of the attack and no one could prove differently. Neither Ivor nor Pauline picked out White in a line-up and the evidence against him only of the other two conspirators could mean the trial would collapse in unprovable allegations and counter-allegations. There was enough to imprison Stroud and Evans, but not White.

Fortunately, Rae Smith was prepared to testify that White had boasted to her that he would receive a £30,000 payoff for killing someone for Stroud and Evans. It was enough for the Crown Prosecution Service. Norman White was re-arrested at the gates of Shepton Mallet jail on 16 June 1992, when he had just been released from his prison sentence for the attack on Rae Smith. All three were eventually sent for trial, each on two counts of attempted murder.

The trial began at Bristol Crown Court on 9 March 1993. Alun Jenkins outlined the prosecution's case, that Ivor Stockle was to be killed for the £138,900 insurance money, and Pauline Leyshon was to be killed with him to make it look like an accident. Jenkins explained, it was a 'cold, calculated and horrific offence . . . The purpose was very simple: to claim insurance monies on the death of Mr Stockle . . . It would have been a sum of money which would have paid off the mortgage of Miss Stroud's home, and paid for the man who was involving himself in the killing.'

White was living with Rae Smith when he started to see Evans and Stroud to plan the killing of Ivor Stockle and Pauline Leyshon, on one occasion ordering Smith out of her own home so he could see them in private. She gave evidence that he received telephone calls from Stroud and Evans several times. He eventually explained to Rae Smith that 'Sheila had offered him £30,000 to kill some guy off.' White told her he had refused to kill him but would seriously harm him. As Alun Jenkins remarked, you do not get payouts on life assurance for seriously hurting somebody. He had to be going to murder Ivor Stockle.

The jury was taken to the site, at Barrow Wake, and to the bungalow at Staunton where the kidnapping took place. The prosecution argued that Stroud and Evans had got the idea of the murder from a violent American film, *Fighting Mad*, in which a couple involved in a land dispute were attacked by three intruders and put in a car which had petrol poured over it, was set on fire and pushed into a quarry. The jury were shown the relevant fifteen minutes of the film, which starred Peter Fonda.

Mrs Leyshon, a learner driver, was put into the driver's seat of the car, on which L-plates were already fixed, to give the impression she had lost control while practising driving.

People attending the case were shocked to see how badly burned Ivor Stockle and Pauline Leyshon still were when they gave evidence. Pauline suffered burns to her face, neck, back, shoulders, arms, chest and stomach. By the time of the trial, sixteen months after the attack, she had already undergone twelve operations and would have to undergo more. She remarked that having the skin stapled down during skin grafts was more painful than anything she had suffered during the fire.

She appeared in court in a headscarf and with surgical stockings on her arms. She had no hair on top of her scalp. Her hair was particularly badly affected because she was wearing hairspray which had made her hair burst into flames. She was also carrying a cigarette lighter which exploded. She had been proud of her attractive hair and its loss was an exceptional blow to her.

Ivor Stockle's injuries included a fractured skull and 25 per cent burns but his skin was fairer than Pauline's and did not heal so well. The right side of his face still showed red scars. At the trial he still had to wear pressure bandages on both his arms and mittens on his hands to protect the skin. He said he had burst into tears when he saw himself in a mirror a few months previously. The blow on the head left him deaf in one ear though, curiously, his sight was improved and he no longer needed to wear glasses.

Sheila Stroud's defence was that Norman White had committed the offence with no help from her; he had attacked Leyshon and Stockle asking for bank books and cheque cards. She had been 'terrified' and did not know what to do. She claimed White later threatened to slash her face if she told anyone about the incident. She said that after it had happened she drove around aimlessly and felt like committing suicide.

Norman White claimed he knew nothing about the incident. Sheila Stroud and Mark Evans had asked him to beat up Ivor Stockle for 'a couple of hundred pounds', but ten days after he had agreed to this, he said, 'They came and saw me again and said they don't want him beat up. They want him dead. I told them no.' On the night of the crime he claimed to have been asleep at his cousin's home after watching television and smoking cannabis.

Mark Evans would testify, however, that Norman White was sitting in a chair in Sheila Stroud's bedroom in an all-in-one wet weather suit. When asked what he was doing Evans said White had told him he planned to wear the suit to a disco. Evans did admit to having driven White to the bungalow where they smoked cannabis while the meeting between Sheila Stroud, Ivor Stockle and Pauline Leyshon took place in the Air Balloon pub. Evans claimed to have been too afraid to intervene when White attacked the couple in the bungalow, asking for cheque books. He had tried to escape from prison, unsuccessfully, while awaiting trial. His barrister remarked that he had a low mental age and was led astray by others. The judge, however, was unmoved and remarked that he had shown 'a good deal of native intelligence' in the witness box.

After the seventeen-day trial, the jury was out for the surprisingly long time of three-and-a-half hours. When each unanimous verdict of guilty was read out, people in the public gallery cried out 'yes'.

Mr Justice Swinton Thomas sentenced each of them to eighteen years in prison, saying the crime was 'in the higher echelons of wickedness', with all three playing equal parts. Stroud was the leader, White was a hired hitman and Evans 'played a full and particularly repellent part'. Stroud stayed emotionless; Evans shook his head and White kept his chin rested on the dock, as he had through much of the trial, as if he were too weary to pay any attention to it. None of them showed any remorse.

After the trial, Pauline Leyshon and Ivor Stockle talked to the press in the living-room of the bungalow they shared.

It was expected to take another five years after the trial before they would be able to function normally again. They were being treated at the Frenchay Hospital, in Bristol, where staff made sure they went in for operations at the same time and had adjoining beds.

Ivor's fingers were so badly burned he lost his fingerprints and for some time to come would have to wear pressure bandages to protect his hands. He tried to put the horror behind him, saying of Stroud and Evans, 'Being locked up will hurt them more than anything I could do. They both come from the travellers' fraternity and they will find it intolerable.'

Pauline, living a life of constant medication from painkillers and other drugs connected with her treatment said

Maybe they are locked away but they still have a certain amount of freedom. They can still walk in the sun in the prison yard. Ivor and I are sentenced to stay out of the sun forever because of our burns . . . Every night before I go to sleep I curse them and I do the same again when I wake up in the mornings . . . One good thing is that our love is even stronger because we came through this together.

They were intending to marry at a quiet ceremony.

★ ★ ★

Pauline Leyshon, who had known Sheila Stroud since they were children living on the same caravan site, probably gave the best assessment of her personality when she said, 'She's always been a spoilt brat. She always had to go one better than you. She wouldn't just buy a pit pony, she had to have a thoroughbred.' She wanted the horses, the land and the house at Staunton, even when their income could not maintain the mortgage. She wanted her own way, even to the extent of trying to keep the money which Ivor Stockle represented when she no longer wanted him as her lover. When she could not achieve it by any other means, she plotted murder.

They may have a further nemesis in store, for White would not even have been approached by the police had Stroud and Evans not both informed on him. A man like White is unlikely to forget such a bad turn, and it may well have been just the thought of revenge which kept him solidly sitting at the trial with his chin on his hand, seemingly oblivious of what was going on around him. Even after their release, Stroud and Evans will spend the rest of their lives looking over their shoulders.

Team Efforts

THE complexity of insurance frauds makes it very difficult for an individual perpetrator to insure the victim, commit the murder and tie up all the loose ends. This is often, therefore, a crime of two or more.

While most of the cases here are 'double acts', in that the crime would not be committed without both of them being involved, there is always a very dominant partner and another person who is almost as much of a victim as the person who ends up dead.

Kristina Cromwell was a forlorn woman, alternately encouraged and rejected by her lover Paul Perveler, but they were linked together in a crime of his devising. It has been conjectured that he was setting her up to insure and murder as well.

This was certainly the objective of Virginia McGinnis in ensnaring her husband, 'B. J.' Virginia McGinnis was the dominant personality wherever she was. B. J. was a sick, frightened man who was never killed for his own insurance because he was too ill to be insured. Still, she had never killed a healthy adult on her own before, and could not have done so without his help.

Michael Kallinger was of course totally dominated by his father but Joseph Kallinger committed few major crimes on his own. Kallinger was a murderer, but it was as if he needed the armature of his son before he would do his worst.

Bill Bradfield was a charming poseur who liked to talk about crime and the power of the intellect. Dr Jay Smith actually was a criminal and had that intellect, and he used it to manipulate everyone, including Bradfield.

The Bradfield-Smith story is probably the most fascinating and horrifying case here, because of the brutality of the crime and because of the prestige of the individuals concerned. Smith had a doctorate, was a high school principal and was a colonel in the reserves. Bradfield was a head of department, a respected teacher and the son of a wealthy family. His friends, who unwittingly helped in the murder, were respectable and otherwise blameless teachers or students.

The Yellow Jaguar

ON 11 December 1966, fire fighters were called to El Sereno on the East Side of Los Angeles. In the pleasant suburban neighbourhood of Ballard Street they found a house in flames. They smashed their way in. A fire was raging in the bedroom but there was no one there. In the living-room, in front of a flickering television, sat the figure of a man. The fire fighters pulled him out through the billowing smoke and laid him on the lawn outside but they could do nothing for him; he was dead. There were also several bullet wounds to show how he had died.

Homicide investigators were called and immediately set to work at the scene. The fire had started in a pile of clothes in the bedroom. The dead man was the owner of the house, 27–year-old Marlin Cromwell, who worked in the catalogue section of Sears department store. He had five bullet wounds, two in the head, two in the chest and one in the shoulder. Near the body was a white towel with a hole in it surrounded by blood. The killer had clearly used the towel as a crude silencer for the first bullet, which had been fired into Marlin Cromwell's head. There were no signs of forced entry into the house. Somehow, the killer had got close enough to catch Marlin unawares. The victim probably did not know what hit him. The first bullet from a .22 revolver killed him, the second was perhaps to make sure. The next three, shot into an already dead body, were gratuitous acts of viciousness.

On the television tray next to the chair where Marlin had been sitting was a life insurance policy for $15,000 with Metropolitan Life. Next door, on the dining-room table, were five boxes of personal papers, including the recent marriage certificate showing Marlin's marriage to Kristina Cromwell just two months previously.

There was a clear mystery: if the fire had been started by the murderer to destroy evidence of the killing, why had it been started in the bedroom when the body was in the living-room, where the murder had certainly taken place? The most obvious explanation was that the murderer wanted the fire to attract attention, so that the body would be found, together with the clues of the insurance policy and the marriage certificate. In other words, the object was not to destroy evidence, but to reveal it.

This was all too obvious. To the officers investigating the crime, it felt as if they had stumbled into the set for a Do-It-Yourself detective magazine. It was so obvious that the assailant was the victim's wife that it could not possibly be the case. It was more likely that someone had set up the murder and the clues in order to implicate Mrs Cromwell. On the other hand, perhaps that's what the detectives were supposed to think, and it was a clever double-bluff.

Kristina Cromwell was twenty-six in 1966. Her father was a supervisor in a soft drinks bottling plant, her mother had wanted to be an actress, but had only been an extra in B-movies and later worked in an estate agent's. Kristina was loved and encouraged but she always felt overshadowed by her glamorous, younger twin sisters. She was a fat child who became a fat teenager in a culture where nothing was adored so much as a thin body. Life was passing her by when she met Marlin Cromwell, who was a friend of her sister's boyfriend and was an unexciting stock clerk in the mail order section of Sears department store. They married, had a son, and settled into a peaceful if unexciting existence of lower-middle-class suburban life. Her constant criticism of Marlin was that he was not ambitious enough. In April 1965, her mother-in-law, who had never liked her, slapped Kristina in the heat of an argument. Marlin did not speak up in her defence and she left him, intending to divorce him. The divorce came through on 2 August 1966.

Meanwhile the fat, dowdy Kristina Cromwell had been undergoing a transformation which accelerated with her separation. She had been a five foot two, fourteen-stone beachball of a person with mousy hair and spectacles, who made little attempt to make anything of her appearance. Over a matter of months, she changed into a beautiful woman. She lost weight, became a blonde, started wearing contact lenses to show off her blue eyes to their best effect, had her teeth capped and started wearing mascara and lipstick. She started meeting men in singles bars where she never had to wait long for company.

She would inevitably see Marlin Cromwell often, because of their young son, and somehow the two of them got together again. On 1 October 1966, two months after the divorce came through, Kristina and Marlin remarried.

It was this glamorous widow who confronted homicide detectives after the body of her husband of two months had been found dead. She had been told by telephone of Marlin's death, as she was spending the weekend at her friend Vicky Stowe's home at Twenty-nine Palms, east of Los Angeles, with her four-year-old son. It was the first time she had seen Vicky in eighteen months. When she received the call, in Vicky's kitchen, she slumped against the refrigerator and closed her eyes. She told her friend the bad news and, instead of rushing to get back to her home to see what damage had been done, said they should make the day as normal as possible for the boy, and take him riding as she had said they would.

When the police finally got to interview her there were two things which interested them in particular: Marlin Cromwell's insurance details, and Kristina's possession of a .22 calibre revolver.

She said a .22 calibre Hi-Standard revolver with a white bone handle had been given to her by an insurance salesman called Dick Scott whom she had met in a singles bar. She had returned it to him because it didn't work, she said, though a story she told at another time was that she had returned it because she did not like to have guns in the house. The gun could not be traced, via the store owner or anyone else, and neither could Scott, who, she said, was tall, of muscular build, dark-skinned and who drove a blue Chevrolet.

As well as the $15,000 Metropolitan Life policy which had been found conveniently close to Marlin's body, he also had an Allstate fire insurance policy for the house, plus damage insurance on personal belongings. There was also a profit share scheme with Sears, which meant some more money would be coming to the widow, and a mortgage redemption policy on the house. In the event of Marlin's death, the remaining mortgage, around $18,000, would be paid off. The policy which really interested them, however, was a $20,000 policy with the National Life Insurance Company, with a double indemnity clause which included murder. If the insured suffered such an untoward death, the widow would receive double. This generous policy was applied for on 6 October 1966, five days after their remarriage, and issued on 25 November 1966, sixteen days before Marlin was murdered. National Life were suspicious, and kept investigating the claim, but Metropolitan Life paid up.

Detectives investigated Kristina Cromwell and her associates for weeks before they called in to the Southern California Automobile Club where she used to work as a claims processing clerk in the insurance section. One of her former workmates remembered that Kristina had had an affair with an insurance assessor called Paul Perveler, a fact which Kristina had omitted to tell them. The police questioned this dark-skinned young man of muscular build with an easy charm who told them he had, until recently, been driving a blue Chevrolet. Kristina Cromwell had done something very foolish: she had lied where the truth was innocent, giving rise to suspicions that she had something to cover up. The police decided to keep a watch on Cromwell and Perveler, and to check his background.

Perveler, who was twenty-nine at the time of Marlin Cromwell's death, came from a well-off Jewish family from Forest Hills, New York. His father, Sid, was a self-made man, having become wealthy dealing in the motor industry. Paul Perveler was an only child and had always felt he was a disappointment to his father whom he desperately tried to please. As a child he had developed food allergies — eating disorders are a characteristic way for disturbed children to control their families. He ran away from home at the age of twelve and reached as far as Texas. He was obliged, against his wishes, to go to an orthodox Jewish school where he was academically indifferent in a hothouse world of educational achievement. He rejected Jewish culture and disliked his mother who he felt dragged his father down.

As he grew into a young man, Perveler found his good looks and easy charm made him successful with women. He enjoyed the company of men, too, and spent his time in card games, drinking beer and driving fast cars. He went to a small college, then to the University of Southern California. He had a shaky career at university, could get good grades if he worked, but he was not willing, or able, to maintain the effort. He was thrown out, then drafted into the army, and promoted twice to sergeant, only to be reduced to the ranks both times for misbehaving.

Like many people with low self-esteem, Perveler became a racial bigot, developing a hatred of black people. He was also ashamed of being Jewish and used to claim he was Italian. After leaving the army he went to Los Angeles, where he took a low-paid job as junior salesman for a freight company.

In 1961, Perveler met Lela Hensley, a teletype operator for Pacific Telephone. Hensley came from Michigan and was of lower class origins than Perveler, but actually fitted with the class he had now become. Americans are proud of the fact that theirs is a nation where class is fluid and people like Perveler's father can move up from nothing to the wealthy middle class. The other side of this equation, however, is that rapid decline is also possible. Paul Perveler had gone the other way from his father. Part of the reason for his social success was that his wealthy background, his college status and his extravagant lifestyle (subsidised by his father) could impress the people in whose company he now moved. He was always speaking about how he was going to be a millionaire before he was thirty-five, but with no indication of how this would be achieved. The East Coast professionals who had been his school fellows would have recognised him for what he was: a spoiled, flashy, under-achiever.

Perveler was with Lela Hensley for six years in all. They were going to get married twice: once he called it off and once she did, saying she was frightened of him. Eventually, in 1964, they did marry. It was a sexually unsatisfactory marriage with Perveler a harsh and selfish lover who was too prudish to discuss his failings. Later, Lela would find out that he would stay up late and masturbate in front of violent television films.

He had gone through a series of low-paid white collar jobs, then became a policeman in 1962 at the age of twenty-seven. It was a job he enjoyed, since it allowed him to indulge his love of guns. His attitude towards black people worsened and he had ample opportunity to display his prejudice. He developed extreme right-wing views. He told lies, which bordered on the anti-Semitic, about how awful his parents had been to him as a child. He was eventually thrown out of the police force after being an intermediary for a colleague who needed to arrange an abortion for his girlfriend. For a while, he worked for a firm of private detectives, then started working as a claims investigator for the Automobile Club and attending law school. At law school he met the only black man who was ever his friend: Jack Dodd, who also worked in insurance. It seemed that Paul Perveler could not even be counted upon to be consistent in his prejudices.

At work at the Automobile Club Perveler met Kristina Cromwell. A liberal, tolerant individual who wanted America out of Vietnam, and supported black civil rights, she was not an obvious match for him. She did have a deep-seated insecurity, however, and Perveler was able to reassure her, to encourage her independence and the creation of the new, glamorous Kristina who was developing.

Paul Perveler and Lela's marriage had suffered its ups and downs, to put it mildly, and Lela seemed to be accident-prone. One day in August 1965 a car leapt off the kerb and hit her, almost killing her. She suffered severe concussion and bruising but could not identify the driver, who was not apprehended. Her health insurance company gave her a $5000 cheque for pain and suffering in excess of her medical expenses. She signed it over to her husband, who was pleased. It got them out of the debt into which his spending had led them.

After she had recovered, Perveler said that the accident had troubled him so much he had dropped out of law school. In fact, he had dropped out some time before, as she discovered by checking with the administration.

Soon after, she was again hit by a car which came directly at her, pinning her to her own small Volkswagen, breaking her pelvic bone and damaging her legs. When she was out of hospital she received another $5000 cheque from the insurance company which she again paid over to Perveler. She now considered leaving him, because she feared he was behind the attacks on her and because she thought he was having an affair.

She began seeing a former boyfriend, and one day Perveler followed her with his hunting rifle and parked outside the motel where she met the man. Out of sight, Perveler aimed the rifle at him, but did not shoot and neither of them knew the danger they were in.

Less than a week later, Perveler climbed into Lela's car as she returned from an innocent formal evening out. He beat her up, tried to strangle her and, dragging her out of the car, smashed her head on the pavement. He tried to get her back in the car but she gripped the top of the vehicle and held on, sure she would be killed if he got her back in there. He took her head in his hands and beat it repeatedly against the car. He then seemed to come to his senses and walked off, leaving a passing motorist to pick Lela up and take her to hospital, where the emergency room staff found severe bruising and cuts with her jaw bone broken in three places. She was literally unrecognisable — so much so that pictures of her in this state were later mistaken for pictures of another woman.

The police picked Perveler up later that night and he was charged and bailed immediately in his own security.

When he got to see Lela in the hospital, he pleaded his pitiful childhood and his unfulfilled life and the usual whining grief which wifebeaters habitually iterate. Of course, she dropped the charges, to the horror of the police.

Perveler's parents, Sid and Miriam, had moved to California, and Lela convalesced at their home after all three assaults. They were somewhat awkward and suburban but there is no suggestion that they behaved any differently towards Perveler than other parents did to their children. They seemed set for accidents, too, though. When they drove on holiday in Ensenda, Mexico, from a hotel their son had recommended to them, a car followed them on to the highway. It was driven by a woman and a man was in the passenger seat. The man aimed a rifle at the Pervelers' car and shot once, then drove off at speed. Sid Perveler suffered a head wound but it was just a scratch.

When she was recovered, Lela went to see her parents in Michigan. The day after her return, when she was so careless of her own safety as to return to live with him, Perveler asked his trusting wife, who had $12,000 insurance via her company, to go up into the San Gabriel mountains to do some target shooting, a hobby in which she had no interest.

When they arrived and she was sitting on the grass, he was nervously waiting for something, she thought, and he kept looking round him for something to happen. Nothing did. They passed a peaceful afternoon and he drove them home, in some indignation, she felt. Anyone might reasonably ask why Lela kept going back to him but the question could as well be asked about any woman who keeps returning to a husband who beats her. Familiarity probably has a great deal to do with it — the difficulty of leaving a domestic situation which has been built up over years. There is also a question of mere choice: the violent man chooses a woman who will be passive in the face of aggression; the victim chooses a violent man.

Lela finally decided to divorce Paul Perveler, and on 5 November 1966, moved out of their flat, not because of the violence but because she found out that he was seeing Kristina Cromwell.

She had discovered this by tracing the number of telephone calls he was making from their home telephone — something she was easily able to do as a telephone company employee. It is a strange world in which repeated murder attempts are considered less serious than adultery.

Kristina Cromwell is alleged to have boasted to a former boyfriend about her part in these attempts on Lela's life: how she picked up Perveler in his own car after he had run down Lela in the stolen one. She is also said to have boasted to the same man of a plot to shoot a woman up in the mountains, but the man would not testify against her, and Kristina Cromwell faced no charges in this connection.

Marlin Cromwell was murdered the month after Lela left Perveler. Police observation showed that Kristina Cromwell was later in frequent contact with Perveler, leaving messages at his message service under the codename 'Miss Walther', which was the brand name of his favourite gun.

After the murder, Perveler was boasting that he was soon going to come into money and he had an extravagant New Year's Eve party for 100 people at the Biltmore Hotel in Los Angeles, for which he did not pay until the hotel sued him.

In general, he was spending more freely, and with large notes, spending much in excess of his $580 a month salary. Police watching Cromwell found her withdrawing large sums. In February 1967, the couple flew to Nevada, using aliases, and enjoyed some high living in expensive hotels: the Stardust, the Thunderbird and the Desert Inn. Perveler won some money, then lost a lot — so much that he was invited to return as the Thunderbird Hotel's guest, free of charge, so he could lose some more.

Telephone calls made to Perveler were monitored and some were found to come from Cromwell's number. On 9 March 1967, she left the message, 'Definite word on policy tomorrow.' Finally, she filed a suit against National Life for the $40,000 double indemnity payout, which they were resisting because of the suspicious circumstances of her husband's death.

On 26 April 1967, police launched a combined raid and searched the apartments of Kristina Cromwell, Paul Perveler, and that of Perveler's parents, who found the ordeal deeply distressing. No further evidence was found, but Perveler and Cromwell were arrested for the murder of Marlin Cromwell, and questioned. Perveler easily fielded the questions and Cromwell refused to say anything. They were released without charge. The only evidence against them was that they had spent insurance money together. The police knew Perveler was laughing at them.

He became more politically extreme, believing there would be a racial civil war, and started carrying even more weapons. It must have been a common delusion among maniacs in California at the time — the mass murderer Charles Manson, a contemporary, believed the same thing.

With his new apartment, complete with pool, things were looking good for Paul Perveler. He leased a new car, took up riding again, and found a new blonde, the stunning Debbi Simmons, a would-be actress. It surprised this much sought-after young woman that Perveler was not very interested in sex — he liked to be seen with women rather than to do anything with them. He was looking for another wife, and in the space of a year he proposed not only to Debbi Simmons, but to a student called Marjorie Huebner, to another woman called Barbara Gutman and to a gym instructor called Cheryl Davis. He also proposed again to the long-suffering Lela. Police would conjecture that he was looking for another wife to insure and kill, and that it did not matter who she was. This would be particularly sad for Debbi Simmons; she really did love Perveler, who did not only want her body as so many men did. Although perhaps he wanted her body in a rather more venal way than most: he wanted it dead so that he could claim the insurance on it.

Perveler's seduction line, for those gullible enough to swallow it, and who were impressed by that sort of thing, was that he was a hit man for an organised crime ring. Debbi eventually moved in with him and he spent her money. He was always talking about how he was going to make it big, how he had a plan which would set him up for life or leave him dead. He would talk about how perfect murders could be committed; that he was involved with the wrong type of people; that he had done, or would do, terrible things; that they would be reading about him in the papers. If all this seems ridiculous, it needs to be said that he fostered his delusions about his superior intellect by surrounding himself with stupid people.

For Kristina Cromwell, things were not so good. The fire insurance on the house was going to the mortgage holder. Marlin Cromwell had failed to maintain payments on the mortgage redemption policy so the lump sum was not paid off on his death, and she still had the debt of the mortgage which she allowed to be foreclosed against her. The most she got from the fire was $1300 for personal property loss. The National Life Insurance Company finally paid out the basic policy of $20,000 without the double indemnity.

Perveler had, by now, managed to buy a bar, the Grand Duke, in San Fernando Road in Burbank, which was successful after a slow start. He kept up his job at the Automobile Club, however, until he was sacked for frequent absences and for making two fraudulent insurance claims. In one, he borrowed Lela's car (she was still seeing him) and had crashed it, and paid a couple of people to witness the 'accident'. He then persuaded a chiropractor to produce fake X-rays, supposedly taken before the accident, and actual ones taken after, and testify that a congenital minor spinal defect in Perveler had been the result of the crash.

In the second fraud, he had a minor criminal he knew from the bar steal his car and drive it to Mexico, take it apart and sell the parts. A friend at the insurance company, Michael Brockington, whom Perveler relied upon to back him up, simply could not betray his employer and told his superiors, who sacked Perveler. Perveler did not know he had been betrayed by Brockington, but simply assumed he had gone too far in the insurance schemes, so he did not pursue them.

Brockington managed the accounts in the bar for Perveler and served there some nights. He was drawn to the eventful and dangerous life Paul Perveler seemed to live. Perveler's talk was all bluff and threat and boasting, but with an element of truth. He certainly drove exciting cars and dated exciting women.

An attraction of friendship with Perveler for Brockington was that he got the women with whom Perveler did not want to do anything, including Debbi Simmons. Brockington was a true friend to her, and successfully leaned on Perveler to give her back the money he had stolen from her when he was supposedly going to marry her.

Perveler had other ways of making money, however. When one of his oldest friends tearfully told him he was getting divorced, Perveler persuaded him to give $5000 dollars in savings direct to him for safekeeping, so his wife could not receive it as part of the settlement. The friend did this, only to be threatened with violence when he asked for written evidence of the transaction, and told, 'You got taken.' Perveler also suggested a deal: he would blow up the man's shop and kill his wife, if the insurance payment was right.

The man went to the police despite the threats, and they added this to the list of Perveler's wrongdoings in which they were already interested. Perveler seemed compelled by his nature to take greater and greater risks: he did not need this money, his bar was now doing well, and he was a good manager. Whatever his past had been, Perveler had an opportunity to be a successful businessman if he performed no more criminal acts in the future. Later, Perveler confessed to Michael Brockington that he had killed Kristina Cromwell's husband. It was an unnecessary confession and was probably only made because Perveler enjoyed the sense of danger it gave him.

Perveler leased a plush new apartment. He introduced Kristina Cromwell as his fiancée to John Miller, manager of the Castillian Apartments. He set about buying another bar, calling it the Grand Duchess, and finally did marry someone:

Cheryl Davis. She was twenty-one, a petite brunette, and an instructor in one of the many fitness clubs in Los Angeles. She was a postman's daughter and her marriage, on 1 March 1968, was against her parents' better judgement. She was more independent-minded than most of Perveler's girlfriends. Perveler gave Cheryl as a present a crystal punchbowl set and expensive luggage which were not exactly new. He had stolen them from Lela, having originally given them to her as a wedding present. When Cheryl kissed her husband on the cheek at the wedding reception, Kristina, to whom he was talking, said, 'Oh no, why did you have to go and do that?' and stormed off. The couple did not have sex on honeymoon. When they did have sex, perhaps for the only time in their marriage, she told a sister it made her feel dirty. Two weeks before her death she was planning to go home to her mother.

Shortly after the marriage a short, stocky blonde woman was seen hanging around the outside of their home. Cheryl complained that she was frightened of this apparent prowler, but she was never identified.

On 20 April 1968, Cheryl went to the Grand Duchess, opened two weeks earlier, and had dinner with her husband. They returned to the bar, then at 10.30 p.m. Perveler told her, 'It's time for you to go home.' He went outside with her for a while, and she left for home in her yellow convertible Jaguar, open to the wind though it was not a warm evening. A few moments after she left, Perveler took a brief call from an unidentified woman. Cheryl had been driving the distinctive car, leased for her by her husband, for just a day.

On the nine-mile journey home, Cheryl stopped for fuel and to see a caterer, whose business was almost opposite her home and who had dealt with arrangements for her wedding.

Back in the car, she pulled into the drive of her home, Castillian Apartments. As she stopped, ready to put the Jaguar into the carport, a figure stepped out of the darkness and fired a .25 automatic directly at her from close range. Cheryl put her hand up instinctively and pushed the gun away. The first bullet tore through her clothes and the flesh of her left breast and embedded itself in the leather of the seat beside her. She knew in her terror that she must defend herself. The attacker's gun had jammed and the dark figure struggled with the trigger to make it work. Cheryl fumbled desperately to open her handbag where she kept her own revolver on the seat beside her. The assailant brought the jammed gun smashing on to Cheryl's head, stunning her, so that she slumped down, then the figure ejected two cartridges manually and shot twice directly into Cheryl's head. As if this were not enough, the attacker smashed the butt of the weapon down on Cheryl's head another six times before making off.

When the three shots sounded into the California night they were heard by the apartment block's manager, John Miller, and another resident, who ran out to find Cheryl Perveler slumped over the seat with blood pouring from her head and chest. She was still alive and gasping for breath in the car with its engine still running and the lights on. Miller called the police and an ambulance. Mrs Miller called Paul Perveler at the bar, but could not bring herself to tell him that his wife had been shot, and said there had been an accident. He was shocked at this and it was only later in the hospital, when he was told that Cheryl had been shot, that he was more calm.

Cheryl had two head wounds, one above her left eye and the other above her left ear. There were also seven wounds on her head, caused by being battered with the butt of the gun, most of them after the shots had been fired. She did not live the rest of the night.

Back in the drive of Castillian Apartments, the forensic team was examining the car. In the blood-soaked Jaguar they found the spent cartridges and the live round which had been ejected, but not much to help them, except what was not present: any discernible motive. Sexual assault had not been attempted; there had been no effort to get the woman out of the car; her money and credit cards were still in her handbag which was open beside where she had been sitting for anyone to see. The absence of obvious motive, and the pointless ferocity of the attack, indicated some personal reason for the killing.

In any crime where the motive is not obvious, the first step is to check the family and business associates. In this case they were the same: Paul Perveler. It did not take detectives very long to find out that, even though Perveler had an alibi, he had a record of wife beating, was a suspect in the Cromwell case and that he was suspected of involvement in the hit-and-run attacks on his ex-wife. They immediately went to see Lela, who told them the whole story of her near-misses. She was devastated that she had not warned Cheryl and wanted to help the police in any way possible.

They later found that Perveler had taken out a life insurance policy for $25,000 on Cheryl with her father named as the beneficiary, then had changed the beneficiary to himself one month to the day before her death. The salesman for Equitable Life was his friend Jack Dodd, with whom he also took out insurance on the bar and on his own life. His friendship with Dodd was a curious inconsistency in the life of Paul Perveler, a man so racist that when Dr Martin Luther King was shot he declared drinks on the house in his bar.

After the police had interviewed anyone who might have had a motive for the murder, they finally got round to Michael Brockington. He told them everything, including information about a trip with Perveler to Santa Fe Springs, to a building where, it was found, Kristina Cromwell then worked, to pick up an envelope full of money which was Perveler's payoff from the Cromwell killing. Police now arrested Perveler and Cromwell, who were refused bail, and the newspapers revelled in a real 'double indemnity' case in which it was suggested that each had killed the other's spouse for the insurance money.

That was not the case, however. Perveler was charged with the murder of Marlin Cromwell, the murder of Cheryl, and with beating Lela. Kristina Cromwell was charged only with the murder of Marlin Cromwell. There was no evidence to link her with Cheryl's murder. As Los Angeles District Attorney's prosecutor

Vincent Bugliosi states in his book about the case, *Till Death Us Do Part*, 'We are a society of due process. Kristina Cromwell was never indicted nor even accused of Cheryl's murder. If the term "innocent until proven guilty" means anything at all to us, Kristina did not commit that murder.'

Bugliosi confides his very real fears that Cromwell would walk free and that Perveler would do so, too, of everything but the assault on Lela to which she was now prepared to testify. Perveler was not charged with the two hit-and-run incidents or the San Diego rifle incident so the jury were not told about them, as it would have prejudiced them against him.

Cromwell, with the help of supportive friends and neighbours, hired the talented defence attorney Melvin Belli, who attempted to have the case against her dismissed, arguing (quite correctly): 'One of the best police departments and one of the best district attorney's offices in the United States have been running Kristina down since December 11th of 1966, and have come up with nothing.

There is nothing such as a fingerprint. There is nothing such as a note. There is nothing.'

The judge denied the request. Perveler had one lawyer, became dissatisfied with him and fired him, then another and did the same thing. Finally, he decided to represent himself, and then decided to have another lawyer representing him.

Bugliosi states in his book, 'We went into the case with no eyewitnesses, no "smoking gun", no fingerprints, no bullet match-ups, no physical evidence connecting the defendants with the crime. If ever there was a classic, textbook case of circumstantial evidence, this was it.'

There were 109 witnesses called in the trial, which started on 18 November 1968 and ended three months later, on 25 February 1969. In court, Kristina Cromwell hugged her mother each morning and asked about her son whom the old lady was looking after. Perveler never even acknowledged the presence of his parents, who came every day.

Two criminals who were now in the state penitentiary said they had sold Perveler a .25 automatic that jammed, which they had taken in a robbery. They also sold him a diamond he had set in a ring for Cheryl, and which she was wearing on the night she died, and which she wore when she was buried.

Michael Brockington told the court that Perveler had confessed to killing Marlin Cromwell. He said that he did not go to the police with this piece of information because 'I didn't want to have my head blown off.'

Under cross-examination, Brockington admitted his subservient relationship to Perveler: he worked part-time as a bar manager for him and ran errands for him, got his cleaning, did his shopping, got his car washed and drove his girlfriends around. When Perveler had no more use for his girlfriends, Brockington would himself go on dates with them. The defence tried to demonstrate that Brockington had killed Cheryl because he was jealous of her relationship with Perveler.

The evidence against Kristina Cromwell, though scrappy, was, in total, compelling. There was her evasiveness about knowing Perveler; giving him half the insurance money in a conspiratorial manner; spending some of the money with him under an alias. Witnesses could say they had heard Perveler speaking to Kristina on the telephone saying things like 'Don't let the police department rattle you. They can't prove anything. We have got this far. Don't blow the deal now.'

The curious case of Jack Dodd's relationship with Perveler came out at the trial, too; of how Dodd, a respectable and upright family man, had originally testified that it had been he who had persuaded Perveler to take out the policy on Cheryl, despite Perveler's protestations. As Brockington, who was present, would demonstrate, that was not how it had happened. The policy went through quickly and was made out at Perveler's instigation. The reason for Dodd's support of Perveler, given by two witnesses, was that Dodd wanted to show the ultra-racist Perveler that a black man could stand by him and be his friend when all others had deserted him. Perveler had obviously divined this desperate need in Dodd to prove himself and filed the information away, keeping in contact with the man for future use.

Bugliosi conjectured that while Perveler had been outside the Grand Duchess with Cheryl for a while on 20 April, it was to set her up for the killing. He had perhaps told her to park in the carport rather than on the road as she often did; had perhaps told her to keep the convertible hood down. He told her to stop for fuel to delay her, and to call in at the caterers so that the killer could get a good look at her and take up position. As Bugliosi said to the jury, the killer had to be waiting for Cheryl to arrive at the carport. 'Who else knew when Cheryl was going to arrive at the Castillian Apartments, exactly where she was going to park, and even though it was the very first day she had the Jaguar, the type of car she was going to be driving except Paul Perveler?' He had either committed the murder or conveyed the information to someone else who did so.

For most of the trial it was considered that Perveler had had an accomplice do the killing. During the trial, however, a man called Walter Wasson who lived near the scene came forward to say he had seen a man like Paul Perveler hurrying away from the murder scene with Perveler's distinctive shuffling walk.

It had been considered that Perveler did not have time after being last seen in the bar to get home, kill Cheryl and get back to the bar. Early evidence had shown Perveler had been away from the bar for only ten or fifteen minutes after Cheryl left, only just long enough to drive home at maximum speed, do the killing and drive back. It was possible but far from probable. Later evidence, however, found that he had been away for twenty-eight to twenty-nine minutes — time in which he could easily get home, hide in the darkness and kill Cheryl, especially as she stopped twice on the way.

Perveler was found guilty on all counts: the murders of Marlin and Cheryl and the attempted murder of Lela, and was sentenced to death. Cromwell found guilty of Marlin's murder and was sentenced to life imprisonment.

Michael Brockington later married Lela. Perveler tried to escape three times without success. He never confessed or repented. In 1972, all death sentences in the US, including his own, were commuted to life imprisonment.

Kristina Cromwell was paroled in 1976. She got a job and went to college and continued to live the blameless life she had led before she ever met Paul Perveler. The most sympathetic rendering of this story is that this sociopathic man destroyed three generations of the lives of those around him. The parents of the two victims, Kristina Cromwell's parents and his own were devastated by the deaths. Kristina Cromwell's son lost his father and also his mother during her term of imprisonment. All the people Perveler had considered to be friends or girlfriends were contaminated by him and Kristina Cromwell, though culpable, was also a victim.

She maintained contact with him because she had genuine feelings for him, which he sometimes gave the impression of reciprocating. He was linked to her because of the killing of Marlin but he may well have been setting her up even more as a victim. Introducing her as 'my fiancée' suggests that he intended to marry her, and his wives were destined to die. Perhaps he desisted from this course because the death of heavily insured Marlin Cromwell followed by the death of his widow similarly insured would have been just too suspicious.

The fact that Perveler did not marry and kill Debbi Simmons is still something of a mystery. She was certainly compliant and would have done anything for him. Bugliosi suggests that Perveler did have real feelings for her, probably because she was so genuinely devoted to him. He just cared for her too much to marry her.

Brockington was asked at the trial if he thought Perveler loved Cheryl, to which he replied, 'I don't think Paul is capable of love, as we know it.' Everyone would have been better off if he had shown such perception earlier in his relationship with Perveler.

The Ice Lady

BIG SUR is an area of the western Californian coastline known for its rugged beauty. It is a popular spot with sightseers who stand on the towering cliffs and look out to the Pacific Ocean or down to the seals basking on the rocks below.

Down the wild and lonely road from one of the many viewing posts, a fat woman with long auburn hair came running one windy April day in 1987. She was out of breath when she reached the Coast Gallery, a small art shop, but managed to gasp out that a girl had fallen over a cliff nearby. She dialled the emergency services from the shop, then the manager of the gallery, Deborah Cross, drove her back up to the lookout point above Seal Bay.

The big woman was talking all the while about the girl. 'She was taking photographs and she tripped. She has high, spiked heels on. I asked her to take them off, that she'd trip and fall. To please change into a pair of sneakers or just take your shoes off. She refused to, she absolutely said no, she wouldn't do it. She didn't want to take them off. I wish we'd taken Highway 101 up the valley, not the seacoast route. But we wanted to take her up the coast to see the scenery. How am I going to tell her parents what happened? How can I face them?'

The police arrived first, then a Search and Rescue crew, and they assessed the scene, which was already becoming crowded with onlookers and a television crew. Two men from the rescue team abseiled down the cliff side, finding first one blue high-heeled shoe, then another, then blood, still wet. Four hundred feet down, on a ledge, was the body of a young woman wearing jeans and a windcheater. Her head was covered in blood and one leg was twisted out of shape. The two officers confirmed her dead and placed the corpse in a body bag, radioing for a helicopter to take her away.

Deputy Coroner David Dungan quickly

established that the body, which was winched up from the level ground where it had come to rest, was that of twenty-year-old Deana Wild. She had been staying in San Diego with the woman who raised the alarm, Virginia McGinnis, and her husband Billie Joe, universally known as B. J.

They did not seem tearful or even very worried. A witness remarked that, on being told Deana was dead, Virginia and B. J. seemed to register 'relief rather than grief'.

In response to Dungan's questions, Virginia said that she had become cold on the cliff edge and was going back to the car. B. J. followed her. They had looked around and Deana was gone, without even a sound. She gave David Dungan the telephone number of Deana's mother in Kentucky, and said she would telephone her to break the news to her.

She was asked a routine question: 'Do you know of the existence of any insurance on the deceased or that the deceased may have taken out on herself?' She said she did not. B. J. was asked the same question and also replied in the negative.

At midnight, David Dungan called Mrs Bobbie Roberts at her home in Fincastle, Kentucky. She identified herself as Deana's mother and he told her Deana was dead. Her daughter seemed to have slipped and fallen down a cliff at Big Sur.

The next day, Virginia McGinnis called and commiserated with Bobbie Roberts. She said what a beautiful person Deana was, and that she understood Bobbie's grief because she, too, had lost a daughter. She promised to send on Deana's things, and a roll of photographs which they had taken at Big Sur before Deana's death.

Less than a week later, Virginia McGinnis called in to Mac McCain's insurance agency in the Chula Vista area of San Diego, where she lived, and went through to Mac's office. He noticed she had her arm in a sling. 'She's dead,' said McGinnis, putting an insurance policy on his desk.

McCain considered it a memorable visit. He had issued the life policy on

Deana Wild on 1 April 1987. By the afternoon of 2 April, Deana Wild was dead.

'When do we get the cheque?' said McGinnis.

★ ★ ★

Bobbie Roberts went through life in a daze after the news of her daughter's death. There was also a technical problem, for which her experience as a high school teacher had not equipped her. She summoned the courage to talk to a lawyer who worshipped at the same church as her.

After the service at the Second Presbyterian Church in Louisville, Kentucky, corporate lawyer Steven Keeney chatted to other members of the congregation. The nervous Bobbie Roberts, not used to asking favours, approached him and requested his help. Her problem was with the insurance on her daughter Deana Wild. She had died in a fall in California in April. Bobbie's schoolteacher's insurance covered funeral expenses for the death of her children, and Deana's funeral had cost $3500. But the insurance company would not pay up, even though it was now well into July. Would Mr Keeney please help?

Keeney found it hard to refuse a request from a single woman who was obviously not well off, particularly as he was in church, and he consented to make some telephone calls and write a few letters. He anticipated it would be an easy job to recover a matter of a few thousand dollars from the AmEx Insurance Company. In fact, as he was to discern some years later, this insurance only covered children under nineteen, so there was no way they would pay up in any event on the death of a twenty-year-old. By the time this was discovered, however, other events had long since given the case its own momentum.

Keeney quickly found the immediate source of the problem: the office of the Monterey Coroner, in whose jurisdiction the death had taken place, would not issue a death certificate. The cause of death, they said, was still pending. This surprised Keeney, as did the knowledge that there was a $35,000 insurance policy on Deana Wild, made out to one James Coates, a man Bobbie Roberts had never heard of. It was taken out with the huge State Farm Insurance Company. The coroner's officers were perfectly forthcoming in explaining to Keeney why they were suspicious: the same persons who had obtained the insurance policy the day before Deana's death had also been the only people at the scene of Deana's fall. Virginia McGinnis was also the mother of James Coates, the beneficiary of the policy, who was recorded on it as 'fiancé' — a somewhat improbable relationship, as Deana was already married.

Keeney, a meticulous investigator, collected all the evidence about Deana's death. The pathologist's report found her death to be caused by a 'basal brain laceration . . . due to basal skull fracture', meaning that getting hit on the head had been the principal cause of death. Perhaps she hit her head on a rock on the way down? Perhaps she was hit over the head before she went down? The other injuries were a fractured shin, knee and thigh bone and two fingers, all on the left side; and cuts and grazes to her arms. These alone would not have caused death.

Her blood tested negative for alcohol or narcotics but did contain nortriptyline and amitriptyline, components of a drug marketed as Elavil which was a 'mood elevator' used for depression, including post-operative depression. There was no potential for abuse, however, as the side-effects were unpleasant, particularly when first starting the treatment. Physicians' desk references note that these chemicals cause 'drowsiness, dizziness . . . may impair alertness . . . patients should be warned of the possible hazard when driving or operating machinery'. Bobbie Roberts had no idea why her daughter might have been taking such a drug, and the pathologist had not specified the quantity of the chemical which Deana had in her.

At Steven Keeney's suggestion, Bobbie Roberts called Virginia McGinnis and secretly taped the call. She called ostensibly as a concerned parent but the real object of the call was to elicit information from McGinnis. After some general questions,

Bobbie asked why her daughter had been taking Elavil, which Bobbie knew about from the pathologist's report. McGinnis said it must have been from a prescription given to B. J. a long time previously for sleeping after he had an operation. McGinnis attempted to explain:

Well, it's on the order of aspirin, but they are a coated type of medication. And they're approximately the same colour and I know that they were in the medicine cabinet. I don't know if she took one by mistake, but all it would do was make you more excited or hyper or more — it didn't make you sleepy; it just made you feel happier. I don't have a medical book here right at my fingertips to give you the side effects. But basically they are a non habit-forming drug used most generally on a short-term basis. There was a lot of it used when they were starting to take people off Valium and lithium. And as I say, it was not a depressant, and it wasn't anything that would make you sleepy or drowsy.

This was hardly a reassuring comment when she had already said that B. J. was prescribed it to help him sleep.

Deputy Coroner David Dungan's report read that

[Deana] Wild was visiting the area of Big Sur with friends, Billie and Virginia McGinnis from San Diego. Wild had been staying with the McGinnises for only a couple of months when she was dating their son. She stopped seeing their son and moved in with the McGinnises. Mr and Mrs McGinnis knew that Wild had never seen much of California and offered to take a trip which would include San Francisco and the Monterey coastline.

The McGinnises left San Diego early on 2 April and travelled up State Route 1. Periodically they would stop and take photographs and ate lunch in San Luis Obispo. They stopped along Highway 1 near the Coast Gallery to take photos of the sunset and the ocean.

131

The report continued that B. J. McGinnis was standing about two feet from the edge of the cliff next to Deana, and Virginia McGinnis was taking their photograph. B. J. walked towards the parked car. 'He and his wife were walking when they turned around in the direction from where Wild and Mr McGinnis were standing and Wild was nowhere to be seen. Both looked around and then walked back to the site. Neither could see her but looked slightly over the edge and saw a highheeled shoe over the edge about twenty feet below. They looked further and saw Wild lying on the rocks at the bottom of the cliff.'

So Deana had moved in with the McGinnises when she stopped, not when she started, going out with their son; and no cries for help or sound of struggling had alerted them to Deana's fall; and Deana's body was said to be visible from the top of the cliff though none of the professionals there could see it. Despite the inconsistencies, the deputy coroner wrote reassuringly, 'In the initial and subsequent interview with the McGinnises I found nothing to even slightly indicate foul play.'

The photographs were also interesting. Most were of views, some had people. There were two pictures of Deana showing her full length, including the fateful blue high-heeled shoes. She had a willing smile, as if asking for affection. Six of the photographs showed B. J. McGinnis, an overweight, stocky man, with Deana beside him on a cliff edge with the cliffs and the ocean in the background. Six showed scenes without people. One, the only one obviously taken by Deana herself, showed the backs of Virginia and B. J. McGinnis, walking away from her.

One of the pictures of Deana and B. J. showed her slumped against him as they stood against the backdrop. Bobbie Roberts confirmed in a telephone call to Virginia McGinnis that the pictures had been taken just prior to Deana's death, on Big Sur just above Seal Beach. The last picture with the two of them in it showed Deana looking decidedly shaky, with her knees locked together. B. J. had his arm on her back. Perhaps he was supporting her.

The evidence of the photographs did

not fit with McGinnis's account of taking them. The last photograph was supposed to be of B. J. and Deana and while they walked away after taking it, Deana was found to be missing, so Virginia McGinnis ran to raise the alarm. In fact there were four more pictures taken after the picture of B. J. and Deana. The others were all general views. It was as if Deana had gone down the cliff and they had waited around, shooting off the last of the pictures, to make sure she was dead.

Another consideration about the scene on the afternoon of Deana's death was that McGinnis had spoken to Deborah Cross, the manager of the Coast Gallery, as if Deana were already dead: what would she tell her parents? How would she face them? This implied that she knew Deana was dead. A more normal response would be to be hoping against hope that she was alive, that she had fallen on a ledge near the top, that she had sustained only minor injuries and the rescue team would recover her.

Examining the autopsy photographs was a grim task. Deana's body had been photographed, first as it was brought in, then naked, then as it was being dissected. There were two interesting facts: the first was that she seemed to have slid down the cliff limp, putting up little resistance. This implied that she was already unconscious before she went over. The other was the state of her hands: all her false fingernails were broken, and the back of her hands were bruised. These were more likely to be defensive wounds than injuries caused by a fall. It was easy to picture Deana fighting someone who was trying to push her off the edge.

★ ★ ★

Deana had been a difficult child for Bobbie Roberts to bring up. She was the daughter of Bobbie's first marriage, which broke up when Deana was three. Her educational ability was low and she was said to be a borderline case for having, in the jargon, 'learning difficulties'. She was a socially active girl, with a lot of friends, though her relationship with her mother was often stormy. Without warning her

135

mother she left home in September 1986 at the age of nineteen and married her boyfriend, Jay Wild, who had joined the navy. She went to San Diego where he was stationed and discovered that the life of a navy wife is very dull, with their husbands away for long periods at a time.

The marriage very soon broke up under this strain, and Deana met a man called James Coates, freshly free from jail, who introduced her to his mother, Virginia. She took a shine to Deana, and kept her as a house guest even after James Coates violated his parole terms and was sent back to prison.

Virginia McGinnis seemed to have been in trouble throughout her life though she had never been in prison. She was born Virginia Hoffman in a family of poor dairy farmers in Tomkins County, New York. It was a squalid home, where Virginia was probably sexually abused and was certainly physically abused. Her father's behaviour was strange, to say the least, and visitors to the farm recall that he had a row of stuffed children's toys like rabbits and teddy bears nailed to a tree directly outside the house. He once shot Virginia's pet horse and sold the carcass to the glue factory.

Her mother was aloof and snobbish, considering herself better than her neighbours, and Virginia adopted the same high-handed attitude, though she was, if anything, poorer than children from the neighbouring farms.

Her first fire was set when she was sixteen when she burned her father's barn, for which he collected the insurance. When she was seventeen she became pregnant and married Dick Coates, a boy two years older than her from another farm. Virginia had a fierce temper and went for him with a knife several times. Their first child, Ronnie, was born in 1955 and the second, Jimmy, in 1956. As the marriage progressed, Virginia's manners became more refined and she developed her taste for fine clothes and jewellery, which she stole. In fact, she stole all the time: cutlery from neighbours, a steel vice — anything she could reach from shops. She was also highly sexually promiscuous and fire seemed to follow her around. She set two more fires in houses where she was living with her young husband. At twenty-two, she was convicted of charges related to shoplifting and passing forged cheques.

The marriage broke up in 1966 when Virginia, now aged twenty-nine, went back to live with her parents in their home which soon burned down. Some months later, Dick Coates was called by a local insurance agent who wanted to pay over the $10,000 for a barn which had burned down. This was an insurance, and a fire, about which Coates knew nothing. Virginia had taken out the insurance in his name.

Virginia married again, in 1971, to a naval engineer called Bud Reardon, and lived with him in Louisville, Kentucky, with her two boys, his son Butch, and her daughter. This was Cynthia, a girl born in 1969, whose second name was Coates but who was not Dick Coates's child.

One wet Wednesday afternoon, on 6 December 1972, police answered an emergency call to the Reardon home to find three-year-old Cynthia Elaine Coates almost certainly dead. She was given mouth-to-mouth resuscitation but was pronounced dead on arrival at hospital. Virginia said she had let the child go off into the barn and when she went in she found Cynthia hanging by some twine from a seven-foot high rafter. She ran for her father to cut Cynthia down. It would seem that the child had climbed on a small tractor and had got her neck caught in the string.

The police officer who dealt with the case, R. D. Jones, had been so concerned about it that he had not thrown away the evidence as he was supposed to after a period of time had elapsed. Fifteen years later, he could still show Steven Keeney the twine on which McGinnis's three-year-old daughter had been found hanging.

Several things did not add up in this scenario. Jones was suspicious about the lack of deep ligature marks on the child's neck. It was as if she had been strangled, then put in the twine. Her semi-sitting posture on the tractor with her head in a noose was also a difficult position for the child to achieve alone; and Virginia's claim that she had been preoccupied with preparing the pony for the child to ride sounded unlikely, too, on such a dismal day. Virginia's lack of an emotional response to what one might think was the most desperate of tragedies was also suspicious. But there was not enough evidence to justify investigating further, and the case was closed.

Virginia was a good-looking though unexceptional woman who always dressed well, and her home was filled with attractive objects. She claimed to have received them via the will of a woman she looked after when she worked as a nurse in California, but no more is known of this episode in her life. She certainly had some medical knowledge. She seemed to have a happy and successful life with Bud Reardon, who was a good man.

Bud Reardon developed a cancer which spread and he was sick for a long time. He was ill for so long that he had exhausted all sick pay available to him and applied for leave without pay. He still had a Federal Employees Group Life Insurance policy, however, which would pay out on his death.

On 7 September 1974, Virginia explained to sixteen-year-old Butch that his father was not going to be alive much longer. Then she told her two sons, who were older than Butch, to take the boy out on the town, and gave them $20 to enjoy themselves. When they returned, Virginia told Butch his father was dead. She set about claiming the civil service death benefit due on her former husband, and the insurance.

Butch himself did not wait to be insured. He left a few days after his father's funeral, an event to which neither his mother nor his brothers were invited.

Jimmy Coates married a woman called Debbie Abell who had a baby, Jackie. Virginia played the doting grandmother, to the extent of encouraging Debbie to take out life insurance on the child. Debbie was not keen on the idea, and Virginia offered her $500 to adopt her daughter. Debbie said no.

There were two fires at the Reardon household within a matter of weeks of Bud's death, and Virginia and the boys left for California. The trail becomes rather murky after this, which was presumably Virginia's object in moving so frequently.

Steven Keeney mounted a five-year investigation to uncover the truth behind the death of Deana Wild and McGinnis's other crimes. It is the subject of David Heilbroner's book, *Death Benefit*, detailing the frustrations and triumphs of this dedicated lawyer who was not even working in his own field when he was assembling a murder case.

In April 1984, Virginia married B. J. McGinnis, a former navy man who had spent his life in swindles. In earlier years he had been a debonair confidence trickster. He was homosexual but this did not stop him from marrying women. Virginia, indeed, was his fifth wife. One of his marriages lasted only three months. He would charm women, marry them and spend their money, then make off with whatever he could. A divorce settlement alone would give him half their possessions. Like all such con-men, he would have to give the impression he was wealthy. With Virginia's expensive clothes and jewellery, she gave the same impression. Each of these swindlers was marrying the other for what they could get, and all they got in the end was each other. For once justice had been done.

Virginia introduced her new husband to the world of insurance fraud. They had moved to a house in Palo Alto, near San Francisco, which in June 1985 caught fire and was half-destroyed. State Farm Insurance settled for $80,000, which was to be paid directly into the rebuilding of the house. In July, after the Coates boys had been seen piling their mother's best furniture into a truck and driving it away, the house burned down. This time State Farm Insurance paid out $127,255.

Virginia moved to Chula Vista, San Diego. She did not believe in allowing her home insurance policy to lie fallow. In March 1986 she claimed $1169 for wind damage to the house; in October she claimed $9079 for an alleged burglary; and later that month $885 for water damage. That same month her Datsun pick-up truck was stolen and set on fire, and that was an insurable loss too.

The boys had grown up to be a credit to their mother's values. In Kentucky they had a number of juvenile convictions for such things as drink driving and assault, but Ronnie, more seriously, was charged with kidnapping, robbery and burglary. He fled the state and had to be hunted down and returned, and was convicted of burglary and criminal conspiracy. In California his convictions included receiving stolen property, burglary, possession of drugs, forgery, and assault with a deadly weapon. Finally, in 1985, he was sent away for five years on a charge of assault with a deadly weapon, having originally faced a murder charge.

Jimmy Coates, Deana's fiancé-to-be, had been in trouble with the law for most of his life, including assault, hit-and-run, burglary and receiving stolen property. In 1977, he shot dead a San Francisco drug dealer and was convicted of murder. He received parole in 1982 but early in 1983 he was re-arrested for receiving stolen property and then, after another offence committed while he was awaiting trial on this one, was arrested for burglary, for which he received a four-year sentence. This was the person Deana met, and who introduced her to the folks back home while he was out on parole in late 1986 or early 1987. He was picked up for theft again in February 1987.

He was clearly going to receive his fourth prison sentence, this time for offending while on parole, and he did receive a sixteen-month sentence in March 1987. In the preceding weeks, however, it was obvious that he would be in prison when Deana's insurance policy came through and it was time for her to die, according to Virginia McGinnis's plan. No one could accuse him, the principal beneficiary, of being at all involved in the death. All his affairs, however, had been handed over to his mother under power of attorney when he realised he would soon be inside again. The insurance money might be his, but she was the only one who had access to it while he was in prison.

Mac McCain, running an insurance office in Chula Vista, the rundown area of San Diego where McGinnis lived, remembered Virginia, B. J. and Deana coming to see him in mid-February, as did his son Art. They remembered the improbable story that Virginia McGinnis wanted to buy a life insurance policy on Deana so that they could obtain a visa to go to Mexico. In order to obtain a visa, McGinnis said, they needed a social security number and in order to obtain a social security number they needed life insurance. This was a crazy set of statements. As Art McCain said, they needed the social security number for the policy anyway, so there was no deal.

Several days later, on 27 February, Virginia, B. J. and Deana came in again. Deana needed insurance, Virginia said, because she was going to marry her son James. It was more usual for two young people intending to marry to take out insurance in each other's favour, but Virginia said this was not necessary, James had enough insurance. Deana and B. J. both wanted policies. Deana hardly spoke until her medical history was asked for. She did not even say in what sum she wanted to be insured or who the beneficiaries were to be.

Deana had signed the insurance in her maiden name of Deana Hubbard. The primary beneficiary was down as James Coates, who was thirty, her 'fiancé'.

Next in line was Virginia McGinnis, who was fifty, and her relationship was said to be 'Mother-to-be'. Forty-seven-year-old Billie McGinnis was next as 'Father-to-be'.

The McCains were suspicious and would not issue the policies, but sent them to State Farm Insurance's head office for approval with a 'red flag' letter. This was a memo which literally had a small red flag motif on it, and indicated that the McCains wanted special attention paid to the applications for these policies before they were issued. State Farm approved Deana's policy, but not B. J.'s on account of his medical history. He was uninsurably ill.

Virginia McGinnis's explanation for Deana taking out the insurance, when she was questioned by Bobbie Roberts in the secretly taped telephone conversation, was:

B. J. had wanted to increase his insurance, uh, because he had quit the Veteran's Administration; he'd taken out one. And she said, 'Well what about me, am I chopped liver?'

And we laughed and said, 'Well, an insurance policy, what would you want with one at your age?' And the insurance agent agreed and said that, you know, at her age, that he wished someone had urged him to take one out. That it would have matured and made a nice tidy income. I think it was one of those things where you pay twenty years or something like that.'

On 1 April, the McGinnises and Deana arrived to pick up the policy. Virginia paid the $68 premium with a cheque drawn on an account using her previous name, Virginia Reardon. Mac McCain handed the policy to Deana but Virginia grabbed it and asked for confirmation that it was in force. She left but looked back to ask if it covered accidental death. It did, but not with double indemnity.

Mac and Art McCain next saw Virginia McGinnis when she came in to say Deana was dead and to ask when she would get the cheque. Mac McCain explained they would be sending her a claim form.

In his cell, Jimmy Coates heard of his

fiancée's death. Virginia wrote to him, 'Last Thursday 4-2-87 we were going up Highway 1 coast (near Big Sur) and had stopped at a lookout point and took some pictures, and to see the view. Deana was with us and slipped and fell down the cliff.' The letter ended, 'P.S. The dog is fine and we are okay.'

Steven Keeney, working with his secretary Sarah West, spent months compiling a dossier on the case, collecting documents and interviewing witnesses like Deborah Cross of the Coast Gallery, the McCains, and police officers. Finally he organised it into a vast memorandum to the Monterey County District Attorney's Office. Another followed after further research.

They responded with a letter which said, 'All the events which led to the demise of Ms Hubbard-Wild only point to one reasonable interpretation. However, our major stumbling block is criminal agency . . . ' Investigation was said to be continuing, but a brief reply couched in negative terms did not augur well for the case.

Keeney was hampered by several

factors. Principally the problem was the unwillingness of the authorities to take any action, feeling that there was not enough evidence to go to trial. In the United States, the scales of justice are weighted against the prosecution in that an infinite number of minor rulings conspire to prevent evidence from being presented. The question was not really whether Virginia and B. J. McGinnis were guilty, or even whether there was the evidence which would prove beyond reasonable doubt that they were guilty. The question was whether there was sufficient evidence which could be placed before a jury.

Political factors also conspired against Keeney. It was not only the usual bureaucratic inertia. The Monterey District Attorney's office also suffered low morale because of their ignominious failure in the courts in two high-profile cases. They did not want a third. The next time they went into court in a blaze of publicity they had to come out the victors and there was no such certainty in this case.

Another factor was the reluctance of natural allies like State Farm Insurance to go the distance. A State Farm employee actually told Keeney that $35,000 was one of the smallest life claims they had dealt with that year. The implication was obvious: it would cost less to pay up and forget it than to fight.

The resolution of the case was hastened by Jimmy Coates, who was released on parole, at which time he began legal proceedings against State Farm Insurance for withholding the payout on his fiancée's policy. Steven Keeney knew he had a very good chance of being successful. Though State Farm had been diligently investigating Virginia McGinnis, their legal justification for holding on to the money wavered between thin and non-existent. Virginia might be as wicked as they come, but the only thing she had done wrong with Deana's insurance was to forge the name of her next-door neighbour (which she spelled incorrectly) as a witness on the claim form asking for the payout.

State Farm's position was one blow to Steven Keeney's crusade. The next was that the Monterey District Attorney finally decided to take no action over

Deana's death. Keeney was at the end of the line. Not only were the guilty going to walk away from a murder laughing, they were going to be paid for it.

Finally he decided, with Bobbie Roberts, that if the authorities would not prosecute the murderers, they would do it themselves. Steven Keeney filed a civil case for wrongful death against Virginia and B. J. McGinnis. This would mean that at least they would have a trial, and all the publicity this would generate.

Keeney made out a complaint alleging wrongful death and filed it with the Superior Court of the State of California for the County of Monterey. The complaint was served on Virginia and B. J. McGinnis and they simply ignored it. In the absence of a defence, the complaint had a victory by default, but no McGinnises answering questions on the witness stand, which is what Keeney wanted, and what the criminals wanted to avoid. At least a judgement allowed them access to private documents like the McGinnises' bank accounts and property ownership details.

When the case was heard, on 4 April

1989, the judge awarded Bobbie Roberts $285,000 in damages and condemned the McGinnises' 'incredibly violent and despicable conduct'. Of course, there was no way of actually recovering the money, and debts meant nothing to the McGinnises, particularly B. J., who was now in a nursing home, having had a stroke.

Virginia McGinnis had a new home in the neighbourhood of Pittsburg, California. Investigation of the records, however, showed that before the civil judgement against her she had given this house to her son Ronnie Coates. There was no judgement against his property.

The next bright idea came from an unexpected quarter: a San Diego detective called Jack Haeussinger who had experience of Virginia McGinnis's family suggested to Steven Keeney that if the District Attorney for Monterey, where the murder happened, would not take action, why not try the District Attorney for San Diego? The insurance policy had been bought there, and it was clearly part of a conspiracy to murder. This was more of a long shot but

Haeussinger, armed with Keeney's impressive file of evidence, now running to more than 600 pages, badgered the San Diego District Attorney until he was prepared to look at the case. It was eventually given to Deputy District Attorney Luis Aragon, probably with the intention that he would bury it and forget about it. In fact, Aragon was hooked, and he booked himself in for the job, and the services of a full-time investigator.

The investigation went over much of the ground Keeney had covered. It examined the suspicious death of Virginia's mother, who had died, supposedly of a heart attack, some months after the old lady had bought the house in which they were all living in San Diego. There was also the keen realisation of how much B. J. was under Virginia's control. It was even suggested that she had kept him in a drugged state, and no one doubted that if he had been fit enough to be insured he would not have lived long.

Virginia and B. J. McGinnis were arrested at their separate addresses on 15 September 1989. The bail was set at $5 million each. B. J. was watched particularly carefully as he was expected to breakdown and inform on Virginia but he did not. Given his state of health, there would be no benefit to him in confessing to a minor role in the murder in order to gain a reduced sentence. Whatever the sentence he was likely to die in prison. It would be more sensible to protest innocence and hope for an acquittal.

The seriousness of the crime, 'murder for profit', merited the death penalty in California, though the District Attorney had to file an application for it. Doing so was a grave mistake. The courts understandably expect a far higher standard of evidence when a defendant's life is at stake. They also make far more resources available to the defence: two lawyers and four investigators to each defendant, with an unlimited budget. This meant the McGinnis side would range four lawyers and eight investigators against Luis Aragon and one investigator.

With the number of delays, appeals and stays of execution, which happened even when a death sentence was passed, a 53–year-old woman like Virginia McGinnis and a 50–year-old in poor health like B. J. would probably end up dying of natural causes in prison, even if they were sentenced to death.

The delays started immediately with the 'death qualified' lawyers arguing for extra time to prepare the new case. They also moved to have all previous evidence of deaths and all of Virginia McGinnis's arson and insurance frauds excluded from the trial; it might prejudice a jury against her. The judge agreed and excluded everything excepting the household insurance claims made while McGinnis lived in Chula Vista, San Diego.

The insurance claim was settled with Coates finally accepting $7500, representing the interest on the lump sum, and Bobbie Roberts receiving the $35,000. Again it was a case of blind justice. Bobbie Roberts would rather no one received the money for her daughter's murder. She had pitched in not to get the money herself but to deny it to the killer and her family. In the end she got it, but they were paid off too.

Another dreadful mistake shook the

prosecution when B. J.'s medical records were ordered. The hospital accidentally sent his psychiatric records which are forbidden to the District Attorney under regulations governing psychiatrist-patient privilege. Luis Aragon read them, learning nothing of interest, and gave them to the judge, who was angry at Aragon's misconduct. He could have dismissed the entire case; instead he demoted it: it was no longer a death penalty case, but all the benefits of a death penalty case would remain to the defendants.

Another blow to the prosecution was the suicide of Virginia's first husband, Dick Coates. He threw himself off a bridge on to a dry creekbed. Many people thought the pressure of the impending case, where he was going to give evidence, and the number of investigators he had seen, had taken their toll on his morale.

Innumerable delays meant it was more than two years after their arrest before the couple were facing trial. Then, in December 1991, a month before the trial was due to begin, B. J. died in prison from an AIDS-related pneumonia, still without a confession.

The trial itself, after the jury selection, commenced on 6 January 1992. Virginia McGinnis's hair was freshly dyed and she was softly made up. She was wearing bright colours and even her weight seemed to give her a matronly air. She did not look like a guilty woman.

The prosecution's case was that insuring Deana and taking her to Big Sur had been the premeditation for the murder, which also included giving her a tablet of Elavil. She was not betrothed to James Coates, since she was already married.

The defence made an issue of the fact that Deana's behaviour in San Diego could not be considered that of a married woman, so it was understandable that Jimmy Coates would not know she was married. The prosecution called witnesses who would say things like, 'She would fuck everything, including a rattlesnake.' The notion that a victim's sexual promiscuity can be a justification for her murder is a contaminated argument which the jury showed no sign of endorsing.

158

More compellingly, the defence argued that Deana took all sorts of drugs, and taking an Elavil to see what it did was characteristic. Deana used to smoke dope and 'pop pills'. Kindly, maternal Virginia McGinnis gave her a safe haven of respectability from a life of drugs and sex.

Jimmy Coates, tattooed and needle-scarred, testified convincingly that he wanted a wife because he knew he was going back to prison and a wife had special access. He wanted someone who would smuggle drugs in for him and provide sex when private visits were allowed, presumably as a reward for good behaviour. Deana, he claimed, was prepared to do this.

On the other hand, with her marriage having broken up, and her seemingly directionless life, perhaps it was suicide. The array of different arguments were a classic smokescreen defence: give alternative reasons for suspicious events, none of which have to fit together; question the credibility of the prosecution's evidence. For all the witnesses who remembered Deana in Kentucky as a church-going girl who nursed a single drink all night, the defence could bring one who remembered Deana hanging round bars in San Diego with a bunch of drug takers, having sex with any of them.

It was agreed to take the jury 500 miles to see the spot where Deana had died at Big Sur. The prosecution argued that this cliff was not a sheer drop, but for some distance was a slope. No one would go over with just one false step; it was more likely that an already unconscious body had been thrown down there. The defence argued that a slip was a perfect possibility, particularly in unsuitable shoes. There was an iron spike near the edge which it would be easy to trip over. Moreover, there was a house overlooking that point above Seal Bay. Would a carefully planning murderer really commit the act where she could be so easily seen?

Virginia McGinnis did not give evidence. When the jury returned on 2 March 1992, the sixth day after they had retired to consider their verdict, she

160

was as emotionless as she had been throughout the trial. The jury members had nicknamed her 'the Ice Lady'. On all four counts — of murder, conspiracy, insurance fraud and forgery — she was found guilty. Steven Keeney opened the champagne. She was sentenced to Life Without Possibility of Parole, which was the only possible sentence, excepting death, when a prisoner had been convicted of murder for gain.

* * *

As the defence asked, why not kill Deana in Mexico? Why not obtain the insurance from another agency where McGinnis was not known as she was in the McCain agency? It was probably Virginia McGinnis's need for excitement. She had always been daring and brazen in her crimes, even her thefts and arson. It was the sense of danger, the closeness to detection, which really thrilled. Deana could have been killed for money more easily, but McGinnis was not only interested in money — not all of her crimes had even given her a financial reward. She lit fires, then stood and watched them. She was shameless and even ostentatious about crime because it was not just a business. It really excited her.

Kallinger and Son

FOR a while demolition work stopped as the body of a white teenager was fished out of stagnant water under a derelict site at Philadelphia's Ninth and Market streets. Then the hammers started again and the workers continued to pound the building into rubble. The body was taken to the city morgue and police investigators tried to identify it. It was a young man dressed in jeans, sneakers and a shirt, but was too bloated by decomposition in the water to be identified. Trawling through the missing persons register established, three days after the discovery, on 12 August 1974, that it was probably that of Joey Kallinger. This fourteen-year-old was reported missing on 28 July. He was the son of a shoe-mender who lived and worked at North Front Street in the same city.

The father, Joseph Kallinger, was brought to the police station to give more information on the missing boy. He was easy to identify. The broken bones that were detected in the boy's foot had been caused by a fall from a roof, from which he was still limping when he went missing. Kallinger was driven to the morgue and was able to identify the clothes as those of his son: a charred patch on his jeans had been caused by an incident involving petrol some days before he disappeared. Finally, he was asked to identify photographs of the body. It was in too advanced a state of decomposition for the police to allow a relative to see it.

It was difficult to determine even the cause of death. Perhaps he was a runaway who had starved; perhaps it was a sex-motivated murder and the body had been dumped; perhaps he was exploring the derelict site and had slipped and drowned. The family held a small funeral and their grief disappeared in the sea of private misery as the life of the city went on.

Up in the police headquarters, known as the Roundhouse, Lieutenant James F. O'Neill of Homicide Division continued to sift through the evidence. The boy,

Joey Kallinger, had not been a model child. At the age of eleven he had been arrested for shouting obscenities at a policeman who had ordered him to stop dumping rubbish on a pavement; at twelve he was arrested for theft from a railway car, receiving stolen goods and vandalism. At thirteen he was arrested for vandalism on railway property and trespassing. At the same age he was involved with a 34–year-old homosexual. He had been committed to the Eastern State School and Hospital, which was for emotionally disturbed children, and ran away from there at least once. He was diagnosed as a schizophrenic.

On a weekend at home he and some friends again went to play on the railway, and needed to jump from a nearby roof on to the platform. Joey miscalculated and fell three storeys, breaking his foot. He was eventually returned from the State School in May 1974, on the condition that he receive treatment as a patient at a psychiatric hospital. Other Kallinger children had been in trouble with the law on charges including shoplifting, burglary and robbery.

The father was also an interesting case. A 37–year-old shoe-mender, he liked to be called a shoe-maker, and was, indeed, a gifted craftsman of orthopaedic shoes. Two years before Joey's death his father had been convicted of child abuse after assaults were reported by three of his children, including Joey. At the beginning of 1974, however, something had made the children retract their previous testimony and call for a new trial on the charges.

Previously, Kallinger had been charged with arson and had been acquitted. In the 1960s he had collected $26,000 in insurance claims over three years for three fires. And, just weeks before his disappearance, Joey Kallinger had been insured by his father with the Metropolitan Life Insurance Company, who, with double indemnity, would pay $24,000.

On 26 September 1974, police called at Kallinger's home at 4 a.m. and escorted him to the Roundhouse. He was not under arrest, but it was pointed out somewhat emphatically that if he did not come, he would be made to do so. He called his lawyer and went under protest.

Lieutenant O'Neill viewed with scepticism the wiry, darkhaired man's protestations that his rights were being infringed. O'Neill tried every tough policeman's ruse to get Kallinger to talk but he stuck to his story. He had known nothing about his son's death until it was reported to him by the police. The police were now persecuting him because he was taking legal action against them for their prosecution of him on evidence they had fabricated in the child abuse case two years previously. He refused to take a lie-detector test or to make any kind of a statement.

O'Neill knew he was at the end of the line. With an indeterminate cause of death, he could not even prove that a murder had been committed. With no confession or corroborative evidence his prime suspect was going to walk out. He had to let Kallinger go, and at 10 a.m. he walked free into the autumn morning. O'Neill sat brooding over the case. He not only knew Kallinger was the killer, he knew he would kill again. The

Lieutenant would have felt much worse had he known that Joey Kallinger was not the murderer's first victim.

★ ★ ★

The father of the dead boy, Joseph Kallinger, had been an illegitimate baby who was given up for adoption to the Catholic Children's Bureau. He was adopted at two years old by Anna and Stephen Kallinger, middle-aged Catholics from Central Europe. Stephen was a shoe-maker who owned his own shop and the house above it, making the Kallingers better off than their neighbours in the poor district of Philadelphia where they lived.

They were childless and, as they never ceased to remind Joseph Kallinger, had rescued him from the orphanage only so that he could be a shoe-maker, inherit the family business and look after them in their old age. They frequently threatened to send him back to the orphanage. They had a guilt-ridden attitude to sex which they imposed on the child — the denial of sex seemed to be the only subject on which this couple was passionate. They urged the child from the age of six to be impotent, telling him his penis became stiff because of a devil inside him, which they thought would make him avoid any sort of sexual behaviour. Joseph was subjected to cruel and unusual punishments, including being forced to kneel on sandpaper; regularly having his hands burned on the kitchen stove, and being hit on the head with a hammer.

Neighbours testified to the way the Kallingers would keep Joseph in, making him work all the time and not letting him out with other children. The family had all material benefits, however, and to show his value to them he was insured, even at the age of two, for $1000.

In early adolescence, Joseph started feeling the overwhelming urge to 'do something wrong' and he would steal or vandalise things. Once he slashed the other children's coats in the school cloakroom. Masturbation fantasies later focused on the shoe-maker's knife which his father used, and he reached orgasm by using a knife to cut holes in pictures of naked women, or stabbing the penises in pictures of men. As a twelve-year-old he would use a knife to terrorise other boys, forcing them to expose themselves to him.

Perhaps surprisingly, at fourteen he met a girl and had a normal, nervous courtship and first had sex at fifteen. There was nothing out of the ordinary about this relationship. He left school at sixteen and moved out of his adoptive parents' house though he continued working in the shop. He became an excellent cobbler, his work won prizes and he had a personal following from people who would come long distances for his shoes.

Part of his life, like his work and courtship, seemed perfectly normal, but Joseph would also have religious visions and at times of stress his body started taking on twisting and turning movements and his head jerked from side to side. A deep laugh would also emit from him, over which he had no control.

He married at sixteen and moved into a house his parents bought for the young couple and he paid the mortgage back to them. They had two children and were happy for the first year of marriage before things began to go wrong. He complained that his wife was slovenly and a poor mother, she complained that he was crazy and in the end left him for another man, leaving the children. He moved back with his adoptive parents, the children were placed with the Catholic Children's Bureau, and he divorced his wife before either of them were twenty.

At twenty-one, Kallinger married a factory worker called Betty Baumgard, who he had met over a long period of waiting at railway stations for visits to his children. They rented a house and took the children. They had an apparently normal life, though Kallinger could only achieve sexual satisfaction by keeping a knife close to the bed. His wife did not know it was there. He soon became domineering, forbidding her to drive and then even to leave the home except to go to work.

He now worked for a shoe repair chain. At work he was known as 'Crazy Joe' and his boss, Richard Kimmell, said that Kallinger had once turned to him and said about a customer, 'I'd like to take this knife and cut her tits off.' Kimmell once went to the Kallinger home and saw that he had an X-ray machine in his living-room to X-ray people's heels to provide a better shoe fit 'and relieve pressure on their brains', as Kallinger had told him. Kallinger knew he was not entirely normal, but he was convinced his mental problems could be 'corrected' by orthopaedic footwear, by harmonising the angle of his feet to his brain function. 'The heel controls the mind,' he would say, believing that different pressures on the heel produced changes in posture which led to chemical changes in the brain.

He later brought heavy shoe-making equipment into the living-room and spent all his free time working on heel adjustments. He performed 43,120 such experiments between 1951 and 1972. As time went on, his theories became more grandiose and he came to believe he could heal the world with his footwear. 'If we all had the correct adjustment of shoes to feet, there'd be no more wars' was one of his many remarks on the subject.

In a curious incident, he got lost one

day, wandering to a town seventy miles north of Philadelphia where he was taken to hospital and diagnosed as amnesiac. He was eventually traced and returned, recovering his memory. His wife, who thought she had been abandoned, left him and went to her mother's but came back when he did.

Kallinger liked collecting electronic junk and making it work. He filled the house with broken television sets, speakers, record players, washing-machines and vacuum cleaners. He dug a vast hole in the kitchen, eight feet in circumference, supposedly as an air-raid shelter but in fact for the overflow of his junk.

His behaviour lurched from the eccentric to the destructive when he one day went home in his lunch-hour and set fire to a shed which caught his house and gutted it. On later reflection he said, 'The fire at Janney Street was my first fire. I collected nineteen hundred dollars in insurance money because nobody — not even Betty — knew how the fire started.'

Kallinger set fire to this house, and claimed insurance on it three times. The fourth time he did so, there was no insurance on it and the family had moved out. He was tried for this fire, in 1967, but was acquitted. At the trial this respectable craftsman and shopkeeper had as character witnesses Harry Comer — his representative on the state legislature who had known him since he was a child — and a Philadelphia Court of Common Pleas judge.

The trial judge said, 'Where there is no testimony as to motive, we must give the defendant the benefit of the doubt,' and let him go. Much later, Kallinger said he had had a vision which commanded him to start at least one of the fires. Mere destructive rage against the world is motive enough for most arsonists.

In 1967, Stephen Kallinger retired and Joseph Kallinger returned to his adoptive parental home and took over the store and the house. He now had five children living with him. A sixth had been returned to her mother, Kallinger's first wife, after a court battle. With the move he developed a new vigour to his experiments, now believing the right adjustments to shoes would bring superhuman powers of endurance. He tested his endurance on long walks at night while the children were sent out to scavenge for junk.

The children were often kept up at night. Kallinger would wake up his eldest daughter, Mary Jo, to pick winning horses according to a formula he had that was based on tides and the phases of the moon. At one minute past midnight each year on the day of his birthday he would awaken all the family for a party, the party he had never had as a child. Indeed, his adoptive parents had never even given him a birthday present.

The family would all go to bed at 7 p.m. – 8 p.m. as they knew that Kallinger would be getting one or more of them up in the middle of the night so they had to make sure they got some sleep.

Life with Kallinger was strange and adventurous for the children. He and his son Joey once went out spraying graffiti on the side of Joey's school. He was also paranoid, barring up the house with excessive security measures. He believed the CIA watched him from the office of the politician Harry Comer, across the street.

In 1969, Kallinger bought a new house to use as a warehouse and a secret refuge at 1808 East Hagert Street, Philadelphia. He had his children, aged between five and thirteen, dig a twenty-foot deep hole under one room, working regularly over a period of two months. He would climb into the hole and be alone there when he was feeling weird. There he would chant in a private language which had no meaning. Squatting in the hole, he decided it was necessary to 'punish and reform' his children.

He set up what was called the 'torture chamber' by the children, because it was. On a metal table in the cellar he lined up heavy rope, two feet of rubber hose, a box of straight pins, strips of leather and a cat o' nine tails. The children were not punished for specific misdemeanours but whenever an 'itch' in Kallinger's hand told him they had misbehaved and, in ten-year-old Mary Jo's case, for not picking winning horses.

In general, the children were delinquent, and were frequently thrown out of school, when they bothered to attend. Some of the children had been involved in theft, including a snatch theft of a purse in the street, shoplifting, setting fires and stealing from freight cars. Stevie, the eldest, was already being accused of robberies. Mary Jo was dating older boys and Joey was having homosexual sex. One time when she was twelve and he was eleven they sold blow jobs to fourteen boys on a roof. Mary Jo collected the money and Joey fellated them for fifty cents each.

Stevie, the eldest, was punished with having a hot lightbulb held to his legs. After he ran away one time, Kallinger handcuffed and footcuffed him to a bed and beat him over a week-long period. Mary Jo was once punished by being stripped and having wire nails thrown at her.

As they never knew when punishment would come, the children stayed away from home as much as possible and became more delinquent, though Mary Jo retained her love for her father, later saying that she felt he abused her because he was mentally ill.

One night, Mary Jo and Joey did not return and Kallinger went to find them with a .45 automatic. When he did he brought them home and sent Betty and the two younger children, eleven-year-old Michael and nine-year old James, out of the room. He handcuffed Joey to the refrigerator. He ordered Mary Jo to strip to her underwear and burned the inner part of her thigh with a spatula which he heated for the purpose. He did this at least twice, until the flesh was charred. He then beat Joey all over his body with the haft of a hammer. Afterwards, he gave them both some money, summoned the others back, and the whole family sat down to a late meal of pizza.

Mary Jo, Joey and Michael now filed child abuse charges against Kallinger and he was arrested on 30 January 1972 and charged with beating and threatening the life of Mary Jo, who was twelve, Joey who was eleven, and Michael who was ten.

Kallinger was unable to raise the bail money and spent seven months in jail awaiting trial. His friendship with the state representative Harry Comer, eventually helped him to be released on a reduced bail. Comer testified to Kallinger's 'excellent reputation' and to the disruptive effect on the neighbourhood of the children.

Old Stephen Kallinger had died a few years earlier but Anna Kallinger, predictably, felt Joseph Kallinger had done nothing wrong, telling her injured grandchild, 'Your father should have burned the other thigh too. You are a very bad girl, to do this to your father, who loved you and worked hard for you.'

Kallinger was eventually found guilty of the assaults on Joey and Mary Jo. There were behind-the-scenes attempts to keep Kallinger locked up by people who realised what a danger he was. The uncertainty of diagnosis was, however, a hindrance. The court psychiatrists generally concluded that Kallinger was not sane but the diagnosis oscillated between paranoid schizophrenia and personality disorder. He was eventually given a suspended sentence for the attack on Joey and four years' psychiatric probation for the attack on Mary Jo. He never received psychiatric help. He was now thirty-six years old and about to enter his most dangerous phase. In the opinion of Flora Schreiber, who wrote the book *The Shoemaker* about Kallinger, psychiatric treatment even at this stage could have prevented the crimes which followed.

Crazy or not, soon after Kallinger had been sentenced, when he had re-established himself in the home, he did a deal with the children. He summoned the three who had accused him and told them how the accusations had hurt business, because customers shied away from the shop. This was in addition to the months when no money was coming in because Kallinger was in prison. Now the family was on welfare. The children did not have the clothes or the food or the money they used to have.

Now, if they would recant their allegations about him before the court, he would be able to clear his name and business would pick up and they would have all the good things in life again. This sounded like a good deal to the children. They were proud of their father's self-employed status and boasted of it to other children: no one told their Dad what to do. They also saw that they would be financially rewarded by this course of action, and enjoyed the idea of tying the police and the courts in knots. Over several months, therefore, Joey and his father constructed a fake diary covering a period much wider than the assaults, detailing progressively how Joey and Mary Jo had conspired to lie about the child abuse. At the beginning of 1974, the children testified in court for a re-trial and Joey's fake diary was submitted in evidence. The family was now together again, with the delinquent Joey out of the Eastern State School and staying with the Kallingers on the condition he receive treatment at a psychiatric hospital. In the summer of that year, Kallinger took out on Joey not only the insurance for $24,000 with Metropolitan Life, which Lieutenant O'Neill was to find out about, but also a policy with the John Hancock Mutual Life Insurance company which would pay Kallinger $45,000 for the accidental death of his son. It carried triple indemnity.

Kallinger had started taking Michael, now twelve, by bus to the suburbs, where Michael would break into empty houses while his father waited outside. Michael committed twenty-four robberies from winter 1973 to summer 1974, then insisted that his father come in with him, and together they entered houses in fourteen towns in Pennsylvania. Kallinger later said he would receive the command to steal from God, who told him it was the precursor to a massacre which would destroy mankind, for he had failed to heal mankind with his orthopaedic wedges.

When friends asked Michael where he had been when he returned from these burglary jaunts he would say, 'Listen, I've been shopping with my Dad, that's where I've been.'

One day, Kallinger explained to his son, 'Mike, I have a strong desire to kill people.' Thus it was that on 7 July 1974 Kallinger went out looking for someone to kill. He later claimed that he took Michael with him, an allegation Michael will neither confirm nor deny.

Kallinger found a Puerto Rican boy of about nine or ten, called José Collazo, who was playing by himself in the street. He lured him to an abandoned factory where he killed him while sexually mutilating him. When there was newspaper coverage after the child's body had been found, Kallinger acted the outraged citizen while he discussed the case with his friend Harry Comer.

Now it was time to kill Joey. Michael and Joey hated each other, as siblings of their age often do, and it was no great problem for Kallinger to enlist Michael's help. Kallinger intended to fake an accident where Joey would fall from a high place: the Grand Canyon seemed a good one, but they missed the bus to the Grand Canyon. They took the next bus out to a high beauty spot, but Kallinger could not summon the courage to throw his son off, and Joey never knew that he was an intended victim.

The next attempt to murder Joey was by burning him in the container of a trailer Michael was to set on fire with petrol given him by his father for the purpose. The procedure was sold to Joey as just a routine act of arson: they would splash some petrol around the trailer then set fire to it. Michael prepared the scene in the back of the trailer and left Joey alone there, supposedly going to get Kallinger. The plan was for him to lock Joey in the petrol-soaked container which he would surely ignite, as he smoked incessantly. Michael closed the container door but did not lock it so he just held it shut with a large milk container. Joey did try to set fire to the petrol by throwing lighted cigarettes at it and eventually ignited it with himself still inside. He ran at the door and smashed aside the barriers Michael had placed there to stop it opening. He leapt out and rolled on the ground to put out the fire on his jeans. Back with his father and brother, he made no complaint about his experiences; it was all part of life with the Kallingers.

The conspirators later wedged him between planks and a ladder in a building under construction, under the pretext of taking photographs, but again Kallinger's courage failed. He said Michael afterwards called him a coward.

On 28 July 1974, the three of them went to a derelict building which Kallinger had suggested would make an atmospheric setting for some photographs.

They took some chains for Joey (he liked to be pictured in bondage poses) and went inside a derelict building on Ninth and Market streets. They descended to the basement, which was flooded with slimy water. Joey consented to being chained and padlocked to a metal ladder and pictured against the running walls. One or both of them then threw the ladder into the water. Joey struggled in the filthy pool and called out, 'Daddy, help me,' then was quiet. They pulled him out of the water, retrieved their locks and chains and went home.

At 11 p.m. that night Kallinger reported Joey missing to the police and over the following days played the part of the concerned parent to perfection, even keeping a tape recorder in his store so that he could record leads about Joey brought to him by people in the neighbourhood. The family published moving pleas for help.

Joey was discovered twelve days later, and identified partly from the scorch marks made on his jeans when he jumped from the burning trailer. Kallinger was interviewed by the police, but the word in the neighbourhood was that Joey had been killed in a homosexual assault and fingers of accusation were pointed at several men, one of whom was taken in but released. Betty was particularly distraught at the funeral that she had not been allowed to see the body, and she resisted the idea that he was dead at all. He was buried next to his grandfather and Anna Kallinger shook her fist at the coffin, saying, 'That Joey took my grave from me.'

Two months after the murder, Kallinger was brought to police headquarters to face Lieutenant O'Neill's questions about Joey's death. They brought him in on Yom Kippur in the hope that his lawyer, Arthur Gutkin, a devout Jew, would not be prepared to be called away from his devotions. Gutkin did come for his client, however and quickly ascertained that there was no proper reason for holding him. Kallinger reacted like a middle-class man with a good relationship with his lawyer, and asked Gutkin to file a civil case against the police for taking him to the police department without a warrant and for detaining him in the interrogation room.

In a small masterpiece of criminal activity, Kallinger now staged a series of set-ups designed to coax the police into arresting him or interrogating him so that he could claim he was being harassed. The first involved Michael, after he had received a bump on his head from a street fight. Kallinger told his son to fall down the stairs in a store, when he was not with him. An ambulance was called and Michael was taken to hospital, whence Kallinger discharged him. That evening, he admitted him to another hospital, where he was known to have been convicted of child abuse. The police were therefore alerted, as a routine procedure, and a case was brought against Kallinger which was easily dismissed: many witnesses had seen Michael receive his injury in the fall in the store.

In the next trick Kallinger told Michael to hide (which he did in his grandmother's basement) and reported him missing. Police then instituted a search for Michael's body, assuming that he too had been killed. They interrogated Kallinger for five hours. Then Michael turned up, checking into a hospital, ostensibly with amnesia.

On another occasion, Kallinger had Michael call the police and give an anonymous tip that someone was breaking in to the house at 1808 East Hagert Street, the one with the pit in it. The boys then went to the house and started acting suspiciously inside it. Police arrived and when the boys refused to open up, they smashed open the door. Joe Kallinger then turned up, and found the police had broken into his house and harassed his kids who had every right to be there . . . he was going to call his lawyer about it.

In yet another incident, Kallinger tried to get arrested, by having Michael make a telephone call that a man carrying a bag of dope was walking with two boys along a particular road near a fairground. The police stopped Kallinger, Michael and Jimmy and asked to see what was in the bag Kallinger was carrying. It was a bag of bones which seemed to be human in origin. He tried to phone his lawyer on the street but a policeman dragged him away from the telephone, handcuffed him and took him to the police station where they put him in a cell.

He was then transferred to the Roundhouse so he could be interrogated again about Joey's death and he again refused to answer any questions. Betty called the faithful Arthur Gutkin, who arrived to have the boys and Kallinger released from cells. The police were still waiting for the result of the laboratory tests on what they now knew were human bones. The Kallingers and Gutkin waited. It cannot have been easy for the police to go back and explain, and apologise to Kallinger. They were old bones, from feet, hooked together with wire: a standard piece of apparatus used by shoe workers like Kallinger.

Arthur Gutkin of course did not know that these were deceptions on Kallinger's part, and genuinely believed the police were harassing his client, whom he defended to the best of his considerable ability. He was convinced of Kallinger's innocence and that he had suffered brutality and indignity at the hands of the Philadelphia police. He was sure he could mount a successful civil rights case against the police department. Kallinger felt that if he did this, the police would not dare touch him again.

Kallinger was undoubtedly troubled by hallucinations and delusions. He was supposedly seeing visions of a disembodied head called Charlie which looked like his drowned son. He had the idea that he had to slaughter everyone on earth by destroying their sexual organs. Undoubtedly, this rich fantasy life had something to do with his behaviour. The question was (and is) did it dictate his behaviour to the extent that he had no control over his own actions?

The final phase of Kallinger's criminal career began on 22 November 1974 when father and son started to go into the suburbs deliberately on the lookout for inhabited houses where they could commit not just burglary as they had before, but aggravated burglary, where injury to women in their homes was part of the crime.

These were leafy suburbs where people knew their neighbours by name and left their doors unlocked, neighbourhoods where the crime of the inner cities had not yet penetrated. The first victim was a woman alone in a house in Lindenwold, New Jersey. Michael approached her under some pretext of selling door-to-door. They both overpowered her, tied her up and Kallinger sexually assaulted her. Finding himself unable to commit rape, he said, 'You just aren't my type, that's all. Goodbye.' They left with a suitcase of stolen property.

The next time, on 3 December 1974, in Susquehanna Township, Pennsylvania, Kallinger used a gun and a knife on a woman and three guests who all arrived independently of each other for a card party. He tied them up, then father and son left with about $20,000 in money and jewels. Kallinger told the victims that if they identified him to the authorities the court system was such that he would soon be back on the streets and would come to get them.

A week later, there was a robbery and sexual assault on a woman living on her own in Baltimore, Maryland, and the following month almost the same scenario in Dumont, New Jersey. Two days after that, on 8 January 1975, Kallinger, dressed in a jacket and tie and with Michael beside him, knocked on the door of a pleasant, timbered house in Glenwood Avenue in Dumont. This well-dressed man accompanied by a boy said he was selling insurance for the John Hancock Mutual Life Insurance Company; were they interested? A woman opened the door fully to apologise, she was not interested. Kallinger pulled out his gun and told her to go inside. He then tied her up, together with another woman and her young son who were also in the house. (An elderly invalid upstairs he left.) Other people came to the door, and as they entered he threatened them, too, and tied them up. After almost two hours the house contained seven people who were being held by Kallinger and Michael: two women upstairs who had been stripped, the four-year-old boy and the invalid. Downstairs were two women, one of them Mrs Romaine, whose home it was, and a man, the boyfriend of one of her daughters.

Maria Fasching, twenty-one, a nurse

and a friend of the family, stopped by to look in on Mrs Romaine's invalid mother as she often did. Maria was slender in build with long dark hair, and was a feminist who was not used to being pushed around. She rang the doorbell and Kallinger answered. She smiled as he opened the door, thinking he was one of Mrs Romaine's guests. He welcomed her, then turned the gun on her when she was in the house. She resisted, asking him what he thought he was doing; there was an invalid in the house and Mrs Romaine's husband was in hospital with a heart condition. This did not impress Kallinger, who tied her up, insisting he was not going to hurt them but just wanted to rob the place.

Kallinger then took the bound man and Maria to the cellar. 'I was always an underground man,' he later explained. He ordered Maria to sexually assault the man. She refused, still bound hand and foot, and he stabbed her in the back, chest and neck. The last words she was heard to say were, 'I thought you weren't going to kill us.'

Now there was no further reason for

restraint by those tied up elsewhere. Additionally, Kallinger's decision to take two victims to the cellar had meant there were eight victims on three floors of the building, being controlled by two assailants. Emboldened by Maria's screams, Mrs Romaine, still tied up, crawled out of her back door on to the lawn, and shouted for neighbours to call the police. Michael ran down to shout at Kallinger that one of them had escaped. They picked up what they had already stolen, amounting to $80 in cash and jewellery, and ran out.

They ran with some speed and escaped from the scene before the police arrived, throwing away the hunting knife they had used and the jewellery they had stolen. These were found in a garden some days later. They reached Sylvan Park, where Kallinger tore off his shirt, which was covered with Maria's blood. He tried to get the blood out of the shirt in a puddle on the ground but gave up and threw the shirt and tie into a garage, running on with just his jacket covering him. They caught a bus for Manhattan where Kallinger waited in a toilet and

Michael went to buy him a new shirt. They then returned home.

An artist's impression of them was put out, based on the description of witnesses. They were described as 'nomads and highly mobile', which could not have been further from the truth: they lived over a shop with their name on the door, and their mobility depended on buses — Kallinger had never learned to drive.

Luckily, a woman out walking her dog had seen Kallinger trying to clean the shirt and she told the police of these suspicious people answering the description of the murderers. The area nearby was searched and Kallinger's shirt and tie were found. The shirt had a laundry mark which detectives endeavoured to trace, by visiting every laundry in the region. The one which matched was at Bright Sun Cleaners, a block from the Kallinger shop. They put individual customer identification marks on every item of laundry, and this one had the mark of the Kallinger family.

On 17 January 1975, nine days after he had killed Maria Fasching, officers from the FBI and police from three states broke down the door of the Kallinger house in North Front Street. Kallinger and Michael were sitting looking at their coin collection, a picture of family peace and happiness, except that in this case the coins father and son were examining had been stolen from one or another suburban house they had burgled.

Lieutenant O'Neill had the great satisfaction of arresting Joe Kallinger, his only regret being that he had not got him earlier. 'I knew you were going to kill again,' he said to him.

Police found a stereo set and jewellery which had been taken from the burglary in Dumont two days before the killing of Maria Fasching. Later, they would also discover $600,000 in cash together with jewels that had been prised from their settings, which were discarded while the jewels were stored in the back of the large machine which was used for finishing and polishing shoes.

Over the remaining days of January victims identified Kallinger and Michael and they were charged in three states with crimes including murder, rape, robbery, assault, and possession of offensive weapons. The community around Kallinger's shop was shocked. Harry Comer, who, after serving twenty-two years, was now no longer on the state legislature, said, 'It's just hard to believe, that's all.' Another neighbour said, 'He was a nice man who worked hard and didn't bother nobody.'

Asked by a reporter about her life with Kallinger, Betty said, 'He's always thoughtful. He never hit me. He never even raised a hand to me. I wouldn't have stayed with him . . . He also makes me feel good . . . I just can't even go into the bedroom with him gone. I just try to sleep on the couch.'

Michael Kallinger was sent to a series of correctional centres, then sent to foster parents. He was put on probation until he was twenty-one under the condition that he finish high school and that he did not write anything about the case. Betty Kallinger wept when he was made a ward of court.

Kallinger was tried first in Pennsylvania, for the burglary, robbery and false imprisonment offences at Susquehanna Township, in which he had tied and robbed the four women who were meeting that morning to play cards. The trial began on 19 June 1975 but there was a mistrial: one of the court staff talked to the jurors about the case, communicating her belief that he was obviously guilty. A new trial started on 8 September 1975. It was suggested by the defence that the accused was not responsible for his actions because he had been inhaling toxic chemicals, principally toluene from the glue used in shoes. Evidence was brought forward to show that toluene can cause intoxication and brain damage.

Kallinger testified that he was one thousand years old and had been a butterfly before he received his present bodily form. These admissions had first been extracted by the use of the 'truth drug' sodium amytal.

Betty Kallinger testified that her husband frequently heard voices, saw things in front of him which were not there and said that he was receiving instructions directly from God. On 16 September, he was found guilty on all nine counts after the jury had been out for just an hour. Judge John Dowling said, 'You are an evil man, Mr Kallinger, utterly vile and depraved,' and sentenced him to a minimum of thirty years in prison, and a maximum of eighty. He later said that what had moved him to impose such a stiff sentence was Kallinger's involvement of his son in crime.

Kallinger's trial, in New Jersey, beginning in August 1976, was for the murder of Maria and other offences, including armed robbery and sexual assault in the Dumont and Lindenwold crimes. Feelings against Kallinger were so strong that people entering the courtroom were screened for weapons in case they tried to kill him.

This time, the defence rested on the 1843 McNaghten Rules which relieve a defendant of criminal responsibility if he was unable to tell right from wrong at the time of the crime. There was no toluene defence this time, the brief was that Joseph Kallinger was barking mad. As the judge was going through the procedure for selecting the jury, Kallinger obliged with a demonstration. He wailed, moaned, sang and chanted.

He chanted 'Aah' at different pitches, calling out 'Maa' and 'Oh aw raa' and making loud sucking sounds. His head jerked and stayed in motion all the time and he indulged in shadow boxing and miming piano playing. He chirped like a bird and stuck his tongue out at the judge. He kept this up for fifty minutes until he had to be removed.

When he was more subdued and was allowed into court again, he took glass from his reading glasses, which he had broken, and tried to cut his wrists in the court. He was stopped before he could do any damage. He had also tried to cut his wrists on the zipper from a pair of trousers.

In his prison career in New Jersey he had started to smear faeces on the walls, throw food into the walkway outside, and he stuffed the toilet so that it overflowed. He claimed that it was the ghostly head 'Charlie' which compelled him to do these things. He mounted a defence against Charlie by filling cups with water and standing them in rows just outside his cell. He also claimed there was blood in his urine which on examination turned out to be plum juice.

Kallinger's behaviour caused a problem for the defence, it was so obviously bogus. One of the expert witnesses, a psychiatrist called Dr Irwin N. Perr, said that Kallinger had 'faked behaviour he may view as being crazy' in recent days and months, but that did not mean he was sane. He was insane and could not tell right from wrong, but had taken care not to be detected because 'he had an awareness that these acts were illegal and likely to get him into trouble'. Dr Perr said that Kallinger had 'a psychosis in which there is a veneer of rationality'. His diagnosis was that Kallinger was a chronic paranoid schizophrenic.

Perr was one of two psychiatrists to testify that Kallinger was insane in their opinion. The prosecution had four to say the opposite. One of them, Dr Joseph F. Zigorelli, said, 'I feel that this individual never was a paranoid schizophrenic and still isn't.' He had a personality disorder and was antisocial.

The jury was not convinced with the insanity defence. The jury foreman, a white-haired housewife, added for the record after the verdict, 'As for the question of whether he was insane on January 8 1975, the answer is no.'

On 14 October 1976 Judge Thomas F. Dalton sentenced Kallinger to life for the murder, consecutive with thirty years for the robberies. He would therefore never be released, however much remission of sentence he received. Kallinger kept his eyes down during sentencing and made no display of emotion.

In August 1977, he was tried in Camden County, New Jersey, for crimes committed while breaking into two houses in Lindenwold: breaking and entering, robbery while armed and assault with attempt to commit rape. Insanity caused by chemical means, and for psychiatric reasons had been tried, his defence now was that Kallinger's madness had an organic base. Kallinger asked to be examined for Huntington's chorea, a nervous condition causing twitching and brain deterioration. Doctors found he did not have this condition, and a jury again rejected an insanity plea. He was sentenced to not less than forty-two nor more than fifty-one years in jail.

In jail, he made two other suicide attempts, by setting fire to his cell and by trying to choke himself with the plastic cover of his mattress. He started to chew the flesh of his fingertips. He was responsible for two more jail fires, one of which caused serious damage and led to an evacuation of the cell block. In 1978, he almost killed a 23-year-old man serving a sentence for burglary with a carefully crafted home-made strangling tool and a pair of scissors. It was only after this attack that he instructed his lawyer to drop all suits against the Philadelphia Police Department for their alleged persecution of him. He had finally realised it was a lost cause.

Sometimes he would speak of his son Joey in heaven with his own private nurse, Maria Fasching. Michael Kallinger now lives under another name.

★ ★ ★

The case of Joseph Kallinger is truly perplexing. As the prosecution in his murder trial conceded, anyone who did these things had to be abnormal to some degree. But was he mad? The defence offered two paradoxes: a madman feigning insanity; and the question of whether a person knows something is wrong when he certainly knows it is against the law.

Flora Rheta Schreiber of the John Jay College of Criminal Justice, New York, spent many hours in conversation with Kallinger over six years. Her book, *The Shoemaker*, treats him more as victim than criminal, as a victim of child abuse and of destructive parental attitudes. She found him 'verbal and analytical, charming, intelligent, and poetic. Extraordinarily sensitive, he was also a murderer who could not tell the difference between his visions and reality.'

Schreiber builds up a picture of a man who has to kill because of his delusional fantasies about murdering the whole human race by chopping off their sexual organs. She describes how he claims these delusions led him through his crimes. Many people have perverted fantasies, however, and if they do nothing about them the world is none the worse for it. The evidence that Kallinger was not completely out of control was that he in fact did not act out his fantasies to a lethal degree.

Altogether, Kallinger had seventeen victims under his control: José Collazo, Joey, the four women at the card party, three individual women and the eight in the Romaine household. Sexual mutilation did not happen to any of the women. Attempted rape and forced fellatio happened, and robbery of goods in the victims' homes together with their personal jewellery. Of the seventeen victims, only poor José Collazo was sexually mutilated and he was the first victim, so it was not as if Kallinger was leading up to a hallucinatory crisis.

Care has to be taken in writing about this subject, as neither Kallinger nor Michael were tried for José's murder. The lack of trial evidence means we have to take the word of Kallinger in his confession to Flora Schreiber as to what happened. It is his statement that Michael sexually assaulted the boy (directly leading to the child's death) at his insistence. This would at least concur with the evidence of other attacks, that Kallinger's perversions compelled him to order others to commit sexual mutilations; he did not do it himself. It should be emphasised, however, that Michael Kallinger neither confirms nor denies that he was involved in any way with this murder, and that it occurred when he was twelve years old and was under the direct supervision of his father.

It is interesting that Kallinger's hallucinations of world massacre did not involve attacking adult males in the street, who might fight back. He was not so mad that he would attack anyone, just women and children.

Was he even a crazed lunatic who had to kill? If he were really driven to kill, he had seven bound and defenceless women whom he could have killed in the four aggravated burglaries before that of the Romaine house. In fact, he expressed his perverted sexual desire with them, and displayed his inadequate personality by binding them and ordering them around. Even the last killing, of Maria Fasching, was not perpetrated because of some psychotic delusion of a global massacre, but because the brave woman refused to injure another victim's genitals, which is what Kallinger had ordered her to do.

What he did do in these homes, apart from the assaults on the individuals, was to steal whatever valuables he could find. It is not coincidental that the burglaries, including those conducted by Michael alone where there were no assaults, were all committed when business was bad at the shop. This was due to Kallinger's inability to work resulting from his imprisonment on the child abuse charges, and the decline in business resulting from the bad publicity surrounding it. Moreover, whether it is literally true or not that he believed himself to be under divine guidance, the mode in which Kallinger and his son operated was identical to that of burglars who could not claim a direct relationship with the Almighty.

Kallinger thus was many times in a position to put his obscene ideas into practice but did not do so, probably because they were not so strong as his greed, for which he stole, or his lust, which led him to commit acts of sexual abuse.

Why, then, did he kill José Collazo? The reason, ugly almost beyond the limits of imagination, is that it was practice. Kallinger had not killed anyone before, and he wanted to see if he could do it. He did find killing difficult — he tried three times to kill Joey before succeeding on the fourth. For this important murder, of his son, he had to get it right. Like the craftsman he was, Kallinger first did a practice run . . . on material which was of no value to him.

So why did he kill Joey? Partly for the insurance money, and not out of mere greed: Joey owed it to him. Kallinger had been tremendously proud of the way he worked in his business, of the way he had built up a clientele and had always provided for his large family. The child abuse charges had all but destroyed his business and for this he chiefly blamed Joey. His attitude to child abuse was the same as that of any other abuser: to deny publicly that such a dreadful thing had ever happened, and to assert in private that they had deserved it and he had a right to do it anyway.

By killing Joey he asserted his right to his control over his children, and with the insurance he recovered some of the money he had lost. Joey paid him back. He had already induced the boy to retract the charges in court. Detectives dealing with the case thought to warn at least Mary Jo that she would be next, and when Michael supposedly went missing they thought it confirmed their fears.

Though Kallinger was undoubtedly insane by any accepted use of the term, this does not mean that he was beyond control or responsibility for his actions. Does someone who believes the world is going to end in a holy massacre insure their victims first? It is not without Biblical precedent for God to tell a father to kill his son, but are we seriously to believe that God told him to take out accident insurance on the boy too?

Cruel Lessons

ON a busy, hot Saturday night in August 1978, a couple of teenagers sat by the side of the road in a Pennsylvania shopping centre eating and chatting. Their attention was suddenly caught by a car driving slowly into the car park in front of them. It stopped by a Chevrolet van and a tall man left the car and peered into the van. Over his head was a hood and in each hand he carried a gun.

The couple crept away, shocked to the core at what they had seen, and immediately called the police. As an officer interviewed them by the car park, they saw again the hooded man's brown Ford Grenada. 'I think that's the car,' the young man shouted.

Within minutes a call was out for the car. Lieutenant Carl Brown from the Tredyffrin Township police and his sergeant, sitting in their squad car, saw the brown Ford Grenada driving

210

erratically down the Valley Forge Road.

They pulled the car over with signals and flashing lights. The driver, a middle-aged man, stood by the side of his car as the officers approached. They fixed him in the beams of their flashlights. They asked for his driver's licence and he said it was in the car. The sergeant had walked the other way around so he was behind the man, who reached into his front seat and pulled out a .22 calibre pistol which he raised towards Carl Brown.

'Drop it,' shouted the lieutenant, raising his own weapon. The flashlight showed the pistol rising. Lieutenant Brown realised with horror that he could not shoot. The sergeant was right behind the man; if he fired he would hit his partner too. His finger froze on the trigger. 'Drop it now,' he shouted as the man's gun stayed poised at him.

'Oh my goodness,' the man suddenly said, and dropped the weapon.

They handcuffed the man and read him his rights. In the car, on the passenger seat, they found a bag with a .38 calibre, .22 calibre and .25 calibre gun. There was a hood mask, a bolt cutter and other tools for breaking into cars. There was also an oil filter adapted as a home-made silencer for the .22 calibre pistol.

There was a syringe in the car and another in the man's pocket. Both contained ethchlorvynol, a tranquillising drug known under the brand name Placidyl. Apparently more innocent items in the car included black rubbish bags, tape and gloves.

Just as surprising as the finds in the car was the identity of the hooded man. On 19 August 1978, Lieutenant Carl Brown had arrested Dr Jay Smith, the principal of Upper Merion High School, and a colonel in the US Army reserves.

Smith was all charm after his arrest. He knew he had done wrong but it was in a good cause. He had been looking for his daughter and son-in-law who, he feared, were being held in the Chevrolet van by drug dealers. The syringes belonged to his son-in-law.

Smith, at fifty years old, was a dark-haired and fleshy man with reptilian eyes. Born in 1928 to the Pennsylvania family of a shipbuilder and union organiser,

Smith was an excellent scholar, whose education was interrupted when he was drafted into the army at the end of the Second World War. He flourished in the army and was a member of the army reserves the whole of his life. By the late 1970s he was being considered for promotion to general.

He married Stephanie in 1951. She was some years older than Smith, and came from a similar poor background. She waited for him while he served in the Korean War, and she worked hard to put him through college. Their work paid off when he began to move up through the education system.

His promotions eventually led to his taking over as principal of Upper Merion High School in 1973. It was a school with a good academic record in an affluent area twenty miles northwest of Philadelphia. He took a doctorate in education while he was principal.

His staff considered Smith a sinister figure, who mixed high intellectual ability with blatant sexual suggestiveness. They could not dispute that he was academically strong, with an exceptional memory — he could remember whole sections of books and the names of all the students. He was also secretive and locked himself in his room alone for long periods, and for some reason no one ever asked of him, he brought his black plastic rubbish bags to work to put them in the school's dustbins.

Smith kept his personal life secret, including even details of his family. Most of his staff could not have even said whether he was married. He lived in a suburb close to the school called King of Prussia. His wife, Stephanie, was a blonde with a fine figure who liked to wear short skirts, but whose face showed the ravages of time. She worked at a dry cleaner's, an unusually menial job for the wife of a school principal.

Stephanie was concerned about his extreme sexual tastes. Smith was having sex with two teachers, one black and one white, who were not from his school. Smith enjoyed telling his wife about his unusual sexual exploits with them. When Stephanie Smith ventured into his private, locked basement room, she found items for dressing up, handcuffs, an enema bag, and two dildos: a small pink one and a large black one which could squirt water. Stephanie would also say that Smith had found a way to watch his daughter (also called Stephanie) and son-in-law having sex.

Stephanie found a letter he had written to another school principal in a neighbouring county:

Lovewoman, Our relationship has been the greatest thing that has ever happened to me . . . No matter what we've done, I still love your blowjobs the best, and get red hot looking in the mirror, watching my cock go in and out of your precious lips . . . Even though I got your arse virginity and we'll do some fistfucking this summer (where did you get the idea of fistfucking?) I prefer your mouth to your cunt or your arsehole.

His private life seemed to have few restraints, but he kept it to himself.

An event which was not marked as being of great significance at the time was that Smith's daughter, Stephanie, and her husband Eddie Hunsberger, both drug addicts, went missing in February 1978. Jay Smith told Eddie's parents that he had fled to California because there was a warrant out for his arrest for forging drug prescriptions but when they checked with the police they found this was not true. Stephanie Smith confided to a friend that she thought Jay had killed them, cut up their bodies and destroyed them with acid.

Smith had been apprehended in criminal activity before his arrest in August 1978 — he had been caught shoplifting more than once but had managed to get out of it with a caution. Stephanie Smith left her husband before the arrest, and filed for divorce. To complete her unhappy story, she had stomach cancer and had only a short time to live.

In the police station, Jay Smith asked for his right to a telephone call and spoke to his friend, librarian Harold Jones. He told him to call at his house and, 'Get everything out of the basement, especially the file cabinet.'

Jones, watched by two detectives in

an unmarked car, entered Smith's house and picked up cartridges for the weapons found in Smith's possession, another two weapons and about a pound of marijuana in two plastic bags.

Police obtained a warrant to search the house and in the basement they found more marijuana; a great deal of pornography including magazines featuring bestiality; seventeen bottles of pills including Placidyl, Valium and librium; five oil filters adapted as silencers for pistols; and another identity for Dr Jay Smith. He had the security badge and identification card of a Brinks security guard, and parts of a security guard's uniform. In this guise he went under the name of Carl S. Williams.

When they checked the records for crimes supposedly committed by Carl Williams, rather than Jay Smith, it became apparent that the teacher and soldier had another, completely different career. 'Carl Williams' was on file as a bogus security guard who would appear at stores where Brinks were just about to pick up the day's takings to convey them to the bank. 'Williams' would show his security card and sign the register, would take possession of the sacks of money and walk out of the store. Staff at a Sears Roebuck store in Abingdon had handed over $100,000 in cash and personal cheques to Williams/Smith. Another Sears store in St David's had been relieved of $53,000 worth of cash and cheques. It was only when the real Brinks guard came that they realised they had handed over the money to an impostor. In another store, the cashier had been suspicious and Smith had grabbed his identity card back and run away. Smith was easily identified by staff from the stores in line-ups arranged by the police. One woman said she would never forget his eyes.

Smith may have been guilty of other crimes — he was certainly well equipped for armed robbery — but he was never accused of further offences. The only obvious crime he was found to have committed related to the school: another search of his house found a number of items stolen from Merion High, including reproductions of famous paintings, various pieces of office equipment and four gallons of nitric acid.

Smith was held in Chester County Prison. He was suspended by the school board amid the usual recriminations about how such a man could possibly have reached such a position of seniority in the education system. While in prison he received a letter from the head of the English department at Merion High, William S. Bradfield, comforting him in his predicament. Smith raised the $50,000 bail required, and was released. Bradfield's relationship with Smith continued, and he started visiting frequently.

Bill Bradfield, an enthusiastic and gifted teacher, was a tall and well-built man with light hair, piercing blue eyes and a ragged beard.

He was the son of a corporate executive with Western Electric and had a comfortable childhood though his father's work had meant that the family was obliged to move frequently. His mother doted on him but his father was overpowering and never seemed satisfied with him. People who got close to him found him always pondering on the deprivation of his childhood, the things he had not been given by his parents, though to any objective examination he had a privileged background.

In Haverford College, where Bradfield studied, he met and married a woman called Fran and they had two children. They later parted, and he married a woman called Muriel, and had another child. She looked after all three children in a house he owned in Chester County, Pennsylvania.

It is telling that in describing a woman he knew as a teenager whom he called the love of his life, he said that when he talked about Homer, 'she would listen in just the right way'. He did not want a woman who would do or say anything herself, but one who would react in the right way to him. This girlfriend doubtless existed, but the various romantic deaths he described for her to different paramours have something less than the ring of truth. He was holding her hand when she died of polio in an iron lung; he called at her house one day to find she had died of cancer . . . probably, she just threw him over for someone with a little more substance.

Bradfield had a passion for the American poet Ezra Pound, who is chiefly of interest not for his own work but because of the notable writers he encouraged in the first part of the twentieth century. Pound turned traitor during the war and made many broadcasts in Europe on behalf of the Nazis and Mussolini's fascists. After the allied victory he was arrested. A trial would have been an embarrassment so he was declared insane and imprisoned in St Elizabeth's Hospital for the Criminally Insane in Washington D. C., where Bradfield visited him and ran errands for him. From then on, Bradfield determined to be a poet.

Bradfield taught in a school for disadvantaged children before he moved to Upper Merion High in 1963, when he was thirty. He was exceptionally good at encouraging enthusiasm for academic subjects in his pupils, which is no small gift for a teacher to have, and Bill Bradfield would have had a happier life if he had been satisfied with it.

He had some knowledge of Latin

and Greek, though it is not clear how much. Some would say the especially keen students whom he tutored in these subjects learned very little. On other subjects in which he affected to be proficient, like Eastern religion, he could easily be caught out by people who had genuine knowledge. He could deliver an incisive opening statement on any subject, but if the person he was talking to did not fall silent in wonderment at his brilliance, it became clear that Bradfield had nothing to add. There was no depth, and no scholarship, behind his words.

Bradfield was an intellectual poseur of the type it is easy to find in a community like Merion High. Academically, it was not a high-octane place, and Bradfield played the part of a big fish in a small pool. On a university campus he would soon have been seen to be out of his depth.

Sue Myers, who was twenty-three when she first met Bradfield, found him 'the most brilliant teacher I'd ever met'. Soon they were dating, though Sue Myers was to find that Bradfield's magnetism was linked to a very low level of sexual performance. She thought he would marry her, which was unlikely as he was married to either one or two people already. It was years before she understood his marital status. Their relationship was a secret, and a very well-kept one.

The main reason for secrecy was so that Bradfield could continue to have affairs with other people unimpeded. Finally, in 1974, after being together as a couple for most of a decade, Bradfield and Sue Myers started living together. Soon after this they stopped having sex.

He continued to harbour the urge to be a poet but in the fifteen years he was with Sue Myers he wrote just three poems. For someone with pretensions to great learning, he was also curiously reluctant to read books. He owned several thousand books, including a great many expensive ones, but Sue Myers almost never saw him read. His chief cultural activity at home was watching television comedy shows. He would buy himself expensive presents like a first-class tennis racket though he did not play, and a $3000 piano. He took lessons for a while then stopped, never to play again.

He used to keep all scraps of paper, presumably in the thought that one day his biographer or research students would have need of every detail of the Bradfield archive in assessing his importance to English literature.

His stories included adventures as a guerrilla in Cuba, garotting a guard and blowing up a ship. Sometimes the story changed, and he stabbed or shot the guard, though it was not clear whether he was on the side of the pro-Castro revolutionaries or the Americans. He was extremely right wing politically, so presumably should have been anti-Castro, but the story used to involve his blowing up an American ship loaded with explosives. It is not so much Bradfield's lying which is interesting, as his inconsistent lying. It is as if he wanted to be found out.

His girlfriends were pleasant, shy women, who often seemed insecure. One such was Susan Reinert, a petite, mousy teacher who wore large spectacles and dressed in sensible clothes. She had two children, Karen and Michael. She had a master's degree and had only ever wanted to be a teacher.

As her diary showed, she was already having difficulties with her marriage when she came into Bill Bradfield's orbit. Bradfield's attentions to Susan Reinert, and her increasing infatuation with him, accelerated a split between Susan and Ken Reinert. Bradfield offered to marry her when the time was right, but in the meantime wanted it to be a secret.

He was now living with Sue Myers but had lied about this to Susan Reinert. Reinert was desperate for more physical contact with Bradfield. She used to write such things as, 'This morning I awoke with aching pubic area and erect nipples as usual. My breasts yearned to brush up against your chest. My legs wanted to curve over yours . . . My body smiles and opens to receive all of your love, you can touch any part of me and I am ready . . . Bill, I ache for your comfort and love and tenderness and passion and strength.' This letter was found in 1974 by Sue Myers, who challenged Susan Reinert over it, and doubtless explained a few facts about Bradfield which had hitherto escaped her rival's notice. The relationship between Bradfield and Susan Reinert now cooled, and he turned his attention to other young women.

From September 1975, Bradfield was also seeing Joanne Aitken, who had been an admissions officer at a nearby college but who became a graduate student in architecture at Harvard University. At one point Bradfield and Joanne were staying in a hotel in Philadelphia under the name Mr and Mrs Bradfield. Like Reinert, she became increasingly dependent on him.

By the end of the decade Bradfield was also betrothed to Wendy Zeigler, a nineteen-year-old former student who he had found he could draw into his net of dependent women. She wrote, 'I miss you so terribly, I sometimes think that if I can't feel your hands running through my hair, or have you pull me into your arms and kiss me, I shall scream.' They used to go to motels where the 45–year-old Bradfield and his young friend would kiss and cuddle, but not have sex. After she had graduated from college they were going to be married in a cathedral in France.

Sue Myers knew about his other women and tried to battle them off, but there was always a net of lies and obligations involved in his relationships, and there were always seminars and conferences for him to attend in other towns. He threw off her suspicions about his relationship with Susan Reinert by saying that she was a neurotic woman chasing him, she was pathetic and he felt sorry for her.

He also had male friends; the most important were Vince Valaitis and Chris Pappas, though Bradfield kept his different groups of friends apart from each other. Shy, bespectacled Vincent Valaitis, whose chief interest was in horror and fantasy films, came to the English department in 1974 and was befriended by Bradfield in his overpowering, bear-hug manner, demanding total loyalty and no criticism. He moved in to the apartment above Bradfield and Myers. Valaitis was a Roman Catholic, which appealed to Bradfield, who would expostulate at length on the virtue of the church's attitude to chastity.

Chris Pappas was a former pupil of

Bradfield's who returned to Merion High to work as a substitute teacher. He had an important place in Bradfield's scheme of things, as he could help Bradfield to complete practical tasks, at which Bradfield had no skill.

Bradfield was eager to make money in order to finance a sailing boat which he wished to take around the Mediterranean in the path of the classical Greek hero, Odysseus. In 1977, Sue Myers, Vince Valaitis and Bradfield opened a gift and crafts shop, Terra Art, in a nearby shopping mall. Bradfield put up $40,000 for this by mortgaging his house in Chester County where Muriel and his three children lived. The shop did not prosper.

Jay Smith discerned Bradfield's weakness and treated him with contempt when he first moved to Merion High. Bradfield was the teachers' representative and was often delegated to meet Jay Smith on staff business. Smith would bludgeon the younger man with his intellectual superiority, using words he did not know and even making them up, sure that Bradfield would not recognise the deception until later and then feel humiliated by it.

After Smith's arrest and bail, however, they became friendly and Bradfield would be seeing the former principal up to three nights a week. He claimed to have met Smith on the day Smith was supposed to have been stealing from the Sears store in St David's dressed as a Brinks guard. Bradfield had met him, he now recollected, on the shore in Ocean City on 27 August 1977. If Smith had been with Bradfield, he could not have been in St David's to do the job. 'It's my moral responsibility to tell the truth,' said Bradfield, and his acolytes admired him for it.

He performed another task for Jay Smith, in the company of his friend Chris Pappas. Pappas was kept in the dark about exactly what was happening and just knew that a telephone call was being made which had something to do with Jay Smith and his daughter and son-in-law. Bradfield and Pappas took a detour on a trip to New Mexico and called in at a town called Taos. Bradfield went to a pay phone then they returned home, with no other reason for being in Taos. In the dry cleaner's where Stephanie Smith worked, a workmate received a reverse charge call from Taos. Stephanie could not take it because she was in hospital for her cancer treatment that day. The caller said he was Eddie, and everything was OK with him and his wife, and they should pass the message on. Eddie was, of course, Smith's son-in-law who had vanished with his wife, Smith's daughter Stephanie.

At the end of May 1979, Bradfield appeared in Smith's defence on the second charge, of stealing money from the St David's store posing as a guard. Susan Reinert told friends she felt Bradfield was perjuring himself in saying he was with Smith all day on the day of the crime as actually he was with her. Bradfield defended himself by saying that as he knew Smith was innocent, in telling a lie to demonstrate his innocence he was serving a 'higher justice'.

The jury did not believe Bradfield, anyway, and Smith was convicted. He was out on bail for the next month, and due to return to the court in Harrisburg to be sentenced on 25 June. When he did so, he was sentenced to two to five years. He was sent to prison in Dallas, Pennsylvania.

★ ★ ★

On the morning of Smith's sentencing there was a suspicious car in a hotel car park. The trunk of the red Plymouth Horizon outside the Host Inn in Harrisburg was open, and it was only a matter of time before someone would take a look in. Two people passing the night before had noticed something white poking out of the trunk. They thought it was a plastic bag, and thought perhaps they should close the trunk so that no one would steal from it. They then thought better of it and walked past. Finally, after it had been there all night, a police patrol officer, thinking the car might have been stolen and dumped, checked its registration and found that it belonged to one Susan Reinert. Someone called the police to say there was a 'sick woman' in a car outside the motel and an officer finally came and opened the trunk to find the naked, bruised, battered body of Susan Reinert lying in a foetal position with her knees drawn up. The white object which could be seen through the open trunk was one of her hips.

Detective Jack Holtz, aged thirty-two, was called to the scene. He arrived early in the morning of 25 June 1979 to find the body being moved, with the disturbance of evidence that would cause. He had the hands bagged to retain any evidence which was on them, and let the car with the body be moved away.

There was little to learn from the scene. The car was three spaces from the entrance of the hotel, the hatchback had been open displaying a part of the body, there had been a telephone call attracting attention to it. You did not have to be a detective to tell that someone wanted the body to be found.

When the car could be examined three unusual items were found inside: a rubbish bag which was under the body, a blue comb with the insignia '79th USARCOM' and a 'strap-on' rubber dildo.

An examination of the body by the duty pathologist found it to be a woman in her thirties who had been severely beaten and chained so that the links bit into her flesh. She was five feet two tall and weighed just over seven stone. There were defensive wounds on her arms where she had tried to protect herself, and her face was badly beaten.

There were red fibres in her hair and her mouth had been taped. She had been injected with morphine. The pathologist concluded, wrongly, that she had been drugged and strangled. In fact, she had been injected with a lethal dose of drugs.

Detectives contacted her husband, Ken Reinert, now remarried. He had married Susan when he was in the air force and they had had their two children. When the eldest, Karen, was five, in 1971, Susan went back to work, taking a job at Upper Merion High School. He was called at his work as a personnel manager in a bank and went to the morgue to identify the body.

It was not until the evening of Monday, 25 June, when Ken Reinert was being interviewed in detail, that he wondered who was looking after the children. Were they with friends or neighbours? This was the first time Jack Holtz and his team had heard that the whereabouts of the children was not known. They had assumed, like Ken, that the children were somewhere safe. Frantic telephone calls discerned the terrible truth: they had gone missing at the same time as their mother.

The last time Susan was seen was by a neighbour on Friday, 22 June 1979, at about 9.30 p.m. She had left her attractive, suburban home at Ardmore during a hailstorm with Karen who was eleven and ten-year-old Michael. Neither she nor the children were dressed for the weather, suggesting that she had rushed out in response to a telephone call. It was later discerned that certain documents were absent from the house, which implied she had taken them with her. These were her insurance policies, her will and an investment certificate.

While Holtz was checking her house for clues, something happened that was against all regulations: the body was released to an undertaker under instructions from Susan's family. It was immediately cremated with whatever evidence it contained.

This awful fact, the loss of the most important piece of evidence they had, utterly dismayed investigating officers and threw the investigation off balance.

Within the first day or two of the investigation, after the television news had covered the finding of the body, an agent from the New York Life Insurance Company called to say that Susan Reinert was more than generously insured.

It was possible the destruction of evidence was deliberate, one of the detectives conjectured, and that the body was not that of Susan Reinert. She had gone off with her children, to join her lover later, once he collected on a large amount of insurance policies. The battered body was that of some poor woman who had been murdered because she looked like Reinert. It fitted the facts as well as anything else, and was actually rather more probable than the truth.

The name of William S. Bradfield kept cropping up, whenever the police asked about Susan Reinert. When her mother died in October 1978, and Susan Reinert inherited $34,000 and some land, Bill

Bradfield had started to take a renewed interest in her, cloaked in his usual secrecy.

In March 1979, Bradfield finally asked her to marry him, and she gave him her mother's valuable diamond ring to reset as a wedding ring, and $25,000 of her inheritance. He was going to invest it to pay for her children's education in the future. He would match it with another $25,000 so they could buy a high interest $50,000 bond.

She later told two friends, separately, that Bradfield was going to marry her in summer 1979, when he had finally managed to effect a separation from Sue Myers. They would go to England, but Susan had to keep this a secret in case her husband found out. He might think they were going to England permanently and would go to court to have the children taken from her. She had an abiding fear of losing the children which was quite unrealistic; she was a good mother and her husband was happy with the arrangement they had.

From March to June 1979, Susan Reinert started to insure her life. She tried to obtain half a million dollars worth of insurance policy, naming her 'friend' William S. Bradfield as beneficiary but the United States Accident Insurance Company judiciously decided this would be over-insurance.

She tried to have New York Life insure her for $250,000 but was first turned down, and offered $100,000 worth, which she accepted. She now tried USA Accident again, this time successfully, with a $250,000 policy with an additional indemnity of $200,000 for accidental death. She named Bradfield the beneficiary, as her 'intended husband'.

She now went back to New York Life, saying she was marrying the beneficiary and he was quite well off, at which they permitted her another $150,000 worth of insurance, meaning she was insured for a quarter of a million with them. She already had a modest insurance, of $30,000 taken out in 1977 just after her divorce, so in total these transactions added up to her intended husband standing to gain $730,000 in the event of her accidental death. 'Accident' in this case included murder.

With the exception of the small insurance policy she already had, all the policies were taken out within 120 days of her death. Two of them were taken out within the month of June. Just in case there was any doubt about the beneficiary, on 5 May 1979, less than two months before her death, she made a new will leaving everything to Bradfield.

Sharon Lee, another English teacher, called Bradfield on 26 July, the day after the body was found. He was taking a course at St John's College in New Mexico. He said he had heard of Susan's death, but wanted to know the details so she told him what she knew. Sharon Lee was under the impression her friend was going to marry Bradfield in England in July, so she was surprised when Bradfield said that he had no knowledge of such a trip, and did not expect to be seeing Susan until the next term started in September. She remembered very clearly something he said, when she mentioned the hunt for the children, 'How old were the children?' It was an odd remark, partly because he knew the children very well, but also because he used the past tense. The entire state was out looking for them and hoping they were alive, but he knew they were dead.

Bradfield had spent the weekend of the murder at Cape May, New Jersey, with Vince Valaitis, Sue Myers and Chris Pappas. The whole trip to Cape May was peculiar, considering that Bradfield and Pappas were on the following Monday going to New Mexico to attend a summer school. To voluntarily do this travelling on the weekend prior to a long trip seems excessive. Pappas and Valaitis thought so too but Bradfield virtually ordered them to go.

When Holtz interviewed Sue Myers and Vince Valaitis at their apartment block after the body was found, they said they had left with Bradfield and Pappas for Cape May at 4 p.m. on Friday, which would put their time of departure well before Susan Reinert went missing.

The proprietor of the boarding house where they stayed, however, had a different story. All four had arrived at the Heirloom in the early hours of Saturday morning, around 5 a.m. The owner, Marian Taylor, remembered

Bradfield paying for two nights but asking for a receipt for four days. Taylor agreed to put Friday on the receipt, thinking it was being done for some minor tax evasion. The drive would have taken them five or six hours; they obviously did not leave in the afternoon but late at night.

Jack Holtz and another detective flew to interview Bradfield and Pappas. They wanted to speak to Pappas alone, first, but Bradfield insisted on coming with his friend, and announced that he, Chris Pappas, Vince Valaitis and Sue Myers were 'in Cape May on Friday, Saturday, Sunday and Monday, the entire weekend of the murder'. He said he had been advised by his attorneys not to give any statement, as had Chris Pappas and Sue Myers who were also represented by the same law firm. They would all refer any questions submitted in writing to their lawyers.

Holtz called the lawyers, to find they accepted his questions, which concerned Bradfield's whereabouts over the weekend of the murder. Bradfield again refused to answer them, but said he would submit them to his attorney.

Frustrated, the police now let selected information out to the press, like the fact that Bradfield was beneficiary of the insurance policies and will, making Susan Reinert's death worth almost a million dollars to him. When Bradfield was interviewed by reporters he kept saying it was 'incredible' that he had been given so much in Reinert's will. He knew nothing about it until the newspapers called to tell him about it.

Vince Valaitis locked himself away. His sole contribution so far was to tell Bradfield to talk to the police, and Bradfield said he would answer any questions which were submitted. Valaitis then just stayed in his room. Finally, some friends coaxed him round to their house and encouraged him to call the FBI.

The FBI came with Jack Holtz, and 29-year-old Vince told his story, that 'Bill Bradfield told me that Dr Smith was a hit man for the Mafia, that he had been threatening a number of people, including Susan Reinert. He said Smith said Susan Reinert knew too much about him and his trash and that Dr Smith was chopping up dead bodies and putting parts of them into trash cans around the high school.'

Bradfield had confided to Valaitis that Smith had killed scores of people. He kept a list of people who did not deserve to live, and one of them was Susan Reinert. Susan Reinert had been having an affair with Jay Smith, she had jilted him and Smith was angry with her.

The detectives looked at each other glumly. It was not only nonsense, it was hearsay nonsense. The District Attorney's office would be laughing at them.

When Bradfield finally returned from his summer school, he cornered Valaitis, who begged him to go to the police. Valaitis really wanted to believe that Bradfield was innocent. Finally he confessed that he had talked to the police. 'You've put me in the electric chair,' said Bradfield. It was the end of their friendship.

When Bradfield was eventually taken to the police station, with a court order demanding that he submit to fingerprinting, he had a question for them. 'How long do the state police stay on a murder case?'

Newspaper coverage of the case became very strange, with rumours of devil worship and twenty to thirty men and women known to Susan Reinert allegedly being involved in orgies. This was all based on the thinnest evidence: the rubber dildo found in the car with Susan's body and the pornographic magazines in Jay Smith's house. A little more than that would be needed for an orgy.

Still, the parents of pupils at Upper Merion High took it all very seriously and when term recommenced after the summer break, they insisted that those involved in the murder investigation — Bradfield, Myers and Valaitis — should not be returned to the classroom. They were all put on non-teaching duties, pending the outcome of the investigation. Bradfield now made his only statement on the case in response to this indignity: that he had nothing to do with Susan Reinert's death and he had no idea of the whereabouts of her children. He was doing everything he could to bring the matter to a speedy and just resolution.

Bradfield was a very long way indeed

from the electric chair. Holtz and another four state detectives, plus eighteen FBI officers had been working on the case. The FBI had moved in arrogantly saying they would clear up the case in two weeks, only to abandon it after three years as 'unsolvable'. It became the biggest investigation in the history of the state.

For his little group of believers, Bradfield had a story that Susan Reinert was dating a black man called Alex of whom she was frightened, and that he was probably the killer. To add verisimilitude, he described the kinky sex the two were supposed to be having. No such man was ever found.

He begged members of the Bradfield club not to betray him to the 'fascists' (by which he meant the police) and attempted to identify himself with his hero, 'Look what they did to Ezra Pound.' It had eluded him that it was Pound who was the fascist, that was why he was punished.

The real break in the case came when Holtz and the rest of the team drew a blank on the bodies of the children and started on another track: they followed the money.

Repeated searches of Susan Reinert's possessions and monetary affairs showed up a photocopy of a receipt demonstrating that the doomed woman had purchased a quarter of a $100,000 investment certificate from a bank. The names on the certificate were fake, however, and it was a crude forgery, typed on an IBM golfball typewriter. This was a model to which Bradfield had access — it belonged to Sue Myers. Susan Reinert's bank withdrawal coincided with notes on her calendar saying 'investment — cash to Bill'.

Bradfield's shop, Terra Art, was doing very badly indeed. Bradfield was in debt for $21,000 at the time of Susan Reinert's death. The pressure of the investigation further eroded the enthusiasm of Sue Myers and Vince Valaitis for the store. Bradfield was now in big financial trouble and he made the mistake of his life.

He had already filed claims on the insurance policies and the insurance companies refused to pay. Now he tried to probate Susan Reinert's will.

Her family contested it and the court appointed a deputy district attorney to safeguard the interests of the missing children in what was called the Orphans' Court. In the only piece of justice so far seen in this case, little Karen Reinert and Michael Reinert were effectively putting William S. Bradfield on trial.

Almost a year after Susan Reinert's death, Bradfield appeared in the Orphans' Court to answer questions about her financial affairs and his involvement in them. The objective of the hearing was merely to sort out the affairs of a person who was dead, but it was still a court and Bradfield was under oath. He denied receiving any money from Reinert. There was no $25,000 and no diamond ring. If anything, he had given her money. Holtz and the other police were delighted. One of the few things they could prove about him was that he had Susan Reinert's money.

In another development, Chris Pappas, Bradfield's former student, was now prepared to talk to police and confess that he had helped Bradfield count and wipe fingerprints off $28,500 in notes in Bradfield's attic which, Pappas said, he kept there because he did not trust banks. The reason given for wiping the fingerprints off was that if Jay Smith killed Susan Reinert, then the police would come looking for Bradfield, as he was a beneficiary of her insurance policies. Pappas's fingerprints were on the money so they were wiping them off to protect him. Bradfield's explanations probably sounded better heard than read. Bradfield used the money for his legal fees.

The long-suffering Sue Myers finally locked Bradfield out and changed the locks, and he went to live with his parents. That was where he was arrested for theft of the $25,000 and conspiracy. Sue Myers talked to the police, handed over Bradfield's love letters from his various girlfriends, and the key to the code he used when instructing someone to destroy the golfball from the IBM typewriter on which the fake investment receipt was written. It was a book code based on Ezra Pound's translation of Confucius.

Jack Holtz and his colleagues, not without internal disagreements, made the strategically daring decision to arrest Wendy Zeigler. She was deeply religious, an assiduous scholar, and really guilty of nothing but being an adolescent in love with Bradfield. But she had covered up for him, hiding the $25,000 stolen from Susan Reinert over the summer. She had refused to help the police in the inquiry, and charging her along with Bradfield was the only way to persuade her to talk. Now she did so, at his trial in December 1982.

A star witness at the trial was James P. Macmillan, the manager of the Continental Bank in King of Prussia, where Susan Reinert had an account. He told a story to chill the heart of anyone working against confidence tricksters. Susan Reinert had walked into the bank and asked for $25,000 cash. It was policy to question people who asked for large amounts of cash as there is rarely any legitimate reason why someone would want cash, but confidence tricksters always do. Mr Macmillan explained this to Susan Reinert and offered to produce a cashier's cheque or a wire transfer to her investor's bank. He tried to pay half in cash and half by wire transfer. He offered to call the person she was supposedly investing with. He gave her the information that no investment bond would be paying more than nine per cent and she said she would be receiving much more than that.

Finally this good man, a man anyone with any sense would listen to, used a legal manoeuvre to permit him to refuse to release cash if he were certain some irregularity was taking place. Despite her protestations, he allowed Susan Reinert to take out only $1500 from her savings account. Several days later, she transferred $11,500 to a current account, and then transferred another $5000. She then opened another account at another bank and transferred everything there. She made five cash withdrawals of amounts up to $10,000, amounting to a total of $25,000 in cash. At least no one could say she had not been warned.

Then Bradfield took the money to his attic with Chris Pappas and the two of them counted it and wiped their own fingerprints off the notes. He gave it to Pappas to hide and eventually to put in a safety deposit box. Pappas then handed it back to Bradfield who gave it to Wendy Zeigler. She placed it in another safety deposit box.

Three days before Susan Reinert's body was discovered, Bradfield asked Wendy Zeigler to remove $25,000 from the safety deposit box she kept for him in case something happened to Susan Reinert that weekend.

The judge had declared inadmissible the photocopy of the fake investment certificate. Police had been unable to find the original, which led them to assume that it was one of the documents taken with Susan Reinert on that fateful Friday night. Luckily, she had taken a photocopy. The photocopy still showed that the fake certificate had been typed on an IBM golfball typewriter like one to which Bradfield had access, which he had hidden with a friend in New Mexico when he went to the summer school there after the murder. The fake signatures of bankers on it also looked like Bradfield's.

The defence, that he may have been given the money by his parents over a long period, was wholly inadequate and Bradfield was found guilty after the jury had been out ninety minutes. He was allowed out on bail pending an appeal but as investigation into the murder again stepped up, the bail was increased so he had to begin serving his sentence of four months to two years in Delaware County Prison.

In 1982, he dropped all claims to the insurance money and the rest of the estate. Now he was backing off. He had given up on profiting from the crime and was trying to save himself from a murder conviction.

Bradfield's native wit helped him in prison, where he made friends with a tough, streetwise black inmate called Proctor Nowell, who was a heavyweight boxer. Bradfield asked Nowell to teach him to play chess. Soon he was receiving friendship and protection from Nowell. He needed the protection because convicts give child killers a rough time. However, Nowell, who was twenty-three, had two children himself. He was interviewed about conversations with Bradfield and was eventually persuaded to testify before a Grand Jury which was investigating whether there was enough evidence to try Bradfield and Smith for the Reinert murders. He quoted Bradfield as saying, 'I was there when they were killed, but I didn't kill anyone . . . None of this was meant for the children, only for Susan.' Nowell was removed from prison to an alcoholic treatment unit after giving testimony against Bradfield.

The Grand Jury finally indicted Bradfield on three counts of murder, conspiracy, solicitation to commit murder, kidnapping and obstruction of justice.

By now Bradfield was out of the prison pending his appeal, Joanne Aitken having raised the $150,000 bail money. He was living in the guest quarters of his mother's house in Downington with Joanne but was arrested on 6 April 1983 in nearby Birdsboro at the house of a friend. It was a moment Jack Holtz had been waiting four years to experience.

Now that all of Bradfield's acolytes, with the exception of Joanne Aitken, were talking, Holtz could make more sense out of Bradfield's trail of lies. It never made perfect sense, as he told a different story to each of his dupes and swore them to secrecy.

Pappas could testify to Bradfield's obsession with Smith and his 'assassination techniques'. He had kept a piece of paper with incoherent notes made by Bradfield on it including, 'lured and killed kids and taped her'.

Pappas had hidden acid for Bradfield, which had supposedly come from Smith, as had a gun from which he filed the serial number. He had also constructed a home-made silencer for a pistol, supposedly according to Smith's specifications. All this was to gain Smith's confidence.

Chris Pappas also described Bradfield's bizarre behaviour. He had an 'assassination jacket', a blue jacket with four large pockets. One pocket contained a ski mask and gloves, another had chains and locks, a third had tape and the last had plastic bags inside. Bradfield explained to Pappas that he wanted to 'enter into a teacher-disciple relationship' with Smith, to gain his confidence in order to confound his evil schemes. For this he needed to practise the techniques Smith used to kill. One night he practised wrapping the chains around Chris Pappas's wrists and locking them together, and testing how fast he could take sticky tape out of his pocket to tape up a victim's mouth.

The object of going away with Pappas, Valaitis and Myers on the weekend starting Friday 22 June was that he needed them for his alibi, he explained to them. As Dr Smith was likely to kill Susan Reinert that weekend, rather than perform the knight protector act as he had allegedly been doing previously, his concern now was to ensure the deed was not blamed on him.

Bradfield should have arrived home to travel with his friends at 7 p.m. on Friday evening, but did not arrive until 11 p.m., which was one and a half hours after Susan Reinert and the children were last seen. Bradfield's excuse was that he had been staking out Susan Reinert's house for signs of Jay Smith: 'I followed Smith around her house fourteen times, then I lost him in the hailstorm.' He said this was the weekend Susan Reinert would die. Presumably, they took no special notice because Bradfield was always saying such strange things and had an almost psychotic preoccupation with Jay Smith and Susan Reinert.

Over the weekend, he was concerned to collect receipts, saying, 'We're going to need every one to prove that we were in New Jersey if Susan Reinert is killed this weekend.' Later, Bradfield suggested that he and Vince go to church to pray for Susan. They did so, and lit a candle for her.

They returned at the end of the weekend and Joanne Aitken drove Bradfield and Chris Pappas to the airport on 25 June, the day Susan Reinert's body was discovered. They flew to New Mexico while she drove to Santa Fe where the summer school was taking place. In the car was Sue Myers's IBM golfball typewriter which Bradfield wanted with him on the summer school, but which did not come back.

The prosecution case was conjecture and circumstantial evidence. Bradfield had probably pretended to Susan Reinert he was going to see a lawyer with her that evening to discuss the details of their marriage, about which Susan was anxious. That was how he had managed to get her to bring all the insurance policies, the will and the original of the investment receipt. He had lured her and the children to a place where they were taken and later killed by an accomplice. The children may have been killed immediately, they were of no value. Susan Reinert was kept alive until he was well away, on his 'alibi weekend'. The accomplice killed her and made sure she was found.

Forensic evidence was scant. There was a fibre found in Susan Reinert's hair which matched fibres in Jay Smith's house. A strand of hair matching Susan Reinert's was found in his basement. A blue comb of the 79th USARCOM, the army reserve unit in which Smith served, was found under the body. As the defence was not slow to point out, this hardly indicated the guilt of William S. Bradfield.

Bradfield, now fifty, eventually went into the witness box to give a watered-down version of the story he had been telling his friends about his relationship with Smith in the period, approaching a year, between Smith's arrest on the weapons charges and Susan Reinert's murder. He said, 'Dr Smith was an unguided missile, and with my being there, at least I could see what he was being guided toward. I was spending more and more time with Smith by Christmas of 1978. I was also spending more and more time trying to be near Sue Reinert . . . to see if she was OK. I was at the point of taking Dr Smith seriously enough that I checked on Susan Reinert, almost constantly.'

He denied having marriage plans or a sexual relationship with Susan Reinert, saying that when neighbours had seen his car in front of her house in the mornings, it was because he had called round early for breakfast.

His explanation of the 'lured and killed' note was that it was a record of comments made by his lawyer about what the authorities were saying about him. If he were so sure Susan Reinert was in danger, why did he go away on precisely that weekend? He had given evidence that Jay Smith said professionals chose holiday weekends to kill. His response was that he could not park in front of Susan Reinert's house for the whole holiday weekend. With all of his supposed suspicions of Smith, he could not explain why he did not go to the police except to say that the police were corrupt and Smith had influence over them.

He had a gun with a silencer to protect himself, he said, in case he was attacked by Smith. 'If Smith were to threaten me while I was in the car, I would have to try to wound or disable him, or kill him. And the first thing that I would do, we agreed, was that I would call Chris, and he would come immediately . . . I wanted to do more than simply disable him. I wanted after that to be able to call Chris and for Chris and me to decide where we were going to take Smith. We talked about what public official we could be absolutely sure we could trust, or whether we should do away with Smith.'

Of course, his determination to speak in Smith's defence, to give him an alibi for the Sears theft, sat poorly with his contemporaneous plans to murder Smith because he was so dangerous.

Bradfield had by now divorced his second wife, Muriel, and had signed a non-cohabitation agreement with Susan Myers. In both cases he had a document drawn up which specifically precluded from each woman the possibility of obtaining a share in an insurance policy payout of half a million dollars. This was despite his having denied all knowledge of Susan Reinert's insurance policies, saying that they were a sick, romantic fantasy of Reinert who had taken them out and named him as beneficiary without informing him.

Prosecutor Rick Guida described to the jury Bradfield's 'murder jacket', where he had chains and locks in one pocket, tape in another, gloves in another, and a plastic bag in another. 'All these items were so that you could mobilise, kill and dispose of the body. What did Sue Reinert's body show? Chain marks, tape marks, a plastic bag under her body. Is it just a coincidence that on this one night in June of 1979, he just happens to put on the exact jacket that was used to practise abducting, killing and disposing of people?'

What was the point of having the car with the body taken to Harrisburg and parked in a motel car park with the body exposed? 'Why would a killer take a chance to do that? Who benefits from that? . . . Do you know why her body was exposed? Because this body is worth, to only one person in the world, seven thousand dollars a pound and it has to be found during the alibi weekend so that he can say to the world, and to a jury, "I couldn't possibly have done it, I was away."

'No one else would have taken this chance unless they did it for Bill Bradfield. Because her body had to be found. Because nobody collects on insurance unless they have a body.'

Joshua Lock, Bradfield's dedicated defence attorney, said, 'The irrefutable physical evidence does not implicate the defendant in any way, and in many ways points the finger at someone else,' meaning Jay Smith.

On 28 October 1983, after an hour and fifteen minutes, the jury returned and delivered the verdict that Bradfield was guilty of conspiracy to commit three first degree murders. He looked straight ahead and blinked several times as the verdict was announced. Given a chance to speak, he again denied the crime. The judge said that there could be no death penalty in this case as aggravating circumstances, that the children had witnessed their mother's death for example, had not been proved. He was sentenced to three life sentences to be served concurrently.

The investigators had been keeping an eye on Jay Smith. Now Jack Holtz turned his full attention on the sinister doctor of philosophy.

Many prisoners had come forward to Jack Holtz, to testify that Bradfield or Smith had confessed to the three murders. Most of them were unbelievable, criminals hoping to receive a reduction in sentence by informing on another prisoner. It was also inherently unlikely that Smith would have actually confessed murder to so many people. He seemed a more cautious type than that. One man, Charles Montione, recalled Smith speaking often about how to commit the perfect murder. 'Never kill anyone unless you can make the body disappear,' Smith had said. He also discussed various escape plans with Montione, who was in prison for armed robbery and burglary. After Bradfield was convicted, Smith became agitated and spoke about the mistakes in the murder. Smith felt that allowing Susan Reinert's body to be found was a grave error. He is reported to have said to Montione, 'Look, five years have passed, two more and she would have been declared legally dead, and the insurance money would have been paid.' In the same conversation he said the children's involvement was a mistake, and that they had only been killed because they were witnesses. He said Bradfield did not even know where the bodies of the children were.

Another convict, a former police officer called Raymond Martray who had run a burglary ring, had kept in contact with Smith, and he was also prepared to testify against him, though the evidence of criminals was rarely very compelling. A Grand Jury, listening to this testimony, were prepared to recommend Jay Smith's arrest. Eventually, Smith was charged in his cell on 25 June 1985, six years to the day after Reinert's body was found. After the jury selection and legal arguments, the trial started on 31 March 1986.

Smith, now fifty-seven, was bespectacled, balding, and wore a dark suit and a tie. He was fortunate in two respects. One was that the judge ruled as inadmissible all the evidence which the police had found in his basement at their searches in 1978: the drugs, plastic bags, guns, acid and so on. It might prejudice a jury against him and that would be unfair. He also had the fortune, and good sense, to be represented by an extremely able lawyer.

William Costopoulos, for the first time in any of these trials, attacked the 'cult' of Bradfield accomplices. He said to the jury, 'You might call them co-conspirators. They slept with him. They gave him sexual favours. They lied for him. They practised killing Susan Reinert with him. This group had possession and control of the instrumentalities of crime consistent with Susan Reinert's death.'

The Bradfield clan were torn apart in court by this skilful lawyer, for removing the serial number of a gun, for secreting ski masks and money, for holding the parts of weapons supposedly to protect

Susan Reinert from Jay Smith.

The former convicts testified against Smith, Martray's testimony being augmented by videotapes of his talking to Smith, taken secretly by the police. It was compelling, not so much because Smith confessed to the killings on tape, as because he was so clearly a criminal, at home in a criminal world and with no feelings for the Reinert family.

Two days after Susan Reinert's body was found, when he was in jail, he wrote to Stephanie, who was dying in the Bryn Mawr Hospital, 'Capri [his car]. First clean it up thoroughly. We will try to sell but not give away.' About the house he wrote, 'We must throw away most of the stuff. Don't keep things because they just seem too good to throwaway. We will replace at an auction or other place cheaply. I can't stress the importance of this. Clean out and then clean up. Things that must go: beds and rugs. Downstairs rug is full of matchsticks, cigarettes, old strands of marijuana, etc. from Eddie and Steph and their friends. Every time I walk on that rug, something new pops out. It must go. I will write more later about disposal.'

The evidence of carpet fibres was more equivocal than it seemed, however. The carpet in the basement was not red, like the fibres found on Susan Reinert's body, but beige. The police officers who had searched the house after Smith's arrest, however, remembered red carpet offcuts in the basement. The delay in Vince Valaitis coming forward and giving information to connect the murder with Smith meant that the house had been sold and the carpets taken up by the new owner before Holtz and the investigators got back there. The new owner, who had bought the house from Smith to move in shortly after he had been sent to prison, as he was sure he would be, remembered the beige carpet in the basement to be soaking wet when she moved in, as if it had just been washed. She cut it up and threw it away.

The theory, then, was that Susan Reinert's body had been laid on the fragments of red carpet which had been removed and dumped after the murder. The remnant of the red carpet was an offcut from the carpet upstairs in the house, which was still there, and which matched the fibres found on the body.

On the twenty-fifth day of the trial, a series of Karen and Michael Reinert's schoolfellows came to court to testify how they had been to the Philadelphia Art Museum. All the children, who were now teenagers, remembered the school trip and the little green pin with a white P on it they had all been given. Just such a pin was found in Jay Smith's car. It was the only piece of physical evidence which could link him with the dead children. One witness could even remember Karen Reinert was wearing the pin on the day she disappeared.

William Costopoulos used expert evidence to demonstrate that the brown hair found on Smith's rug may not have come from Susan Reinert's head; it might have come from the head of any brown-haired person. The fibres in Susan Reinert's hair could have come from any other carpet, it need not have been that one. Philadelphia Museum of Art handed out over half a million green and white pins per year. None of this should be used to condemn a man for murder.

Why dump the body in Harrisburg when he was due to appear there that morning for sentencing, asked Costopoulos. Why leave a comb with the name of his own army unit under the body? Why kill Susan Reinert at all? It was not in order to persuade Bradfield to testify for him, as he had already done that and had been unsuccessful. She had made out no insurances or wills in Smith's favour, and he hardly knew her.

The jury were instructed in the afternoon of 29 April 1986 and the following morning, almost seven years after the body of Susan Reinert was found, they found Dr Jay Smith guilty of her murder.

Smith did not take the stand at the trial, but did at a sentencing hearing after the verdict and proclaimed his innocence, though he said he accepted the jury's 'honest decision' to convict him. He still refused to say where the bodies of the children were. The jury took five-and-a-half hours to deliver a sentence of death on Smith. When the announcement was made, his hands clawed the air and his head went back, mouth open, but he stayed silent.

The usual process of appeals has followed, mainly dealing with the questions of whether the judges had correctly instructed the juries in the two trials. The wheels of the law grind slowly.

★ ★ ★

It was a bizarre set of circumstances which brought these two very different men together in the same crime. Bradfield could make people do things they did not think they wanted to do, and when this gift was used to encourage students to work, he was a teacher of rare quality. Unfortunately, he felt moved to use it to encourage impressionable people, unwittingly, to cover up murder. His gifts of persuasion and motivation were also useful in encouraging Susan Reinert to over-insure herself to an absurd degree and to hand over to him all the money she had on no surety except a promise of marriage. His malevolent power over her is mirrored only by her desperate desire to believe in him.

Bradfield's control over his supporters' club was staggering. It was a year after Reinert's death before Chris Pappas was prepared to tell the police the details of Bradfield's supposed campaign against Smith. Susan Reinert repeatedly made withdrawals from her bank account though the staff deliberately made it difficult for her, assuring her that she was the victim of a confidence trickster. It is unlikely to be coincidence that Bradfield's acolytes were people of diminutive stature while he was tall and well built. He towered over them in every way.

His mixture of daring and vulnerability was immediately attractive to a certain type of insecure woman, desperate to be loved. He was interviewed many times by an attractive journalist, Loretta Schwartz-Nobel, who was writing a book about the case. His letters to her give some idea of the Bradfield charm with which he entrapped so many women, 'I think of you so often day to day in here, and sometimes have long internal conversations with you. I see many things and people and situations through your eyes, and often think that you, like Henry James, would more surely catch "the tone of things" in here than I. I miss seeing you and talking with you. I'd love to see you. Do write when you can. Yours, Will.'

He would keep passions aroused, but not satisfy them. Wendy Zeigler talked about spending several hours 'hugging and kissing' in a motel room before she took the money from him to secrete in a deposit box. He told Loretta Schwartz-Nobel he had never had sex with Wendy or with Susan Reinert. This is a lie as regards Susan Reinert, unless all her letters were erotic fantasies, but it does indicate his ambivalence about sex. He had had a celibate relationship with Susan Myers since 1973 or 1974, at least five years before they parted. He protested his primary relationship with Joanne Aitken was non-sexual. This actually seems likely. While everyone lies about sex to some extent, and big liars like Bradfield tell big lies, his account of his sex life concurs with that of his girlfriends. Denying them sex also acted to keep the flame of desire alive, a trick usually operated by women on men, here used in reverse.

As may be imagined, Jay Smith saw things rather differently. 'Keep friends with all females,' he wrote to Martray, 'even a bad fuck is better than none.' How such a dreadful human being as Jay Smith could find such a number of women willing to indulge his sexual tastes is something of a problem until one reads about his usual behaviour as a school principal. He would make grossly sexual suggestions to all women he had the opportunity to meet. A few, maybe one in a hundred, maybe less, would find this sort of blatant approach stimulating, and he had his catch. He was so arrogant, he did not care about the opinion the rest had of him.

Smith had nothing but contempt for Bradfield; he saw straight through him. But when he was in trouble, he realised he could use Bradfield for an alibi over the Sears robbery. Smith did not realise that Bradfield felt the same way about him, and that Smith's brutality would be harnessed to solve Bradfield's money problems. The only humour in the case is imagining Smith's reaction when he learned that Bradfield had been telling everyone who would listen that Smith was going to kill Susan Reinert, and just how the crime would be committed.

It is difficult to tell why Smith did it. Motive was never proved. He may have had a deal with Bradfield over the insurance payout but there was no evidence of this. More likely he did it for the same reason that he went shoplifting when he was far from poor, and discussed armed robberies that he could commit with Martray: Smith committed crime because he enjoyed it. Blatant theft and creeping around a car park in a mask with a gun in each hand excited him.

The children were the key to the case. Had there been no children involved, it would probably have disappeared by default after a year of investigation. It was anger at the suffering of the children which motivated the police.

Why were they killed? The easy explanation is that they were witnesses to their mother's abduction, though not her murder, which had to happen while Bradfield was away after Smith had kept her alive for at least a day. This explanation does not fit the facts. The children had a loving father and he would certainly have contested Susan Reinert's will on their behalf had they been alive. The only chance of getting the money would be if the children were dead.

Evidence of Bradfield's long-term intention to kill the children is present in the comments of Susan Reinert to her friends. Reinert had long been saying that Sue Myers intended to kill her for her relationship with Bradfield, and also said that she intended to harm her children. Sue Myers genuinely hated Susan Reinert and made no secret of it; she saw Reinert as the principal thief of Bradfield's affections. But she had no feelings of animosity to the children and she was certainly no murderer. The only way Reinert could fear that Myers was out to get her and the children was if Bradfield had told her. It was another Bradfield lie which might be useful to obscure the picture later on.

If the children's being present had been a mistake, Bradfield could easily have backed off, saying one murder was OK, but he would not do three. Even at the last minute when he had lured them to Jay Smith's basement this would have been possible. Nor did he flinch from active involvement. It takes two men to control three people, even people as small as Susan, Karen and Michael Reinert. Bradfield planned and carried out the murder of all three, leaving a trail which, if it led anywhere, led to his accomplice Jay Smith. He then went on holiday and left Smith to clean up the mess.

The Aeroplane Bombers

PEOPLE fear strange things when they fly. They fear the wings will fall off the plane — an almost impossible event. Or they fear that an engine will fail — a rare event but one for which a pilot has training, and there is at least one other engine to do the work. They may even fear that terrorists will hijack the plane and hold the passengers hostage. What they never think of is that they and everyone else is going to be blown out of the sky because of an insurance policy taken out on the person sitting next to them.

In terms of the number of dead and the scale of devastation caused, insurance bombings rank among the major civilian crimes of the century. In the worst case, forty-four people were killed, sending a ripple-effect of grief throughout families in an entire nation. The anticipated payoff for this destruction, which of course also included the loss of a valuable jet plane, was a $37,500 insurance which was not valid anyway, not having been signed by the deceased.

As a direct result of this case, a bill calling for the death penalty in sabotage of commercial aircraft, if the plane crossed a state line, was passed in the US Senate in May 1956. There had been no specific law against it before, it simply had not been considered necessary. The newspaper accounts of these cases are filed under 'Airlines: accidents'. It was literally unthinkable that anyone would do such a thing on purpose.

In the case of Joseph Guay, the judge wept in open court at the infamy of the crime. Despite their scale, however, these cases have much in common with other insurance murder cases. Joseph Guay was, like Warren Green, obsessed with a woman who did not care about him. Both men conceived the same strange idea that killing their wives would solve their problems. Both also propounded an elaborate plan to throw suspicion away from themselves, and put on calculated displays of grief to fool the world at large. Neither of them were very good

Above left: The happy couple. Warren Green and Julie Sillitoe on their wedding day. *(Wigan Observer)*

Above right: The home of the newlyweds. *(Frank Orrell/ Wigan Observer)*

Left: Julie in her uniform as a student nurse. *(Wigan Observer)*

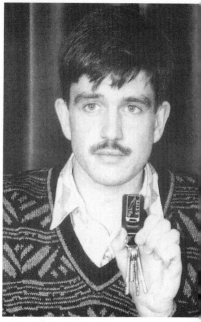

Stuwart Skett, the Cub Scout leader who became Julie's lover. *(Jon Snape/Wigan Observer)*

Warren Green holding a replica of the keys which w to give the vital clue to the identity of the murderer. *(Jon Snape/Wigan Observer)*

The men who solved the case *(left to right):* Detective Superintendents Norman Collinson and Frank Smout, an Detective Inspector Jack Booth. *(Jon Snape/Wigan Observer)*

Above left: Ivor Stockle and Pauline Leyshon pose for a studio portrait some time before the attempted murder. *(Michael Charity/Camera Press)*

Above right: After their horrific experience Ivor and Pauline are burned and battered, but still alive.
(Michael Charity/Camera Press)

Left: Sheila Stroud, Ivor Stockle's volatile ex-lover who hatched the plot to kill him and Pauline Leyshon.
(Michael Charity/Camera Press)

Mark Evans, Sheila Stroud's lover who helped in the murder plot. *(South West News Service)*

Norman White, the hired hit man. *(South West News Service)*

The bungalow where Ivor and Pauline were attacked and bound. *(South West News Service)*

The burned out
wreck at the bottom
of the cliff.
(Michael Charity/Camera Press)

The jury are invited
to see the trajectory
the burning car took
over Barrow Wake.
(South West News Service)

Above left: Susan Reinert, who loved Bill Bradfield enough to give him all her money – and insurance policies.
(UPI/Bettmann)

Right, above and below: Ten-year-old Michael Reinert and eleven-year-old Karen, whose bodies were never found.
(UPI/Bettmann)

Bill Bradfield, the teacher who exerted a mesmeric control over his circle of friends, leaves court after sentencing. *(UPI/Bettmann)*

Dr. Jay Smith: high school principal, army colonel and murderer. *(UPI/Bettmann)*

Kristina Cromwell, the suburban housewife. *(Associated Press)*

Marlin Cromwell, who worked as a clerk in a department store. *(Associated Press)*

The woman Kristina Cromw turned herself into. *(Associated Press)*

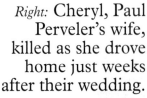

Left: Kristina's new lover, the sinister insurance investigator Paul Perveler. *(Associated Press)*

Right: Cheryl, Paul Perveler's wife, killed as she drove home just weeks after their wedding. *(Associated Press)*

Maria Fasching, the brave woman who was killed when she stood up to Joseph Kallinger.
(UPI/Bettmann)

Kallinger going to court.
(UPI/Bettmann)

The airport machine where John Graham bought insurance on his mother Daisy King before seeing her off. *(UPI/Bettmann)*

Investigators reconstructing the wreck of the United Airlines plane in which 44 people died, including Daisy King. *(Associated Press)*

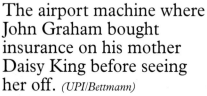

John Gilbert Graham, restaurant proprietor and mass murderer. *(UPI/Bettmann)*

edrick Seddon: property
ner, insurance agent,
eemason. A pillar of
:iety. *(Hulton Deutsch Collection)*

Frederick and Margaret
Seddon (with prison officers
to her left) in the dock at the
Old Bailey. *(Topham)*

e house in Tollington
rk, north London, where
za Barrow moved in as a
lger with the Seddons.
'ton Deutsch Collection)

Ernie Grant, the orphan
who stood to inherit Eliza
Barrow's money – except
that Frederick Seddon got
there first. *(Hulton Deutsch Collection)*

Alfred Rouse, the travelling salesman with a string of women to whom he had promised marriage.
(Popperfoto)

The remains of Rouse's car in which a man died – but was it Rouse?
(Popperfoto)

Police search for evidence near where the burning car and body were found.
(Popperfoto)

saline Fox, formerly the
age beauty and still a
ndsome woman in old age.
dication International)

Sidney Fox, charged with
killing his mother.
(Syndication International)

e hotel room where Rosaline Fox died. The charred
irks under the armchair show where the fire started.
e open door leads to Sidney Fox's room. *(Popperfoto)*

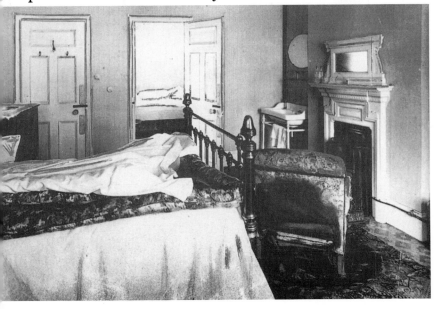

Jeweller Joseph Guay and his wife Rita.
(*Topham*)

Joseph Guay and Marie-Ange Robitaille, the teenager with whom he became infatuated.
(*UPI/Bettmann*)

Marie Pitre, another of Guay's lovers, who became involved in the murder plot. *(UPI/Bettmann)*

The wreck of the Canadian Pacific plane in which Rita Guay and twenty-two other people died. *(UPI/Bettmann)*

Frederick Holt, accused of murdering his lover for an insurance claim.
(Syndication International)

Kathleen Breaks, found dead in the sand dunes on Christmas Eve.
(Syndication International)

at it — Guay was too histrionic to be believable, Green was too cold and controlled. Probably neither of them understood real human emotions.

The case of Arellano and Sierra was an attempt by middle-class people to get richer by killing poor people. The more poor people who could be killed the better. Their main concern was not the suffering of the victims or their families, but how they would tag the bodies so they could be identified after the crash. Like Bradfield and Smith and other insurance murderers who worked as a team, one of these men was self-important, feeling that his respectability would put him above suspicion, and the other was a lying manipulator, a typical under-achiever who wanted wealth without working for it.

The late 1940s and early 1950s were the high point of plane bombings for insurance. Cases stopped in the 1960s and in the early 1970s, terrorist bombings of aeroplanes became the latest challenge to security. Or did they? When an aeroplane has been blown up over an ocean, there is precious little wreckage to testify to the exact cause. Was it really Sikh extremists who blew up an Air India 747 over the Atlantic in 1985? They never claimed responsibility for it.

A Surprise Present

JOHN GILBERT GRAHAM, the 23-year-old proprietor of a drive-in restaurant, hoisted his eighteen-month-old son on his shoulders so the child could have a better view of the United Airlines plane as it flew off into the distance taking his grandmother on her way to see her daughter in Alaska. The plane was headed for Portland, Oregon, where she would change planes. John Graham mentioned to his wife that he had put a surprise present in his mother's luggage.

It must have been heavy, for when they had arrived at Denver airport they had to pay $27 for overweight luggage which Graham insisted they do, saying his mother would need all her luggage, even though the baggage checker said it would be cheaper to take out some things and send them by mail.

Eleven minutes after take-off, on 1 November 1955, the four-engine DC-6B, Flight 629, exploded at 6000 feet.

Eyewitnesses saw a great arc of fire as the plane plunged to earth. A large part of it crashed in a beet field about forty miles from Denver. All forty-four people aboard were killed and wreckage was strewn over two square miles. The tail was over a mile and a half from where the engines fell. A makeshift mortuary was set up in the National Guard armoury in Greeley, where FBI specialists attempted to identify bodies and collect personal belongings pathetically scattered over the countryside. Relatives were brought in to view those not beyond identification.

Airline officials had the terrible task of telling the relatives of the passengers about the tragedy. They were struck by Graham's apparent indifference to the death of his mother, Daisy King, whom he had insured for $37,500 on the day of her death. He had bought the policy from a machine at the airport which took quarter dollars. He had arrived well supplied with them, though he had been nervous and spoiled two policies before he made one come out correctly. He did cry copiously some time after he had been told of the death.

Later, referring to some shells his mother had in her bags for hunting when she reached Alaska, he said, 'Can't you just see those shotgun shells going off in the plane every which way and the pilots and grandma jumping around?'

He told someone working in the garage which was repairing his truck that it was easy to blow up a plane: you would need just two gallons of nitroglycerine and a timing mechanism, which could all be placed in a suitcase and slipped on the carts that carry baggage to the planes. He remarked that if this plane had not been twenty minutes late, it would have crashed into the Rocky Mountains and no one would have suspected sabotage.

A painstaking reassembly of items in the baggage hold to determine which piece of luggage had been at the epicentre of the blast found Daisy King's luggage to be as close to the centre as it was possible to be. Checking her handbag, which was in hand luggage and had survived intact, they found a newspaper clipping relating to a police hunt for John Graham in connection with a forgery case. They started to invest greater interest in him.

Graham was questioned by the FBI who then concentrated their search on him. He claimed that the gift-wrapped package he had placed in his mother's luggage was a present of tools for small work — she enjoyed making jewellery and other items out of shells. The FBI searched his house and found a roll of the thin wire that had been used in the bomb in the pocket of one of his shirts. They also found wrapped packages, gifts for Daisy's daughter, Helen Hablutzel, which Mrs King had obviously intended to take with her but which had been thrown out of the luggage to make room for the package Graham placed in there. He was arrested and charged with the crime. He had placed a time bomb consisting of a timer, a six-volt battery, two blasting caps and twenty-five sticks of dynamite in his mother's luggage. The salesman remembered selling them to him. He had even given his own home telephone number when he had bought the electric timer.

The story of John Graham's miserable background, affluent but starved of affection, was brought out in interviews with psychiatrists.

His parents separated when Graham was eighteen months old and his father died soon afterwards at the age of sixty-three. His mother at this time was thirty-five. She was a generous woman in providing toys and money for her children but spent little time with them and was not demonstrative or affectionate. Graham was placed in an institution and left there even after his mother married a wealthy rancher, John Earl King, who would have been willing to have him at home. Graham would run away from the institution to the King ranch but his mother would send him back.

As a child, he had difficulty in expressing emotions and showed cruelty to animals. This included tying rockets to cats' tails and beating a cow nearly to death with a club because it kicked him. As a teenager he went into rages where he attacked his mother, knocking her down some steps; and his stepfather, almost pushing him down a well they had been working on.

As a teenager, Graham enlisted in

the Coast Guard from which he was discharged because he was 'an exceedingly immature individual who has exhibited poor judgement and who tends to act on impulses . . . He is a dependent person, with strong ties to mother. He tolerates frustrations, even those in the normal course of work, very poorly. Other evidences of his poor judgement and impulsive behaviour are to be seen in some of the infractions he has committed in service life; namely, sleeping on watch, stealing food while on watch, and returning to work drunk.'

Over the next few years, Graham would go from being an emotionally crippled misfit to being a criminal moving from non-violent crime to violence against property. The culmination, of the plane bomb, was a spectacular act of violence against people and property. His earlier offences included forgery on payroll cheques he had stolen from an employer, amounting to $4200. He was saved from a four-year prison sentence by his mother's paying $2500 worth of restitution. His probation report on this case said he 'shows very little concern over his present offence. For the past couple of years he has led a wild life — spent most of his money on drinking parties and women.'

He was subsequently involved in drinking and traffic offences then, as a young man, committed his first major crime. This involved carrying contraband, which ended in his smashing a speeding car through a police road block, being rewarded with two months in jail. Another case, involving arson, was not known about until he confessed to it during clinical questioning during his detention for the plane bombing: he had once been refused a discount on repairs to his car so he broke into the garage at night and set it alight, causing $100,000 worth of damage.

Graham's deep feelings of hatred were well concealed, and he was generally perceived to be confident and cheerful. After his prison sentence he seemed to settle down. He started a course in Business Administration at Denver University and married a woman called Gloria Elson, the couple having two children. His mother, whose second husband had now died, made the down payment on a house for the couple, paid his university tuition fees and purchased a drive-in restaurant for Graham in West Denver for $35,000. She moved in with them and became increasingly interested in the business, particularly as Graham was a poor manager. Her interference was a constant source of friction between them. The business was not a success and it was closed during the winter months.

Graham once caused a gas explosion at the drive-in for the $12,000 insurance payment, and, on another occasion, parked a truck belonging to his mother on a railway line, attempting to collect the insurance money when a train wrecked it. These were his first insurance crimes and were thus important stepping stones on his path towards the plane bombing. At the time of the plane bombing he was working as a mechanic, his 45th job since leaving school.

Inevitably, Graham tried to simulate insanity. He adopted a behavioural pattern symptomatic of a condition known as Ganser syndrome: showing disorientation and answering questions inappropriately in a way which is not characteristic of known forms of insanity. He walked very slowly and stared straight ahead with a vacant expression, rolling his eyes and speaking in a monotone, saying that everyone was against him and they were trying to poison him. He asked if his mother could visit him and attempted suicide by strangulation with two socks tightened with the cardboard core from a toilet roll. He stopped this behaviour when he was told the prosecution knew where he had bought the dynamite, timer and battery for the bomb. Later, after his trial, he admitted it was an attempt to fake insanity.

His motive was more than the money: his complicated relationship with his mother was the motor for the crime. He had argued with his mother over her refusal to stay with his family for Thanksgiving. Her rejection of him in this way made him use the dynamite on her — he had previously intended to use it to blow up the drive-in for the insurance. Her refusal to stay was taken out of all proportion.

I wanted to have her to myself for once [he said]. Since I was just a little kid she would leave me with these people, those people. I wanted to get close to her, every time I'd get close to her she'd brush me off like I was a piece of furniture, as if I didn't mean more to her than nothing. I couldn't get close to her and make her realise that I loved her. If she gave me money I was supposed to realise that was enough. I just wanted to do things with her, to sit down and talk to her — just like everybody else's mother would do.

I had to stop her from going — yet it seemed I had to be free from her too. She held something over me that I couldn't get from under. I can remember watching the plane take off. When it left the ground a load came off my shoulders, I watched her go off for the last time. I felt happier than I ever felt before in my life.

Two doctors commenting on this case remark, 'Much emotion accompanied these confessions but there was little conscious guilt, rather he was filled with fear, anxiety, despair.'

When asked if he felt remorse for planting the bomb which had killed so many people, Graham said

I just felt if it killed someone that was tough. It didn't seem to make any difference. It seemed the odds were big enough, there was more fun that way. I didn't care whether it was against the law or not. I knew I was taking a risk because the plane was twenty minutes late. No, I didn't feel sorry for anyone on that plane or their relatives. If someone said there were forty-four dead ducks in that plane it wouldn't make any difference to me. I guess it's not the right thing to say. I just didn't think about the other people on the plane.

After the trial, which became a television attraction, he refused to appeal against a sentence of death passed against him, and petitioned for the Supreme Court to overrule an appeal entered against his wishes. He was duly sent to the gas chamber on 12 January 1957. He told a warder, 'If any mail comes for me after next month, you can re-address it to hell.'

The Love Bomb

LUCILLE LEVESQUE, a booking clerk at Quebec's Ancienne Lorette airport, remembered Joseph Guay. The 31-year-old, slim, wavy-haired jeweller badly wanted a booking for his wife, Rita, on a plane the next day, 8 September. This could not be arranged, so he had to accept a booking for the day after, but Lucille put him on a waiting list. He also had some other business which she remembered. He took out a $10,000 one flight insurance policy on his wife, which insured her for one-way travel. This was a little curious, as a return flight policy was no more expensive.

Later, Lucille telephoned him at home to say she had a cancellation for the next day, his wife could fly then. He said it was 'too late', and the booking still stood for 9 September. That evening, the couple went to the theatre.

The following day, Joseph made sure she got the flight. At the airport, pretty, dark-haired Rita Guay, who was twenty-eight, was worried about her return journey — she had wanted to get back the same day, anxious about her young daughter. He persuaded her that now they had booked, it did not matter, she may as well go. He kissed her goodbye and she went. Guay stood watching the Dakota looking at his watch somewhat nervously.

The Canadian Pacific plane exploded in flight and nose-dived, crashing in woods near Sault-au-Cochon, twenty minutes after it had taken off from Quebec on 9 September 1949, killing Rita Guay and twenty-two other people, including three small children.

The plane had crashed in a particularly inhospitable part of Canada where it took rescue teams hours to reach the wreckage, and days to recover the bodies. When Guay and his five-year-old daughter went to the airport to ask about survivors, airport officials were so touched by his all too visible and audible anguish that he and the now motherless child were taken to a room in an expensive hotel, the Chateau Frontenac, and a priest was sent for to counsel them.

Despite the difficulty of access, Guay insisted on going to the scene of the accident where he wept hysterically. He arranged an expensive funeral with a five-foot cross of red roses bearing the inscription 'From Your Beloved Albert', which was his middle name and the one he liked to use in love.

All such crashes would be rigorously investigated, though in this case there was particular attention because three of the dead were directors of the Kennecott Copper Corporation, an American company which had large holdings in Canada.

The investigators' first thought was that perhaps there had been a mechanical failure in the plane, or a structural fault, but none were found. Crash investigators found the plane's engines had been running even after the explosion and there was no problem whatsoever with them. Indeed, the engines were still running, ploughing into the earth, when the plane was on the ground.

Eventually, from the shape of the twisted metal, it became clear that the plane had come down because of an explosion. Traces of dynamite were found in the baggage compartment and the way the metal had been blown out of shape from that compartment showed that the explosion had taken place there. The police checked the background of every passenger, and every piece of freight. Everything checked out except one item: they could not trace the person who consigned to air freight the 26-pound box which was declared to contain a religious statuette. Her appearance was remembered at the checking desk: a plumpish woman in her thirties dressed in black. Ten days after the crash, the identity of this woman was still unknown.

Fortunately for the investigation, Paul Pelletier, the taxi driver who had taken her to the airport remembered her. He had carried the air freight parcel down to the cab for her and driven her to the airport. He could take the police to her home address which he did, but they found she was not at home. She was Marie Pitre, a 39-year-old waitress, and when police asked for her they were redirected to the local hospital. She had taken sleeping pills in a suicide bid.

Detectives interviewed her at her bedside. She admitted taking the box that supposedly contained the statuette to the airport at the instigation of jewellery dealer Joseph Guay, who had been her lover. He had encouraged her to deliver the freight — the contents of which she claimed not to know — by saying he would cancel promissory notes which he held in her name. She said she did not know Rita Guay would be on the plane.

After the plane was brought down, newspapers carried stories saying that the police were looking for the woman in black who had consigned the box to freight. Guay visited Pitre and told her she could be identified and she had better kill herself. She should swallow sleeping tablets and turn on the gas and write a note saying she had blown up the plane because she was jealous of Rita. This is what this obliging woman said she had tried to do.

She said she could deny him nothing, even though he had another mistress called Marie-Ange Robitaille, a cigarette girl in the Monte Carlo Night Club who was sixteen when she first became Guay's lover. She called herself Angel Mary and Guay always called her Ange, French for Angel. She called him Albert.

Rita Guay found out about the affair in which her husband was meeting Marie-Ange for sex at a guest-house, and contacted the girl's father. He protested about her having an affair with a married man twice her age, she moved out of the family home and Guay installed her in the spacious flat he had obtained for Marie Pitre to live in. The older woman did not entirely approve of this domestic arrangement but there was nothing she could do, being entirely financially beholden to Guay — he owned the flat and held promissory notes in her name — and she was also emotionally dependent on him. They lived together for a while, then Pitre moved out.

Marie-Ange and Guay had a stormy relationship with Guay beating her and she frequently threatening to leave or actually running away, only to be brought back by him. He made her use a different name, Nicole Cote, to render it more difficult for her parents to trace her. He would not allow her out of the apartment except with him. Once he bruised her face with love-bites which remained for a week afterwards, so she would not try to go out.

His generosity dwindled as the violence increased. There were fewer presents and more beatings. She ran away from him at one time and was on a train about to move off, intending to get back to her parents in Montreal, when Guay ran on. He had told the railway officials he was trying to recover his little sister who was running away from home. He dragged her from the train and into his car where he took her shoes and overshoes so she could not escape.

She later, over a long period, made herself unattractive to him and he finally allowed her to leave. She went back to her parents and got another job in a night club.

He came to entrap her again, however, this time with a gun which he threatened to use on her if she did not come back. She was frightened enough to go with him to the holiday resort of Seven Isles. He spent the journey looking at the terrain below, holding his watch. On this trip their relationship of tears and violence continued. One night he left her out all night during a violent storm and struck her the next day when she packed her bags to leave. As she left he gave her a desperate love letter.

Guay had tried without success to free himself from his passion for Marie-Ange. Finally, he resolved that the only way he could break the power she had over him was to possess her completely. He had to rid himself of his wife so that he could marry Marie-Ange Robitaille and tie her to him. She must be his utterly.

First he thought he could just blow his wife up in a taxi, and he discussed the logistics of this with friends. He then considered another plan. A friend of Guay's said the jeweller offered him poison and asked him to use it to dose a bottle of cherry brandy, his wife's favourite drink, in return for $100. He refused.

Pitre was still under his control, however, and he used her for his next plot. He had her buy ten pounds of dynamite, allegedly for land-blasting work — removing rocks from some land. Suspiciously, she had induced a friend, a Mrs Hector Parent, to pick it up for her. Guay picked it up directly from Pitre. The timing device for the bomb had been assembled at Guay's behest by Genereux Ruest, Marie Pitre's crippled brother who was a watchmaker. Ruest was paralysed from the waist down but made up for his lack of mobility by his manual dexterity. Guay had claimed that the timing device was for dynamite to detonate some tree roots and he gave Ruest the clock face for the bomb.

Pitre was completely under his control, even after the plane was brought down. He told her to summon Marie-Ange to her apartment and she did. Marie-Ange thought the crash had been an accident and commiserated with him on the death of his wife. Guay got her into a bedroom and again made protestations of love and offered gifts which she refused.

This was the story Marie Pitre told the police, and enough of it leaked out to the press to have journalists swarming around the hospital when she left, attention which she relished. She posed for pictures dressed in black and with a black skullcap. The newspapers nicknamed her 'Madame Le Corbeau' or 'Mrs Crow'. Crowds gathered outside her apartment, hoping for a glimpse of her. She was later arrested for attempted suicide — an offence at that time — as a holding charge while investigations continued.

The first hearings of the 'Love Bomb Murder Trial' commencing in October 1949 attracted vast public interest. The accused needed extra police protection because of the strength of feeling against him among the thousands who thronged outside the courtroom. The eighteen-year-old son of one of the dead Kennecott executives, R. J. Parker, was apprehended in Massachusetts trying to get to Canada. He said, 'I'm going to Canada to kill the man responsible for my father's death.'

Guay was committed for a full trial which took place in March 1950. Genereux Ruest disappeared before the trial but was later found not far from Quebec. Although he showed a marked reluctance to testify, he was persuaded to say that he had made up a timing mechanism at Guay's request. He was not, however, willing to incriminate his sister.

Guay's friend, whom he had tried to have poison his wife, not only testified to this, but added that after the plane had come down Guay offered him $500 to say nothing about the poison plot. He claimed that Guay has said 'good riddance' of the death of Rita and had boasted of his insurance of her. Pitre told the full story of Guay's relationship with her and of her part in the planting of the bomb. The high point of public interest, however, was the evidence of Marie-Ange with her tale of Guay's demented passion for her. Everyone was eager to see this exceptionally beautiful young woman, for the love of whom a man had committed such a dreaful crime.

The defence argument was that a mechanism such as the one Guay had rigged up could never work, so the prosecution called a Professor Lucien Gravel who, in front of the court, took ten minutes to assemble a mock bomb with an alarm clock timer with the big hand taken out, a terminal screwed on to the clock face, and another terminal connected to the hour hand. The leads from the termini ran off the battery and a fuse. When the termini connected, as the enrapt court observed, the charge went through the wires and blew the fuse. Had it been a detonator and explosive instead of a fuse, it would have exploded.

The prosecution said that when Guay timed the flight on his journey to Seven Isles with Marie-Ange, it was to establish when a plane on that flight path would be over water and when over land. In the event, his calculation went awry because the plane was five minutes late. The wreckage was there to be examined.

Guay had got the idea of a plane bomb from a time bomb on a Philippine Air Lines converted C-47 which had blown up a cinema owner from Daet on 7 May 1949. He was sentenced to death on 15 March 1950. He was so devastated that Marie-Ange had testified against him that he did not appeal against the death sentence. Without her his life was not worth living. He bowed his head as sentence was passed and when asked if he had anything to say, said, 'No'.

The trials of Ruest and Pitre followed. Evidence was brought forward to demonstrate that they must have known they were assisting in a murder. Ruest had tested the mechanism with a small amount of explosive in his workshop and small traces remained. Both were found guilty and hanged.

After the executions Marie-Ange ran a restaurant in Montreal with the delightful name of Au Petit Coeur (The Little Heart).

Seven Silver Gifts

MIRACULOUSLY, there is one account of what it is like to be in an aeroplane when a saboteur's bomb rips it open in mid-air. On Wednesday, 24 September 1952, seventeen passengers, including journalist Margaret Larkin and her ten-year-old daughter Kathy, climbed aboard a Mexican Aviation plane at Mexico City. They were flying on a Douglas DC3 to Oaxaca, where they would be visiting friends for a few days. As the plane climbed into the sky, Margaret Larkin tried to sleep on what was a routine shuttle flight. She was woken up as the plane was rocked by an explosion, the air was filled with the roar of it and with the tearing and ripping of metal. Something smashed into Margaret's left ankle. Smoke filled the cabin, then a freezing blast of air blew in as the side of the aeroplane opened out to the sky. The passengers were screaming, including

Kathy beside her. Margaret shouted at her to fasten her seat-belt and, in the hell of smoke and flying debris blowing around the cabin, she pulled the blanket around her daughter and sheltered her with her arms.

She wrote:

I saw that she was unhurt. The blanket had protected her bare legs. I had a moment of piercing grief for her — so perfect and beautiful. There was nothing that I could do to save her; my terrible helplessness was more overwhelming than my fear. Yet perhaps there was one more thing that I could do in these last moments — perhaps I could shield her from terror. I rocked her in my arms, comforting her, and myself as well, with physical contact.

Even with the billowing smoke, it was possible to tell there had been an explosion in the forward baggage hold. Through the broken door of the baggage compartment a five-foot hole in the plane could be seen, and the contents of suitcases strewn over the floor. The fuel tank had also been torn open, and most of the plane's instruments had been rendered useless, including the radio.

With a businesslike manner she did not feel, air hostess Lilia Novelo walked past the gaping hole, where the wind was so strong it tore the buttons off her blouse. She ascertained that the situation was desperate, then went back to explain calmly to the passengers not to worry, everything would be all right, they were going back to Mexico City. She then passed out blankets and did what she could to tend the wounds of the passengers, including bandaging Margaret Larkin's ankle where blood was pouring out. Many others had more serious injuries: fractures and wounds where the blast had embedded bits of metal into their flesh.

The passengers gathered at the back of the cabin, congratulating themselves on their survival and comforting the wounded. If they had known what Captain Carlos Rodriguez was thinking they would have been less cheerful. He had decided to land at Veracruz, closer than Mexico City, but below a heavy cloud bank, and he had no radio contact. He could not know, either, how many of his landing instruments would actually work when required.

When the explosion had happened and the fuselage had been blown out behind his seat, he had been speaking to the control tower at Mexico City and had just had time to shout that his windows had broken and he was coming down blind using his instruments, before the radio cut out. His side windows were blown out and the front window had been rendered opaque from the blast. Air currents were tearing at the plane and, with the damaged instruments and weakened controls, it was all he could do to keep it level. Parts which had ripped from the plane by the blast, but had not been torn off, were presenting resistance to the air which reduced the speed of the plane. Once a plane's speed is too low, it will go out of control and plunge down. The passengers were lucky to be in the hands of a former Second World War combat pilot who was able to arrange the dangers in a realistic order in his mind and still make decisions.

If Captain Rodriguez could reach a signal tower at Tulancingo, guided only by his magnetic compass, he could guide himself from there to Veracruz, despite the cloud cover. As he considered the extent of the cloud cover, the fuel he needed to maintain height and speed, and the distances involved, he realised he would not make it. He must think of something else. While he was trying to work out an alternative, he saw the cloud floor thinning. He took a chance, and went down through it, knowing he could not regain height above the clouds. He had one shot.

He began to come down in wide spirals, intending to land anywhere he could. He had gone back towards Mexico City, where he hoped the mist would have cleared enough to provide him with a place to bring the plane down, but he would never reach the airport. Eventually, to his enormous relief, he was lucky enough to find a runway, stretching out in the distance.

He now had to decide whether to bring the landing gear down. If it came down inadequately, tangled in cabling, or collapsed on the side of the blast where the plane structure was weakened, it would be more dangerous than not coming down at all. On the other hand, a landing without the wheels down would be very dangerous indeed. He decided to drop the landing gear, and sent a message to the bemused passengers to ask if anyone had a pair of sunglasses. He was worried that the shock of landing would blow the glass of the shattered windscreen in and distract his attention when he needed it for landing. The co-pilot wore the sunglasses and used his hands to shield Captain Rodriguez from the opaque windscreen while giving him verbal instructions as to what he could see through the broken side windows.

Rodriguez brought the plane down in a perfect, smooth landing, then went through to shake the hands of all the passengers. Soldiers came to help them: he had landed at an unfinished military airfield at Santa Lucia. It was forty-five minutes since the explosion and fortunately the plane had been fifteen minutes late. Had it taken off in time it would have been too far out over mountainous country to be able to return.

Soon a plane came to ferry them back to Mexico City, and brought doctors, crash investigators and company officials. The investigation of what seemed an attempt at mass murder began immediately with questionnaires to the survivors. The North Americans were going on holiday to Oaxaca, but the investigators were most interested in six Mexicans, who did not look wealthy enough to be flying but were in fact travelling to Oaxaca to take up jobs which had been offered them by a Señor Eduardo Noriega. Most of these understandably wanted to take the relief plane the aviation company offered them so that they could take up their jobs in Oaxaca, and five did so.

On arrival, they were disappointed to find no one waiting for them. There should have been a bus to meet them and a man to tell them where to go but there was no one. Moreover, their idea of what their employment was actually to be was very confused. Officials of the Mexican Aviation Company were sympathetic and tried to help but there was no sign of their employers the lumber company, or railway company, or the 'Chicago Company' for which some of them were supposed to be working as domestics in blocks of flats.

The five came from two families. One family had been recruited via Jesus Flores Breton, an unemployed labourer who had gone to a recruiting agency where he had paid ten pesos to be given the address of an employer. He was sent to see Señor Noriega, who employed him and, as a token of good faith, gave him back his ten pesos, earning the man's highest esteem. The other family was recruited by Juan Vargos Vera, in a similar position to Breton, who had placed an advertisement in a newspaper saying that he wished any kind of employment. Vera was telephoned by Señor Noriega, who said he was an agent for the Chicago Company and recruited him. Other members of Vera's family were also invited to come to work. The sixth person who had been supposed to travel to Oaxaca, a Colombian called Ezequiel Camachoe, had decided not to complete the trip after the explosion, saying he did not think there were any jobs and that there was something peculiar about it all.

The bewildered five who continued to Oaxaca, however, were still looking forward to their highly paid jobs, for which they had had to go through such a rigorous examination: providing their birth certificates and marriage licences, certifying that they had no small children, even signing a contract. They were actually given a gift when they signed the contracts, such as a medallion or a belt buckle or keyring with their initials on them. It was explained that it was an American custom to give presents when a contract was signed. The contracts were for four years so the families had given up their apartments and sold their furniture to go out to Oaxaca.

Another person with them, who had also survived the explosion and taken the flight the company provided from Mexico City to Oaxaca, was a timid little man called Ramón Arellano. His nephew, Emiliano Arellano, had sent him to Oaxaca offering him a job as a superintendent of a small warehouse and foundry.

'You will have a house, servants and your food provided,' his nephew had written, a wonderful opportunity for the stooped little man. As the bewildered travellers compared information about the elusive Señor Noriega it became clear that he was in fact 49-year-old engineer Emiliano Arellano. An employee of Mexican Aviation had stayed with them, ostensibly to help them in their plight by paying for a hotel for them and helping them seek their employment. He listened to the story they told and noted it for the investigators.

The Colombian Ezequiel Camachoe, who had left the group, was a smart man, and realised that the lost job opened up another opportunity elsewhere: when he left Mexico City airport, declining to take the courtesy flight on to Oaxaca, he took the twisted piece of aeroplane he had taken as a souvenir and went straight off to sell his story to a newspaper. They printed his story including the fact that 'Señor Noriega' had checked two suitcases on to the plane when he came to wave off his new employees and his uncle. Camachoe soon found himself talking to the police, who held him as an illegal immigrant so that they could keep an eye on him.

The police investigated his story and found that he had been insured for 200,000 pesos. The collective insurance for Señor Noriega's employees was just under two million pesos. When Noriega's address was explored, no such person was living there. However, the porter said that Emiliano Arellano fitted the description. On the insurance questionnaires, Noriega's name was mentioned with Arellano as his agent. The information from the six other passengers, via Mexican Aviation, confirmed that Arellano was a key suspect. His uncle was able to tell them that Emiliano had worked in his father's mines, and so knew about explosives.

Police searched Emiliano's apartment and found a photograph of him, then started a manhunt.

Emiliano Arellano was the youngest of seven children of a German mother and a Mexican father who owned land and mines. He claimed to have been in the

United States, spending a total of eleven years there. He claimed to have studied at the Colorado School of Mines and the Texas School of Mines. He never received a degree, but always called himself an engineer. Arellano had difficulty holding down a job but always had an extravagant scheme up his sleeve, including one for salvaging metal from the bottom of the Gulf of Mexico; one for producing cheap oxygen; one for replacing wooden railway ties with cheaper hollow concrete ones.

He was also the moving spirit behind Post Mortem, a company for insuring people to permit them to have expensive funerals. This was to be organised by docking a small amount of money directly from the insured people's wages, which would be achieved with the collusion of the union leaders who would receive a commission. Eventually, the trade unions sank the business by refusing to co-operate.

Arellano's backer in Post Mortem was Paco Sierra, a 42-year-old prominent singer and impresario. He was the young husband of an older woman, Esperanza Iris, a very famous light opera star. The gossip was that he had married her for her money, and a certain amount of reflected fame, though it seemed a happy enough marriage which had lasted eighteen years. When questioned, Sierra denied having seen Arellano for several months, though the porter at the hotel where 'Noriega' had interviewed the workers said that Sierra had recently been visiting daily. He said, indeed, that he would never have let Arellano run up the rent like that if it were not for his friendship with Sierra who was underwriting the bills.

Sierra soon came to the police of his own accord, via a senior police officer whom he knew well and who acted as intermediary for him. Sierra said he knew Arellano, who was a reprehensible individual, and had little to do with him since the collapse of Post Mortem. However, he had seen Arellano on the night of the explosion and the engineer had given him a package which he now presented to the police. They opened the brown paper parcel to find it contained the insurance policies on the passengers and their legal documents.

Three other people were listed as

beneficiaries of the insurance policies beside Arellano: Gil Madragón, a radio singer and a good friend of Sierra; Sara Gutierrez Tenerio, a friend of his wife and organiser of her fan club; and Concepción Manzano — until recently a maid in his home and who, as it turned out, was expecting his child.

Arellano had disappeared though he did attempt to telephone Sierra, finding that the singer was not at home. The tall, gaunt fugitive took a bus to Jalapa, then turned back and returned to Mexico City, booking into two cheap hotels on different nights as he pondered the newspaper coverage and considered his story.

Finally, he realised he could hold out no longer and went to the police, admitting hiring the workers and 'attaching wires to a clock', but said it had been done under orders from Sierra. The police arrested Sierra, amid a great deal of publicity.

The first time the two former friends recounted their stories in public was at a hearing to determine whether there was evidence to justify holding them for trial. Arellano said he had been summoned to see Sierra and the singer told him he had acquired a hotel and required Arellano to find some workers to help run it. He was instructed not to engage anyone with small children or other close relatives and to obtain their birth certificates and marriage licences. This was all said to be necessary because the hotel was licensed by an American company which was particular about the sort of people who would be employed there. Arellano also admitted attaching wires to a clock which Sierra had given him. He said he was not able to do it until Sierra gave him the tools.

Arellano explained to the court that he had done this curious job for Sierra because, 'He said his father was terrified of earthquakes, and that a friend of his had an apparatus made with an alarm clock, which would register earthquakes, and he wanted to give his father such an apparatus. But, he said, he did not know how to attach the wires so as to pass the current through the clock.' Arellano therefore made such a device, with a terminal on the clock face and a wire leading off it, and the hour hand forming another terminal. He was asked directly if he knew this was to be used as a time bomb and denied it.

Sierra, with many tears and theatrical gestures, contradicted this. He said that six of the insurance policies were made out to people of his acquaintance (Arellano's uncle's was made out to his nephew alone) because he had given Arellano the names of acquaintances of his which Arellano could use for a crooked scheme whereby fake workers could receive end of year bonuses from government departments. He had later argued with Arellano over Post Mortem and cut off contact with him, he claimed, though he did later go with him to purchase an alarm clock which he claimed Arellano's wife wanted. He had bought some tools for Arellano out of the kindness of his heart. He admitted to having financial difficulties with the Iris Theatre which he managed for his wife. His wife was wealthy, he was not. Inevitably, the judge decided there was a case to answer.

Under Mexican law this was not an

offence triable by a jury, so the trial took place before a judge. Part of the evidence, from Ramón Arellano, was that his nephew had taken his small, tattered suitcase and had checked it in. It was only later, after the flight, when he handed in the baggage receipt slip, that he found two suitcases had been checked in under his name. The stooped, impoverished old man was a fine witness, a man too humble and broken by his experiences to say anything but the truth. Arellano's deception of the impoverished old man set the public fiercely against him. He told how he had been offered a good job, had been brought to Mexico City, put up in a hotel and taken to the airport to be sent to his death, all the while praising his generous, thoughtful nephew. It was seen as a particular affront to decency to trick a member of your own family in this way; it seemed more excusable to do it to strangers. The other people recruited by Arellano, now living with friends and relatives and with no homes or jobs, also gave moving testimony against him.

The three friends of Sierra, whose

names appeared as beneficiaries of the insurance policies besides that of Arellano, gave evidence to say they did not know their names were on the policies.

A local carpenter testified that Arellano had come to him to ask him to construct a wooden box in a hurry 'because he wanted to send a battery out of the country'. There was some disagreement as to who had possession of this battery, and whether it was charged up or whether Sierra called on Arellano to have it charged. Evidence of a rehearsal for the bomb, a test explosion, was concealed by both men. Both concealed the evidence of buying the explosives, too, though later Arellano said Sierra's chauffeur Hector had done it at Sierra's instigation.

Arellano used to boast that he was a master engineer with experience of explosives and would never have constructed such a poor bomb, his would have been far better. This probably did little to impress the court.

The most damning evidence, linking the men together in the conspiracy, concerned the little silver gifts for their victims. These gifts had been bought at a shop where Sierra had introduced Arellano. They were for the victims to carry so their bodies could be identified, as all were engraved with their initials: a medallion, a keyring, an initialled bracelet and wallets with small engraved silver plates. The shopkeeper where they had bought them could not remember whether both had participated in the purchase or only Arellano, but they had both been there. One shop assistant remembered Sierra specifically asking for a chain for the medallion which came with a ribbon — something which might be torn off a body in the plane explosion. Sierra had paid for the gifts, attempting to bargain the shopkeeper down in price.

The attempts of the two men to throw the blame on each other rebounded on themselves: if Sierra were the master criminal with Arellano as his dupe, why did he not send Arellano in the plane too, and remove the only witness? If Arellano were the master criminal, why did he use the names of friends of Sierra whom he had not met? The only answer is that they were working together and were equally guilty.

Sierra had all the advantages of friends in high places, and of hosts of admirers who would come forward to testify to his performing abilities and his Catholicism. He called twelve character witnesses. The friendless Arellano called none.

The judge found them both guilty but considered Sierra had been misled by the 'dangerous criminality' of Arellano. Sierra was 'easily susceptible to reform and social adaptation' while the reprobate Arellano was beyond redemption. The judge gave Arellano the maximum sentence, thirty years, while giving Sierra eight.

There was now an interesting change in popular feeling, which had hitherto supported Sierra. Now that his guilt was established beyond doubt, it seemed utterly unfair that the rich and famous man should get off lightly and his wretched accomplice should receive the maximum for the same offence.

They both appealed: Arellano for a reduction in sentence, and Sierra that he was an innocent man wrongly convicted. The appeal court saw no need to alter Arellano's sentence but fully recognised the injustice of Sierra's, and raised his to thirty years as well.

Sierra now went mad or feigned madness, taking on the persona of Father Pro, a famous figure in Mexican history who was executed for his alleged involvement in a bomb plot. The formerly fat singer did not eat and prayed continually. However, this did not have what was presumably the desired effect of moving him to a private mental hospital, and he gradually recovered.

Margaret Larkin actually went into the prison and interviewed her would-be murderers, a fascinating journalistic feat. In the event, it was less revealing than might be imagined. In common with other insurance murderers, Arellano and Sierra were egotistical, mendacious and utterly unrepentant. They had no compassion for their victims, or intended victims, and retained all their emotion for self-pity. She did, however, establish from Arellano why the bomb did not destroy the plane. Speaking purely hypothetically, of course, he said it might have been because the powder was not sufficiently compressed, or because some of the powder had got wet with fluid from the motorcycle battery when it had turned over. Larkin surmised that Arellano, who was neither an engineer nor even a very good amateur technician, was simply incapable of making a very good bomb.

★ ★ ★

This story had an interesting sequel. One José Alfredo del Valle was undeterred by these stiff sentences, and set out to duplicate the crime. He intended to simulate his own death in order that his 'widow' could collect 850,000 pesos in insurance. To make it work, someone who looked like him and a plane full of people had to die.

Del Valle, a gambler, practised making bombs for nine months. He frequently gambled with men in military circles and eventually induced one to sell him some dynamite and TNT. He then encouraged a gambling friend to drive with him from Mexico City to Culiacán. He helpfully loaned his friend some of his clothes and bought him a ticket, in his own name, to La Paz in California. He was going to drive the car to La Paz and he would meet the gullible friend there. In fact, it all went wrong because the flight was too heavily laden and when he tried to check in the 77-pound package with the bomb, they would not take it, but consigned it to fly separately. He made an excuse to his friend, who presumably was growing used to bizarre behaviour by now, and he did not take the plane.

The bomb, however, was taken that day, on 9 May 1953, via Mazatlán airport, where it exploded killing three airport employees and injuring fourteen other people. Del Valle later tried to hang himself in a public park but was arrested and under questioning he admitted the crime. He said he had got the idea from the Arellano-Sierra case and, like them, he was sentenced to thirty years in prison. He continued to try to kill himself, eventually succeeding, on 14 October 1956, with tablets of the barbiturate Nembutal.

Stealing Bodies

THERE was a grisly find in the woods near Saalfield, Germany in September 1928: a man's skeleton with clear signs of violence. He had been shot through the head, his feet had been chopped off and his clothing scorched. In the waistcoat pocket was a watch engraved H. Alberding, Fulda. In the lining of the right sleeve of the jacket was a letter in Heinrich Alberding's handwriting, saying, 'I must now prepare myself for my last journey, I am told. If anything . . . should happen to me, inform the police in Fulda at once. My name and address are: Heinrich Alberding, 24 Markstrasse, Fulda.'

It was not, of course, the body of Heinrich Alberding, a 32-year-old businessman who had disappeared on his way to Frankfurt eight months earlier. Alberding had written a letter to the police in Fulda after his disappearance, claiming he was sending it by the unconventional route of throwing it out of a window and trusting that someone would pick it up and post it. He was being held captive, he wrote, by two business rivals who had drugged and kidnapped him because he had uncovered their narcotics trade. If his body were found, the police should look in the right sleeve of the jacket.

Once this body was found, Mrs Alberding approached two insurance companies and claimed a total of 60,000 marks on policies which had been taken out in September 1927, four months before Alberding's disappearance.

Examination of the spine of the corpse showed it was not the body of a man of thirty-two, but of someone ten years younger. An anatomist from Gottingen, Professor Stadtmuler demonstrated that the dead man could not be Alberding by using a novel method to compare the skulls. He used photographs to make life-sized drawings of Alberding's skull and then made similar drawings of the skull of the corpse. When the drawings were superimposed it was obvious they were not of the same man.

In 1934, police made a sudden raid on Alberding's house. He was found hiding under a bed and was taken out to stand trial for murder. The victim was not identified; he was just some poor wretch who had been killed and mutilated by Alberding who was eventually sentenced to death.

The discovery of the corpse in the woods set the scene for a cluster of similar insurance murders and frauds which happened over the next few years. In each case there was a well-to-do businessman as the murderer; an elaborate plot to produce the deception; and an anonymous victim whose name was not even known by the murderer. The murderers in the three cases which follow all lived lives which were envied by others: they had pleasant homes and jobs, and families who loved them. But they all thought they were so clever they could get away with the murder and mutilation of a stranger. All had such contempt for human life that they could kill someone without remorse, as long as they were poor enough, or, in Alfred Rouse's chilling phrase, 'the sort of man no one would miss.'

A Bogus Funeral

ERICH TETZNER, a travelling salesman from Leipzig, had a terrible car accident in November 1929. He was driving his green Opel along Highway 8 when it collided with a milestone and caught fire. He was burned to death. The sympathetic authorities released what was left of the body to the grieving widow, Emma Tetzner, for a burial which she arranged in the South Cemetery of Leipzig. She also applied for his insurance payments with three different companies. These amounted to the massive payout of 145,000 marks, a remarkable sum for someone of his limited means. The policies had, moreover, come into effect only a few weeks previously.

The least sceptical insurance agent was likely to be suspicious about this death. Why did Tetzner make no attempt to get out of the car? Perhaps he had a heart attack: did he have heart problems?

Perhaps it was suicide, in which case they would not have to pay at all. In the end, under some pressure, Emma Tetzner consented to an autopsy on the charred remains.

An employee of one insurance company, the Nordstern, called on the forensic scientist Richard Kockel at the University of Leipzig, who was interested enough to go to the cemetery. The body awaited burial within an hour.

In the coffin was a badly charred trunk to which was attached the base of a skull, the upper halves of both thighs and part of the arms. There was also, surprisingly, a fresh piece of brain about the size of a fist next to the corpse. There was no soot in the air passages, which showed this man had been dead before the fire started: he had not breathed in any fumes. There was blood in the heart and part of the lung was well preserved, so Kockel took samples. Known changes in skeletal structure in early adulthood led Kockel to deduce that the skeleton was of a man aged around twenty and certainly not more than twenty-two. The skeleton was also that of a light young man. Tetzner was twenty-six years old, five feet eight inches tall, stockily built and even overweight.

Kockel left the chapel of rest with his jars of samples, and let the grieving friends and relatives get on with the funeral of someone who was certainly not Erich Tetzner.

On examining the tissue he had taken away, Kockel found there was no carbon monoxide in the blood, which meant indisputably that Tetzner could not have been killed in a fire. The lungs showed fatty embolisms, however: fat from the tissues driven into the lungs in a manner which was consistent with physical trauma. In Kockel's estimation the man had been beaten to death and then burned. Kockel told the police and advised them to search for the missing parts of the body: the top of the head, which presumably had been removed to hide the evidence of injury; and the bottom of the legs. Perhaps these had been removed for the grotesque reason of making a corpse that had a different height to Tetzner seem to be of the same height. It was later mentioned by one of the policemen who had been at the scene that the piece of brain had been found outside the car, about five feet away, and not even on the driver's side of the vehicle.

The police started to keep a watch on the Tetzner house. The family had no telephone of their own but Emma Tetzner habitually used that of a neighbour which the police tapped. It paid off within days when the detective listening in to the calls heard one from Strasbourg coming in at 8 a.m. He intercepted it before it was routed to the home telephone and played the part of someone taking the call. The caller gave his name as Sranelli. The sharp-witted detective said that Emma Tetzner was not available, but that he should call back at 6 p.m. when she would be.

They traced the call to a booth in the main Strasbourg post office. Police Chief Kriegern contacted the French police to explain the situation, and took a flight to Strasbourg where he was in time to arrest the real Erich Tetzner as he entered the telephone booth. The thick-set, overweight man immediately admitted his true identity.

The story had begun innocently enough: Emma Tetzner's mother was being advised by her doctors to have an operation for cancer. Tetzner advised her against it, then he changed his mind, insured her life for 10,000 marks and encouraged her to go for the operation. She died within three days of surgery and he collected the insurance. This seemed a very easy way of making money.

He discussed with his wife insuring himself and faking his death. She suggested digging up a newly buried body from the graveyard and faking an accident where the corpse would be substituted for him. 'Don't be a fool,' he said, 'there must be blood about.'

He went on to experiment with ways of obtaining a fresh corpse. On one occasion, he advertised for a travelling companion and met a young man who applied for the post, but the man grew suspicious and refused to join him. Then he offered a ride to a locksmith called Alois Ortner on the highway near Ingolstadt.

'I realised that this young man would

338

be ideal to leave in the car,' Tetzner later confessed. 'Passing through the town of Hof I gave him some money, and told him to get a shave and buy himself a collar. I wanted him to look as respectable and as much like me as possible.

'Later I asked Ortner to crawl under the car and look at the oil valve. While he was under the car, I seized a hammer and a pad of ether. When he emerged I fell on him.' He hit Ortner with all his force, striking two terrible blows, to the head and shoulders. Streaming with blood, the young man fought back powerfully and succeeded in running off into the woods where he collapsed shortly after Tetzner had driven off.

Poor Ortner reported the assault to the police but he could not remember the number of the car and they did not believe him, thinking he had been involved in an attempted robbery of a passing motorist in which he got the worst of it. Ortner was still in hospital twelve days later when Tetzner was caught, and he eventually gave evidence at Tetzner's trial. The sceptical police to whom he had told his story realised it tied in with

Tetzner only after the murderer's arrest.

After this setback for his enterprise, Tetzner mused over different plans. He said, 'I now intended to pick up a man in my car, blind him by throwing pepper in his face, then burn him alive while he was helpless.' He would then telephone Emma Tetzner and tell her what sort of clothes the dead man was wearing so that she could tell the police, in order to identify him as her husband.

When it came to the man who was buried under his name, even someone as cold-blooded as Tetzner had difficulty bringing himself to describe what had happened. He first confessed that he had murdered a hitch-hiker who was somewhat younger and frailer than himself: a necessary expedient when he had such trouble with the locksmith. The 21–year-old man, Tetzner said, fell asleep so he drove the car slowly into the milestone and when the man awoke, told him they had had a minor accident. The young man went back to sleep and Tetzner poured petrol over the car from a reserve can he had, set a petrol trail and ignited it to burn his passenger alive. This was ridiculous. How did the passenger get from the passenger seat into the driver's seat? How did part of his brain get five feet out of the car? How was he subdued to stop him waking at the explosion of the petrol? What happened to the bottom part of his legs?

In the event, Tetzner did not stick to this ridiculous story anyway. He concocted an even more foolish one. Five months after his first confession, and before the trial, he withdrew his earlier confession and substituted the following story, given in the words he used at the trial:

On the night of November 29 1929, I ran over a man shortly after passing Bayreuth. I placed him on the seat beside me and drove on until he died. Then I put him in the boot.

While having supper at an inn it occurred to me that here was an opportunity to carry out my scheme without murdering anybody. I drove on and, shortly before reaching Ratisbon, I ran the car into a tree to make it appear as though an accident had happened. Then I sprinkled the car with petrol and set it on fire.

Of course, this new version of events meant that for five months Tetzner had made statements admitting to a murder, allegedly to cover up a case of manslaughter. It was unlikely, to say the least.

This gave an opportunity for the forensic scientists to argue about what had really happened. Hans Molitor, director of the Institute of Forensic Medicine in Erlangen, said the first version was correct and that the fatty embolism in the lungs was a byproduct of the man's being burned alive. Richard Kockel continued to insist that neither version was true and that the unknown man had been the victim of mutilating violence before being placed in the car and burned while already dead. The jury believed this version.

Before he was executed, Tetzner said, 'It was just as Professor Kockel thought,' and explained that his passenger had complained of the cold. He had wrapped him in a heavy rug, with his arms fixed to his body, and had then strangled him. He had then crashed the car and set fire to it. This could not be true either, as it did not account for the extreme injuries which the innocent young man had suffered. Perhaps it was just that Tetzner could not face the reality of what he had done. He was executed at Regensburg on 2 May 1931.

The Murder Camp

ONE morning in 1930 Fritz Saffran came into the Platz Furniture Store, which he ran in the town of Rastenberg, Germany, brandishing a newspaper. 'Have you read the report about this man Tetzner?' he said to his lover Ella Augustin. 'That is how I will do our job, too.'

Saffran, who was thirty, had been managing the store for its owner who had retired and who later blessed the marriage of his daughter and the astute young man. A former schoolmaster, Saffran had made the business pay through the worst years of the depression. His easy-going manner made him a popular man in the shop and the town. He also made sure his credit terms were flexible so the store was always full of customers.

In fact, the business was far from prosperous. By the evening of 15 September 1930 the store's finances had been going downhill for two years. Financial

344

difficulties were blown away, however, when an explosion shook the store and it burst into flames with thirty people at work inside. Nothing could be done — all the furniture and the building were destroyed.

The chief clerk of the store, Erich Kipnik, ran to Herr Platz's home to gasp out that Saffran had died in the fire. They had spent the evening in a café then had noticed a glow in the sky in the direction of the store. When they saw the building was ablaze, Saffran ran inside, saying he was going to rescue the ledgers.

'Without a second's hesitation he dashed into the heart of the burning building,' said Kipnik. 'I have never seen anything so brave in my life.'

A little later, a body was found in the charred wreckage of the store. It had the remains of Saffran's suit on, his rings on its fingers and his monogrammed silver watch in the waistcoat pocket.

The town was devastated by the loss and Ella Augustin seemed particularly distraught, collapsing in the street with grief. This vivacious and open young woman had, since she arrived at the firm six years previously, been madly in love with Saffran and had made no attempt to conceal it. At some time Saffran had reciprocated, either because he was flattered, or he wanted sex, or because he wanted to draw her into his fraudulent manipulations, or all three.

There was no great mystery about the fire, and no suspicion, until a taxi was ordered to take a passenger to Königsberg at 3 a.m. and the passenger who stepped out of Ella Augustin's home was Fritz Saffran. Why he showed himself in this way is unclear. Perhaps they had argued and she had ordered him out. Perhaps the taxi driver, called Reck, was in on the conspiracy — the police certainly thought so for they charged him with aiding and abetting but did not prove the charge. It was, anyway, as a result of his talking about his unexpected passenger that police enquiries began. He had refused to take his passenger to his destination, going only to Gerdauen whence Saffran had to walk.

The police started to take an interest in the business affairs of Fritz Saffran.

They quickly discovered that all was not as it seemed at the Platz Furniture Store. It was in severe financial difficulties. The firm had too many bad debts. The easy manner of the manager persuaded customers to buy furniture on hire purchase but not to pay the instalments. To cover debts, Saffran had been taking out loans at high interest. He had also submitted the same hire purchase contracts to two different finance houses, in Berlin and in Königsberg. Even this was not enough, and he forged nearly 400 sale contracts and raised money on them in the same two cities. He then falsified the balances to make the assets on the firm's books worth 285,000 marks when they were actually worth 25,000. Ella Augustin and Erich Kipnik were both in on the fraud and on Saffran's plot to get them out of it. Someone must have suspected something because, in order to distance himself from Augustin, and imply they were not working hand in hand, Saffran staged a scene in which he berated her in front of her office colleagues for some small slip, making her cry. She was an eager actress, as her performance of grief after his 'death' demonstrated.

The fire would wipe out evidence of their criminal behaviour and provide an insurance sum for those who were left. Whether Saffran could have got his hands on it is doubtful, but it is probable it would have been dealt with by Kipnik, his accomplice. An insurance of 140,000 marks would go to Saffran's wife.

Saffran was now on the run. He was staying with a relative of Augustin's, a carpenter who had a tiny lodging in Lauritzer Strasse, Berlin. He grew a moustache to disguise his appearance and went out only after dark. He had only 300 marks and nowhere else to go to. Finally, confinement in the tiny rooms became too much for him and he left, taking the carpenter's identity papers. He intended to go to Hamburg then somehow catch a boat to Brazil. Instead of going to the main railway terminal in Berlin, which would certainly be watched for any sign of him, he went to the suburb of Spandau. Unfortunately for him, the railway official who sold him a ticket had been in the Rastenberg Rifle Brigade a few years previously, stationed in his own town, and he recognised the formerly ebullient furniture store manager.

The stationmaster called the police, who telegrammed the guard of the moving train and rang the police at the next station, Wittenberg, where Saffran would have to change trains. Saffran was arrested in the waiting-room there, and seemed quite relieved his life on the run was over.

The story which came out at the trial was of the three conspirators driving about the countryside with an almost comic desperation, looking for an innocent man to kill. Once Saffran had persuaded them of how clever the Tetzner case was, they set out to do the same thing and went through the same kind of reasoning, facing the same problems he had.

At first they intended to obtain a corpse from a graveyard but realised it would not be of sufficiently high quality to fool the police. 'So we established a murder camp in the Nikolai Forest,' Saffran said. 'The girl stayed behind in the camp while Kipnik and I, each in his own car, roved the countryside for miles around, looking for a likely victim, then reported to the camp at evening. After a time we all three began to go out on these man-hunts.'

Sometimes they would leave the car in the woods and wait behind hedgerows for a man to come walking down the road. Once they saw a man walking alone along a lane. Saffran shouted to him to get him to approach them but he did not hear, or was afraid of their intentions, as he did not come into their range. One night, they got a pedestrian in the car and were going to proceed with the murder when he told them he had six children. They were moved by compassion and let him go.

Another man was less lucky; they overtook him and asked if he wanted a lift. He got in the car and Saffran drove off at a pace. He slammed on the brakes and at the same time Kipnik smashed the man's head three times with a club. Ella Augustin held the killer back, however. 'Ella lost her nerve,' as Saffran put it, and the man escaped.

They then decided that the original plan, to put the murdered man in a car and burn it, was too risky, and they decided to kill someone and take the body to the store.

The police, too, first thought of graveyards, and spent some time searching graveyards to see if any had been robbed of fresh bodies. The corpse they had found did seem to have been in the ground. They did not have much by which to identify him, but when illustrations of the victim's teeth were published in a dental journal, a dentist saw them and recognised the work as being the same as that which he had done on one of his patients. They checked his address and, as they expected, the man had been missing for several weeks. He was Friedrich Dahl, a 25–year-old dairyman who had cycled from his home near Königsberg to look for work. His widow was sent for and she identified his clothes as similar to those he was wearing when she last saw him. This is odd, as the conspirators claim to have dressed him in Saffran's clothes. They probably left most of his own clothes on — they did seem rather squeamish for this sort of work — and only put some of Saffran's clothes on the corpse, expecting the clothes to be consumed by fire anyway.

At the trial, both men blamed the other for the murder itself and Saffran even said that on the fateful night he told Kipnik to drive back as 'my courage failed me'. They stopped the cyclist on some pretext and one of them shot him in the head. It would not be possible to tell independently who did it; for both carried pistols. They rolled him in a carpet prepared for that purpose, concealed it in a shallow grave for two days, then took it to the store. They then put the identifying jewellery and, perhaps, clothes on it, poured twenty-five gallons of petrol over the floor of the store and set fire to it.

One of the most dramatic moments in the trial came when Frau Dahl, the small, frail wife of the murdered man, entered the witness box dressed in her widow's black. Saffran fell to his knees and cried out, 'Frau Dahl, I share responsibility for the death of your husband. I beg you, I beseech you on my bended knees to forgive me for what we have done. And if you cannot grant me your forgiveness today, perhaps at some time in the future you will be able to sympathise with me.'

Kipnik shouted, 'It is terrible to me when I think of my own poor wife and our boy, and imagine what they would have suffered if what we did to your husband had happened to me.'

Later, when Kipnik addressed the court and tried to lay all the blame on Saffran, Ella Augustin, loyal to her lover to the last, stood pointing a finger at him screaming, 'You are the murderer'.

When Saffran was able to speak to the jury he made a curious appeal to their sympathy. 'Think of my terrible position,' he pleaded. 'I was leading a double life. At home I had to appear cheerful and contented, while my heart was breaking. At night I was forced to go out hunting for men to murder.' Their sympathy was muted, to say the least.

The two men were condemned to death but their sentences were commuted to penal servitude for life. Ella Augustin was let off lightly with five years' penal servitude.

The Sort of Man
No One Would Miss

ON the night of 5 November 1930, two cousins, William Bailey and Alfred Brown, were walking home on the moonlit road after a Bonfire Night dance. It was 2 a.m. and they were turning off the road from Northampton and towards the village of Hardingstone where they lived. Just as they turned, a man scrambled from a ditch. He was breathless and agitated, wore a mackintosh but no hat, and was carrying an attaché case. The young men wondered what a respectably dressed man was doing running about by the side of the road in the small hours of the morning when they noticed a fire a few hundred yards down the road. 'What's that?' one said to the other.

It was the man from the ditch who answered. 'It looks as if someone has had a bonfire,' he said, as he hurried away. They watched him go towards Northampton, then turn and look towards London, then stop as if he did not know which way to go.

The cousins began to run towards the flames which were soaring into the night to a height of fifteen feet. It was a car, but was burning so fiercely they could scarcely make it out. One of the cousins, William, was the son of the village constable, Hedley Bailey, and he ran to wake him. His cousin, Alfred, went to wake another policeman. The four approached the fire. By the time they reached it, the flames had died down so a body could be discerned. They fetched buckets of water and extinguished the blaze.

By daylight they could see the scene clearly. The car was a Morris Minor. The charred body inside was a terrible sight. The trunk was lying over the passenger seat and the face was on the driver's seat. The right arm was stretched behind to a petrol can and was burnt off at the elbow. The left leg was doubled under the trunk and the right leg was burned off below the knee. Near the car was a mallet with a human hair adhering to it.

Police were more eager to get this gruesome sight off the road than to solve a crime — murder was not immediately suspected — so, as soon as it was possible to touch the body, it was wrapped in sacking and taken to the Crown Inn at Hardingstone. Police in Northampton began their investigations by asking in the area if a woman had gone missing, as the corpse was thought to be that of a woman.

A post-mortem in the garage of the Crown Inn showed from a suspected fragment of the prostate gland, that it was a male body. He was aged about thirty and had burned to death. His lungs were pigmented, which may have meant he had been a coal miner. The only piece of cloth which remained was part of the fly of a pair of trousers which had been protected from fire and oxygen by the bending of the left thigh against the stomach. Buckles from a pair of braces were also found.

A check on the registration number of the car, MU 1468, showed it to be owned by Alfred Arthur Rouse, a

36–year-old salesman. On the afternoon of 6 November, police called on Mrs Lily Rouse at the family home in Buxted Road, Finchley.

Mrs Rouse was taken to Northampton where she was shown 'brace buckles and pieces of clothing' which they thought might belong to her husband. She was not asked to identify the charred body as it was utterly beyond recognition and could only distress her to no purpose.

Police were interested in knowing more of the stranger the two cousins had seen leaving the scene so hastily, and they circulated a description of him. Of course, it was a description of Alfred Rouse, as there was little doubt that the man seen running away was him. The burned body fooled no one. This was clearly a case of foul play, not an accident. Had it been an accident, however, Mrs Rouse would have received the £1000 from the accidental death insurance policy her husband had just taken out. She would also have been rid of a husband who was also married to someone else — perhaps to two other people.

Rouse came from a respectable lower middle-class family in Herne Hill, London. His father was a hosier. When he was only six his father had left his mother and taken away the children, who were then brought up by an aunt.

A bright child, Rouse was also musical, athletic and a regular church-goer. Though he was later to claim he had been to Eton and Cambridge, he actually went to the local council school. When he left school it was to be an office boy in an estate agent's, then he worked in a furniture wholesaler's in the West End for five years. He married Lily Watkins, a clerk three years his senior, in 1914, just before he went to France to fight on the Western Front. Here he had an affair with a French girl who had a child by him. After only a few months in France, he was wounded when a shell exploded near him in Givenchy. It was allegedly while he was grappling with a German who was about to kill him with a bayonet, and the shell saved him, though details like this are often added by old soldiers for bravado. Whatever the truth, he was certainly wounded in the head and thigh, and discharged from the army.

The wound in his temple healed and he became a commercial traveller for a Leicester firm which made braces and garters, driving around the country in his own car which he also repaired, becoming a skilled mechanic. He made £500 a year, a very good income. He had a cheerful manner and was a bright companion, and so easily made himself popular in his work and around his home in Finchley. For many people in the South of England the late 1920s and the 'hungry thirties' were a time of prosperity. There was an unprecedented rise in home ownership and many middle-class families could afford cars. Alfred and Lily Rouse were among these prosperous suburban folk, with their pleasant house, car and weekends at the tennis club where Rouse was a talented player with his many friends. His party trick was to sing songs from light opera in his pleasing baritone voice.

Rouse also found his good looks and ready wit were invaluable in picking up girls he encountered in his travelling life and he seduced shop assistants, waitresses, servants and nurses. He posed as a man of means with a wealthy background and several houses, who had risen to the rank of major in the army. One estimate is that he seduced nearly eighty women in his travels.

He also had a child by a fourteen-year-old Edinburgh girl, a waitress called Helen Campbell. The child died at five weeks, then, when Campbell was older, he married her at St Mary's Church, Islington. In 1924 she had another child, called Arthur, and an arrangement was made for him to be raised by Mrs Rouse, who was childless. Lily obviously had a fair idea of her husband's affairs. At one time Rouse was supporting this child, as well as a child in Paris, and there was another maintenance order against him.

The following year, when he was thirty-one, he seduced a seventeen-year-old domestic servant, Nellie Tucker, promising to marry her 'when trade improves', and a child was born to her after which she obtained a maintenance order against Rouse. She later gave birth to a second one of his children.

At the same time another girl, a

teenaged nurse called Ivy Jenkins from Gelligaer in Wales, was also expecting a child by Rouse, and having a difficult time with the pregnancy. He had married her, too, or at least that was what her colliery proprietor father believed. Rouse visited her family as her husband, telling them he had paid £1250 for a house in Kingston-upon-Thames which he had furnished. When his wife was well enough to travel, they would go there along with her sister who would spend the first three months with them. Another child in England was also reported to have been fathered by Rouse by another woman.

Obviously, much of this was kept from the real Mrs Rouse but she cannot have been entirely ignorant of the kind of life he was living. When asked about it he said, 'She is really too good for me, I like a woman who will make a fuss of me. I don't ever remember my wife sitting on my knee but otherwise she is a good wife. I am very friendly with several women but it is an expensive game . . . My harem takes me to several places, and I am not at home a great deal, but my wife doesn't ask questions now.'

Rouse's lifestyle was costing him far too much, considering he was earning £10 a week and the maintenance of the car and the house in Finchley cost him half that. His first plan to get him out of his difficulties and away from his real wife, who seemed insufficiently sensual for him, was to sell the house from over her head, together with the furniture, and make an allowance to her. This would, in theory, leave him free to go off with Ivy Jenkins.

The idea that a crime could be successful, and a smart enough criminal could fool the police, came from an unsolved murder which had happened in summer 1930. The body of a woman called Agnes Kesson was found in a ditch. She had been strangled. Rouse said, 'It was the Agnes Kesson case at Epsom in June which first set me thinking. It showed that it was possible to beat the police if you were careful enough.'

He may have known something of the Tetzner case, too, for the German salesman's car had been found burning nearly a year before Rouse's was, so there was ample time for the travelling salesmen's community to gossip about it, even though the case did not come to trial until after Rouse's. Anyway, Rouse hit on the same plan. He took out the insurance and looked for a double. The insurance was for £1000 and the value of the car, which was said to be £140. It was taken out with the Eclipse Company on 18 July 1930. It was also payable on the death of a passenger in an accident, and there may have been some intention by Rouse to use this clause to keep his own identity and claim the money.

In late October or early November 1930, he found a victim. He met an unemployed man near the Swan and Pyramid public house in Whetstone High Road and offered him a drink. The man was about the same height and build as Rouse. He was a respectable man whose only fault was that he had no work, and this he had tried to remedy by tramping the roads looking for employment. He had been to Peterborough, Hull, Norwich and other places, relying on lifts from passing motorists. In his conversation with Rouse he said, 'I have no relations,' which was all Rouse needed. He arranged to meet him again, making a deceitful offer of help to him.

On the evening of 5 November Rouse was in hospital with Nellie Tucker, who had just borne him her second child. She still thought he was a single man, which was at least doubly if not trebly wrong. She noticed he was very depressed and preoccupied and kept an eye on the clock. She asked if he were meeting someone and he denied it but she believed he was.

He picked up the unemployed stranger outside the Swan and Pyramid just after 8 p.m., offering to take him as far as Leicester. Rouse was a teetotaller, but bought a bottle of whisky for his passenger.

Six hours later, Rouse came stumbling away from the blazing car. He was going to leave the lane, running through a gap in the hedge, but turned back, thinking it was a ploughed field and would leave his footprints. In fact it was a meadow and he could have run on it without leaving prints — and without meeting the young cousins who encountered him at the top of the lane. He was completely thrown by meeting them — he certainly could not have expected to have seen someone else on that quiet lane at night — and made the foolish mistake of the remark about the bonfire. Then, not knowing what to do, or where to go, he made for home in Finchley. He got a lift from a passing lorry and arrived home at about 6.20 a.m. He did not eat or change his clothes. Lily Rouse later said she thought that he had returned earlier in the morning, at about one o'clock and he had stayed for half an hour, and that the car had been burned after he had left her. She was simply wrong. This was one of those curious anomalies which occur in evidence by witnesses, quite innocently and with no intent to deceive.

Rouse seems to have behaved like a frightened child, not knowing which way to run and saying the first thing which came into his head. In fact he was saying a great deal but it was a different story to everyone he spoke to.

He set out to Gelligaer where, as a telegram from her father had informed him, Ivy was very ill. He went to a coach company in the Strand and booked a seat to South Wales, telling the agent his car had been stolen on the Great North Road while he was drinking coffee at a driver's stall. In the coach he sat next to the driver and told him his car had been stolen in St Albans. Later, he told the proprietor of The Cooper's Arms that his car had been stolen after he had gone into a London restaurant for a meal.

He arrived at Gelligaer and pacified the family of Ivy Jenkins, telling them his car had been stolen, but his pretence of normality began to break down when he saw the newspapers. There was a full account of the mystery of the charred corpse in the car, a description of him and an account of his wife's visit to Northampton. He had badly underestimated the news value of the case. 'I did not think there would be much fuss in the papers about the thing,' he later said.

Later asked about it, William Jenkins, Ivy's father, said, 'He said the car did not belong to him at all . . . He said his car was insured, or something like that.' The following morning, Ivy's sister showed

366

Rouse a paper with a photograph of the burnt out car with its registration number and his name. It also gave his wife's name. Rouse folded the paper up and put it in his pocket but he must have given the appearance of a man being comically deluged with newspapers. Apart from the problems of the police wanting to interview him, there was the high risk of the Gelligaer family finding out about his wife in London, and of Ivy's father and brother remonstrating firmly with him.

He was driven to Cardiff by a family friend of the Jenkins who asked him questions about the burning car and received no adequate replies. From Cardiff, Rouse booked a coach to London, which was met, at Hammersmith, by one Detective Sergeant Skelly. The family friend, to whom it was obvious Rouse was the man the police were looking for, had given him away.

'I am glad it is all over,' he said, 'I was going to Scotland Yard about it. I was responsible. I am glad it is over. I have had no sleep.'

Rouse made a statement at Hammersmith police station:

I don't know what happened exactly. I picked the man up on the Great North Road, he asked me for a lift. He seemed a respectable man, and said he was going to the Midlands.

I did not know anything about the man, and I thought I saw his hand on my case, which was in the back of the car. I later became sleepy and could hardly keep awake. The engine started to spit, and I thought I was running out of petrol.I pulled into the side of the road. I wanted to relieve myself, and said to the man, 'There is some petrol in the can; you can empty it into the tank while I am gone,' and lifted up the bonnet and showed him where to put it in.

He said, 'What about a smoke?' I said, 'I have given you all my cigarettes as it is.' I then went some distance down the road, and had just got my trousers down when I noticed a big flame from behind. I pulled my trousers up quickly and ran towards the car, which was in flames. I saw the man was inside, and I tried to open the door, but I could not, as the car was then a mass of flames. I then began to tremble violently. I was all of a shake. I did not know what to do, and I ran as hard as I could along the road where I saw the two men. I felt I was responsible for what had happened. I lost my head and I didn't know what to do, and really don't know what I have done since.

He gave roughly the same story later, but this time said he had picked the stranger up half a mile past Tally Ho Corner in Finchley, and that the stranger had been drinking. He carried a mallet for beating out dents in mudguards but did not know how a human hair had got on it. Asked how the car had burst into flames, he said, 'First of all, I gave the man a cigar, which he would naturally light in one way or other. I presumed he would have a match. Presuming he filled up the tank, he would have put the petrol can back in the car, and he might not have put the cap on, and may have upset some petrol in the car, and then if he had lit his cigar the car would have caught fire.'

His trial started at Northampton on 26 January 1931. His manner was described by one observer as 'jaunty and self assured' as he tried to convey the impression that a man of his calibre would contrive a far better murder than this one, were he to put his mind to it.

Part of the case for the prosecution was to demonstrate that a crime had happened at all. If the stranger died in the way Rouse had claimed he did, there was no one to blame but himself.

The prosecution could demonstrate that the man had been alive when the car burst into flames, though he was unconscious. Tests of his blood and the lining of his air passages showed he had breathed in the flames. Moreover, the fuel system of the car seemed to have been tampered with to make the blaze target the body so as to make it unidentifiable. Specifically: a 'petrol union joint' had been loosened so it would drip petrol on the knee of the man in the car, feeding a flame which would rise from the floor to destroy the features of the face. The petrol-soaked cuff of the right arm reached backwards to the petrol can in the rear so flames from there would travel up the arm and shoulder to the face. The top of the carburettor had been taken off to increase the intensity of the blaze. A small piece of cloth from the man's fly, protected from the flames because his leg had been folded under him, was found to be soaked in petrol, suggesting his killer had doused him in petrol before setting fire to him.

The defence argued that none of this proved murder: the petrol union joint is often found loose after a fire; the carburettor top could have blown off, while the petrol-soaked piece of cloth further demonstrated their view that the man had splashed petrol on his own clothes before accidentally immolating himself.

He was lying face down in the car, sprawled over the front seats. The pathologist Bernard Spilsbury thought this was 'consistent with the man either pitching forward or being thrown down, face downwards, on the seats from the nearside door.' Rouse took exception to this. He could commit a better murder than that. 'I should not throw a man. If I did a thing like that I should not throw him down face forwards. I should think where I put him, I imagine.'

The prosecutor, Norman Birkett, pressed him on the matter. 'If you rendered him unconscious, would you have a delicacy about his posture?'

'No,' said Rouse, 'but I think if I had been going to do as you suggest, I should do a little more than that . . . I think I have a little more brains than that.'

Rouse did his case no good by being so vain of his accomplishments as to demonstrate his familiarity with motor cars. He was visibly shocked when he was handed the carburettor from the burnt car. He knew it could not come off accidentally and the fact that it was off demonstrated that the fire was no accident. He recovered his composure to show the court how it could be unclipped. He also knew that petrol must be lit with a burning rag rather than directly, to avoid the danger of flashback, and described this to the court.

Public opinion, and that of the jury,

was much against Rouse, for his callous treatment of his wife and the other women in his life. The newspapers had widely reported evidence about his 'harem' which had been presented at the Magistrates' Court committal proceedings but was not brought forward at his murder trial.

He also gave a bad impression of himself to the jury by his lack of any spark of sympathy for the man who had died in his car. Any expression of regret would have been enough; instead he treated the wretched man's death as a mere source of problems for himself. He was found guilty, and later explained how the crime had been committed:

He was the sort of man no one would miss, and I thought he would suit the plan I had in mind. I worked out the whole thing in my mind.

During the journey the man drank the whisky neat from the bottle and was getting quite fuzzled. We talked a lot but he did not tell me who he actually was. I did not care.

I turned up Hardingstone Lane

because it was quiet and near a main road, where I could get a lift from a lorry afterwards. I pulled the car up.

The man was half-dozing — the effect of the whisky. I looked at him and gripped him by the throat with my right hand. I pressed his head against the back of the seat. He slid down, his hat falling off. I saw he had a bald patch on the crown of his head.

He just gurgled. I pressed his throat hard. My grip is very strong. I used my right hand only because it is very powerful. People have always said that I have a terrific grip. He did not resist. It was all very sudden. The man did not realise what was happening. I pushed his face back. After making a peculiar noise, the man was silent and I thought he was dead or unconscious.

Then I got out of my car, taking my attaché case, the can of petrol and the mallet with me. I walked about ten yards in front of the car, and opened the can, using the mallet to do so. I threw the mallet away and made a trail of petrol to the car.

Also, I poured petrol over the man and loosened the petrol union joint and took the top off the carburettor. I put the petrol can in the back of the car.

I ran to the beginning of the petrol trail and put a match to it. The flame rushed to the car, which caught fire at once. The fire was very quick, and the whole thing was a mass of flames in a few seconds. I ran away.

I am not able to give any more help regarding the man who was burned in the car. I never asked him his name. There was no reason why I should do so.

It had been the contention of the prosecution that Rouse had stunned his victim with the mallet, and this still seems likely. There was no suggestion that the hairs found on the mallet were not human. It seems just another case of a character like Rouse being totally unable to tell the truth, even when nothing is at stake: his defence and appeal had failed.

Much was made at the appeal of the lack of evidence of motive. A good legal argument was put that in the absence of identification of the victim, proof of motive must be strong. Here the motive was murky. Rouse wanted to get away from it all, to leave wife and Welsh bride and the girls with the maintenance orders far behind him. But he could have done this much more easily by pointing his Morris Minor north (he was well known in the South) and changing the numberplates. Keeping the car would also retain for him his principal means of picking up women, the activity he so enjoyed.

Men walk out on home and responsibilities all the time and this is what he planned to do. So why bother with the murder and the blazing car? The only valid motive, which fits the time he was planning the murder with care, would be that he wanted his wife to receive the insurance money from his death. He was genuinely affectionate, to her and to his children, and to his other women, and he did not want to leave his wife and child in penury.

The mystery is why, when he had thought out the crime so well, he did not make better plans for his subsequent escape. His behaviour seemed to be that of an impulsive criminal rather than one who had planned ahead. Even the date of the murder was an astute one: arsonists have long known that the night of 5 November is a good one for a fire, as the fire services are far stretched and a fire has a better chance on that night than any other of doing its work before a fire engine arrives. It is also the only night of the year when a fire at night is not suspicious. He had his own army identity disc with him, which he forgot to put on the victim after killing him, and which would have identified the corpse from the start as his. He had forgotten his hat, having left it in the car, though he would normally have worn it on a cold night, and the cousins specifically remembered he was 'hatless'. He had intended to go to Scotland, which is why the cousins had seen him dithering on the road, not knowing whether he was going north to Scotland or south to London. He said he went home because he did not want his wife to be upset. Really, he just lost his head.

It may have been that his war injury really did affect his mind. A medical report on the injury said, 'His chief complaint is defective memory, an inability to remember orders in his business. He sleeps badly and has difficulty in going to sleep . . . easily excited . . . talkative and laughs immoderately at times, but he states that he always did so.' He may have had a better plan for his getaway, which his mind lost track of in the excitement of the murder. After his injury he did report dizziness and loss of memory. He certainly seemed to become confused in the witness box, being unable to remember simple dates and jabbering out various alternatives.

In a fascinating sidelight on his baroque sex life, his women were still, after this grotesque murder and the exposure of all his deceptions, willing to make excuses for him. His wife wrote to Helen Campbell in consolation after the court case, '. . . myself I cannot but grieve to think it was only through his head-wounds that made him a sex-maniac . . . ' Two women who had borne him illegitimate children (presumably Helen and Nellie) frequently visited him in his condemned cell, as did his wife, who took lodgings near the prison to be near him. She took up work as a shop assistant in Northampton. She had to sell their house.

Rouse was hanged at Bedford on 10 March 1931. His wife said, 'So poor Arthur has gone, and he could be such a nice man.'

Willing Victims

IT must have occurred to many swindlers that the great impediment to a really successful insurance murder is the recalcitrance of the victims. If only they would willingly consent to being insured and being done away with, the crime would proceed much more smoothly.

In the cases that follow, the murderers persuaded their victims to pretend to be dead after signing all the insurance forms. The next scene was to be a resurrection in which they enjoyed the largesse of the insurance companies. Invariably it was not. Once they had signed all the documents it was easier for them to die.

The criminals involved in these murders were all colourful rogues for whom this caper was the latest, and the last, in a career of crime. The other activities of some of these individuals shows just how much insurance fraud with a murder involved is just another aspect of common confidence tricks. H. H. Holmes actually sold tap water at his drug store by the cup, claiming it had medicinal qualities. His usual means of obtaining ready cash was buying goods on hire purchase and selling them immediately.

In these cases the question is, as in all good confidence tricks, how did the victims allow themselves to be talked into it? It is wrong to think of someone asking to be killed but anyone stupid enough to sign their entire estate plus massive insurance policies over to a known confidence trickster, who offers to poison them but promises he will not go all the way, is perhaps a little too gullible for this life.

The most unlikely people are taken in. Benjamin Pitezel was killed by a friend of seven years' standing with whom he had been involved in many criminal endeavours. Surely he should have guessed. Yet his killer had on at least one occasion, and probably more, played the trick of insuring a person and substituting a fresh corpse for that person. There seemed to be no reason to believe this would not be such a trick. He did not suspect that he would end up a victim. Yet criminals are still criminal even with their friends.

It could be argued that Elizabeth Chantrelle was not a willing victim, or even let into the plot, yet she behaved with apparent indifference as to her own safety. 'You will see that my life will go soon after this insurance,' she said, and she was right. She knew she was going to be killed yet did nothing to prevent it. Perhaps she was a careless rather than a willing victim, not prepared to do anything to save herself.

Remains to be Seen

FRANK GEYER, a Philadelphia detective, walked up the stairs of the ancient, mouldering building at 1316 Callowhill Street, Philadelphia one autumn day in 1894. It was not a routine job. This was the second investigation taking place into a fatal accident in a laboratory. A carpenter called Eugene Smith had found Mr Perry, an inventor and dealer in patents, lying on the floor of his laboratory. He had been dead some weeks and his face had been burned by a caustic substance. An inquest found he had died in a laboratory accident when a retort blew up in his face.

The Fidelity Mutual Life Association of Philadelphia had later received a letter from a Chicago lawyer, Jeptha D. Howe: 'B. F. Perry is, in my opinion, actually Benjamin F. Pitezel of Chicago, who last September took out a policy in your company naming his wife, Carrie

A. Pitezel, also of this city, as beneficiary. Mr Pitezel has for some time been in financial difficulties, and it was for that reason that he went to another city and took an assumed name.'

The company was unable to trace Pitezel via the address given for the insurance policy, which proved to be a vacant lot. The agent who had issued the policy, however, said Pitezel had been introduced by a friend, a Mr H. H. Holmes who lived in Wilmette, Chicago. Holmes was not to be found there, but his wife, Myrta, was. She said he travelled a great deal but she could give him a message when he next contacted her. Thus he was informed of the death and agreed, if his expenses were paid, to travel to Philadelphia to assist the insurance company.

Henry Howard Holmes had to be present because Fidelity Mutual said they would accept Perry as Pitezel only if an independent person would identify the body. When he arrived, Holmes explained to the insurance company investigators that he had employed the 37-year-old Pitezel as a chemist in his Chicago drug store. The lawyer, Howe, also came to the identification, accompanied by Alice Pitezel, the fifteen-year-old daughter of the insured man. She had come rather than anyone else because the widow was said to be prostrate with grief and it was therefore up to the eldest daughter to look after the whole family. Alice was the second eldest of the Pitezel family of five children, so the task fell to her.

The body had already been buried, following the inquest, but it was exhumed and laid out in a shed by the graveyard. It was identified by Holmes by a scar on the leg, a mole on the back of the neck and a bruised fingernail. Holmes astonished the doctor conducting the examination by pulling out a lancet from his own pocket and assisting in such operations as cutting off some of the fingers in search of the blackened nail, which would have to be placed in alcohol for the bruising to become distinct from the marks of putrefaction.

Alice was spared the exercise in dissection but was brought to see the teeth of the corpse, with the rest of it covered up, because her father had particularly distinctive teeth. She thought it was her father, and left the shed crying at the dreadful sight. The insurance company had paid up, though they deducted the cost of identifying the body, on the grounds that the expense was the insured's own fault for changing his name. The company handed over $9715 to Jeptha D. Howe.

A tip-off from someone in jail, however, led the insurance company to speak to detective Frank P. Geyer. He quickly found holes in the evidence. Holmes had told Fidelity Mutual it was his first visit to Philadelphia, but the carpenter who found the body said he had seen him in B. F. Perry's office.

A retort seemed to have exploded into the face of Mr Perry or Mr Pitezel but the detective observed that the corpse had a benign expression, he was not clawing at his burning throat. This suggested that the corrosive substance had been thrown on the face after death. Also, there was no glass in his face. There was glass, however, inside the broken base of the retort. Yet an explosion from within the retort should have made all the glass blow outwards. Mrs Pitezel was said to have heard of B. F. Perry's death from an edition of the Public Ledger, yet Geyer found the edition that carried the story was restricted to the city of Philadelphia; it was not an 'out of town' edition which she might have seen in Chicago.

The policy was interesting, too. Policy No. 044145 was due to expire on 9 August but someone had wired $157.50 to keep it going the day before it ran out. On 7 September, Perry/Pitezel was dead.

The Pinkerton Detective Agency was asked to seek Holmes and tried, but he was missing from his office. The Chicago police already knew a little about him; they had found some oil-soaked rags on the premises of a company of which he was one of the directors. They thought it could be an attempted insurance arson, but no crime was committed, nor was there any evidence of who had placed the rags in the building, so they let the matter drop.

Though he had left the city, enough people in Chicago knew of Holmes and his clever deals. His earlier history was murky, for Holmes had changed his name, having originally been called Herman Webster Mudgett. He was born in Gilmanton, New Hampshire, where his father was a farmer and for a time a postmaster, and his mother was a teacher. As he himself wrote, he was 'well trained by loving and religious parents'. He was a bright pupil, if somewhat aloof from his fellows, and he became a schoolmaster then studied medicine at University of Michigan at Ann Arbor.

At the university medical school a student died and Mudgett picked up $5000 insurance money. How the insurance company could pay out on the death of a previously healthy young man insured by a classmate to whom he was not related is an unsolved mystery. There are at least two versions of this story. One is as reported above. The other is that Mudgett insured a patient, then stole a cadaver on its way to the dissecting room and collected the money on the 'dead' patient. It is possible that these are not two versions of the same incident, but two different frauds, the one involving an actual death being a progression from the first.

He married a woman called Clara Lovering at eighteen, and practised medicine in Mooers Forks, New York. After eight years of marriage he deserted her and their son. He later caused her to hear indirectly that he had been in a train crash and had lost his memory.

Mudgett moved to Chicago in 1886 and now changed his name to Holmes. He must have decided he had no further interest in medicine as his degree was in his own name and he could not practise without it. He bigamously married a woman from a wealthy family called Myrta Belknap. Their marriage broke up after he tried unsuccessfully to swindle her uncle, John Belknap, by forging his signature on a credit note for $2500. He invited his uncle-in-law to the roof of his new house to discuss the matter. Belknap did not go.

The couple were later to make up, and Holmes considered the house where she lived with her family to be one of his homes — it certainly operated as a safe house for him — and he sent her money. Myrta Belknap said, 'In his home life, I do not think there was ever a better man than my husband. He never spoke an unkind word to me or our little girl or my mother. He was never vexed or irritable, but was always happy and seemingly free from care. In times of financial trouble or when we were worried over anything, as soon as he came into the house everything seemed different.'

Around this time an event occurred which Holmes was to boast of and embellish in such a way, with such fantastic coincidences, that it is almost certainly untrue in detail. The bare facts are that Holmes insured himself for $20,000 and bribed porters at a Chicago medical school to allow him to look at the fresh bodies. He eventually found one of about his age and appearance, a young man who had been killed falling from a railway car. He took it away in a trunk and went with it by train to Michigan, arousing a great deal of suspicion on the way because of the smell. He set himself up in the north of Michigan, letting it be known he was a wealthy lumber dealer. One day he went into the forest and did not return. Eventually, a body with his clothes and some papers giving his name was found, crushed by a tree. His identity was traced and the insurance paid — presumably to his wife, or a female accomplice posing as her.

In his own, highly mendacious, account of his life, he refers to this as 'case no. five', which of course implies four similar cases. He noted that the gross profits from his insurance swindles to this date (and he was not yet thirty) amounted to $68,700 with a cost for setting them up of $3950.

At the age of twenty-eight, Holmes was hired by a Mrs E. S. Holton to work as a chemist and manage her drug store on 63rd Street in the Englewood district of Chicago. Three years later he became a partner in the store and was soon accused by Mrs Holton of fiddling the books. Mrs Holton unaccountably vanished, leaving him in control of the business which principally operated selling patent medicines. He lived above the store in a flat, and purchased a vacant lot opposite, on which he had a three-storey building constructed. It was a Gothic-style block full of turrets and bay windows. It was locally known as 'Holmes' Castle' and was to be the site of some of the most depraved acts ever to take place in America.

He used a number of different builders, quarrelling with them frequently and dismissing them. That way only he knew the exact plan of the building. It was full of trap doors and secret rooms. Pitezel acted with Holmes in frauds connected with the construction of the castle. Work and materials were commissioned by the Campbell-Yates Manufacturing Company, in which Campbell was Benjamin Pitezel, and Yates did not exist. Holmes was just an innocent agent for the company. The castle was finished in 1891 when Holmes was thirty-one. They later built another storey and did a fine trade catering for visitors to the Chicago World Fair.

Holmes paid for the work on the castle with loans and mortgaged it to a company of wholesale druggists, who also gave him $2500 and a stack of drugs as part of the deal. He asked them to delay a few days before having the mortgage recorded, which they did, only to find that in the meantime someone else had a deed on the property — almost certainly a fictitious person. They then found themselves in lengthy litigation while Holmes simply collected the rents on shops let on the ground floor of the castle: a jeweller's, confectioner's, restaurant and a dealer in ironware.

Holmes was an attractive man of slight build and medium height with large blue eyes, a pleasing voice and a moustache which concealed his buck teeth. A man of obvious education and sophistication, he always dressed well and spoke softly. He was very popular with women and normally had sex with women who worked in the store. Two such were Julia Conner and her eighteen-year-old sister-in-law, Gertie. Julia worked as Holmes's secretary. She was the wife of Ned Conner, a jeweller who rented part of the store for a watch repair business. Holmes took both women as lovers, and Ned Conner moved out.

'Holmes was always very anxious to have me get life insurance,' Conner later reflected, 'and my wife was always anxious to have me get life insurance for the child.'

Gertie became pregnant and disappeared. Holmes then made friends with a fair-haired teenager who used to come to the store, sixteen-year-old Emily Van Tassell. She usually came in to eat ice cream with her mother. At one time she came in on her own, and she too disappeared. There was no trace of her when anxious relatives and the police scoured the area for her.

Holmes then took up with his new secretary, a strikingly beautiful woman called Emmeline Cigrand who liked to call herself Amelia. She had been procured by Pitezel; she had worked in a clinic where he had been treated for alcoholism. Her arrival stimulated the jealousy of Julia, who took to spying on Holmes, so he rigged up an alarm which rang a bell in the store to tell him when Julia was prowling downstairs. He must have tired of her, for soon Julia and her eight-year-old daughter Pearl disappeared. Again, neither Holmes nor anyone else could tell anyone who asked what had happened to them.

Soon the stunning Amelia was no longer to be seen either, though she had been very popular with some permanent guests who had rooms in the castle, and who asked after her only to be told by Holmes that she had gone away to get married. Her friends did not believe him, but what could they do, she had disappeared.

A member of Holmes's staff, Patrick Quinlan, who was a janitor at the castle, said, 'I left because the job gave me nightmares. The doctor had women all over the house. He had them in every room. Then, suddenly, they would vanish.' A number of staff described it as being like a harem.

It is reasonable to assume that at least some of the disappearances were investigated but reports of missing persons with no obvious evidence of crime are never very thoroughly investigated. If any of the women who disappeared were insured by Holmes, the fact never came to light.

Holmes would often urge his staff to take out life insurance. A washerwoman called Mrs Strowers was offered $6000 by him if she would take out $10,000 worth of life insurance, but wise friends' counsel prevailed and she lived to tell the tale.

Meanwhile, Holmes continued with his current main business venture: selling patent medicines for which he made extravagant claims. He sold the rights to the Holmes Chemical Water Gas machine for $2000 to a gullible Canadian businessman. He claimed it could make an inflammable gas out of water by splitting the hydrogen and oxygen. When he demonstrated the machine, amid the tangle of mock pipes which were seen at the bottom of the tank was one which snaked off underground. It was connected to the gas supply.

Holmes then sold water which had gas bubbled through it as a tonic. He sold Linden Grove Mineral Spring Water for five cents a cup, claiming it came from a spring in his basement. It did; he made the spring by tapping the water main.

Holmes never paid his debts, and when a company came to repossess the furniture from the castle, it was found to be empty. Holmes had put it all in a room which had been covered by a partition and wallpapered over. A builder was eventually bribed by the creditor to give away the hiding place of the furniture. Holmes also ordered a vast safe, and had it installed in a room, then made the doorway smaller. When agents for the owners came to repossess it, he told them they were welcome to it but they must not damage his building in getting it out. They left it.

An employee of Holmes, who worked in his drug store, explained, 'He was the smoothest man I ever saw. Why, I have known creditors to come here raging and calling him all the names imaginable, and he would smile and talk to them and set up the cigars and drinks and send them away seemingly his friends for life. I never saw him angry.' Holmes himself did not smoke, drink or gamble.

His relationship with Pitezel was fruitful for both. When Pitezel was arrested for passing a forged cheque in Indiana, Holmes posed as an Indiana congressman and had him bailed out with another fake cheque.

Another woman, Minnie Williams, was

now living with Holmes. She had property worth more than $40,000. Minnie wrote to her sister, Nannie, that she had married a wonderful man called Harry Gordon and that she could come and stay with them. Gordon was an alias of Holmes. They probably did not get married, but it was an advisable remark to make when writing to the folks back home. Nannie came to stay, and wrote to the family that she was going to Germany to study art. She disappeared. Holmes later claimed that Minnie had killed her by hitting her with a stool in a jealous rage, but this was probably a lie. Minnie stayed with him longer than most of his women, and it may have been that she played a part in his criminal activities. She may indeed have been involved in her sister's death.

Holmes let many rooms in the castle to visitors to Chicago for the World Fair and at least two women who stayed there vanished. After this event, he arranged a fire in the castle and made an insurance claim of $60,000 but the insurance company rejected it. They invited him to discuss the claim and while he was doing so at their offices, a police inspector called on Minnie and told her the fraud had been discovered and she was in trouble. She confessed and the game was up. The company did not take it any further, but Holmes's creditors learned of it and began to pursue him for bills totalling $50,000. Holmes and Minnie went on the run.

Holmes had by now met another blonde at the Chicago World Fair, 21–year-old Georgiana Yoke from Indiana, who had very prominent blue eyes. He made her his third concurrent wife, in Denver, when he was thirty-four, under the name Henry Mansfield Howard, with Minnie acting as a witness. What she thought of it is hard to guess. He may have told her he was marrying Georgiana to kill her after taking out insurance, but in the event it was Minnie who disappeared some months after the wedding. Now Holmes sent Pitezel, under yet another name, posing as a Chicago lawyer, to make use of Minnie's property. He came away with a loan of $16,000, secured on the property.

Deeds signed by Minnie gave Holmes the use of the property which was in

Fort Worth, Texas. Holmes decided to improve part of the property and set about building himself another castle, getting material and work on credit for a three-storey building. He found these creditors less malleable than those he had known in Chicago, and soon they were striving particularly hard for payment. Holmes made a quick getaway from Texas, stealing a horse in the process.

Holmes and Pitezel, with their families, moved to St Louis in 1894, where they indulged in another fraud. Holmes bought a drug store, mortgaged the stock and Pitezel stole it. This time, however, Holmes was not fast enough and he was arrested but bailed out of jail by Georgiana twelve days later. These twelve days were the only period this full-time professional criminal ever spent in prison until his final capture. He had no intention of spending any longer there, and of course jumped bail and left the state.

The period in jail was significant for both Holmes and Pitezel. It was here that Holmes met Marion Hedgepeth, a handsome train robber with an elegant manner. He was currently in for holding up the Missouri Express but his most famous exploit was the audacious robbery of the 'Frisco Express which had been boarded by his gang who blew open the express car with dynamite and took $10,000. He cut a dashing figure, with women queuing to get into the courtroom when he was on trial, and his cell was so filled with flowers from them that he could hardly enter it.

Holmes introduced himself to Hedgepeth, saying he would so like to speak to him, as he had read so much about him. Whereupon, Holmes discussed his next insurance fraud with his new friend. He was going to insure Pitezel, have him apparently killed in a chemical explosion, with a cadaver substituted for his body, and claim the proceeds. He needed a crooked lawyer to handle the business for him and Hedgepeth was able to introduce him to his acquaintance Jeptha D. Howe, his own lawyer's brother. Holmes agreed to pay Hedgepeth $500, with $2500 for Howe and $3500 each for Pitezel and himself.

When he came out of jail, Holmes

rented a house on Callowhill Street, Philadelphia, which backed on to the morgue. Pitezel, as B. F. Perry, put up a sign saying he dealt in patents and began seeing callers on 17 August. A carpenter, Eugene Smith, brought in a device for setting saws which he had invented, and he left it with Pitezel. His device could sharpen any dull saw with a minimum of effort, and he hoped that with the expertise of Mr Perry, he could market it and make his fortune.

On 3 September, Smith came back to see what progress had been made and found the door open. He waited for a while, then went inside. He found no one in the office and so went away, but returned the next day and this time went upstairs and looked in each room. In the laboratory he found a decomposing corpse. Its face was directly in the sun, and had decomposed considerably, but it appeared to be that of Mr B. F. Perry.

The police investigation preceding the inquest found that B. F. Perry had been experimenting with chloroform and had tried to light his pipe close to it. The inflammable vapour had caught and exploded, somewhat singeing the man's moustache and hair. It was an accidental death.

Holmes now made the mistake of not paying off Hedgepeth. Jeptha D. Howe had of course been the first recipient of the money, so he took his sum off immediately, leaving Mrs Pitezel $7200. Holmes now told her that Pitezel had a half-interest in the Fort Worth property and that $5000 was due on it. He persuaded Carrie Pitezel to pay this sum in at a bank, saying that if it were paid, she would receive the rents from the property. Of course, the whole Fort Worth deal was fraudulent, and the money went straight into Holmes's pocket. Carrie also gave Holmes $1700, supposedly as his part of the deal, so she actually realised just $500, most of which must have gone in her later travelling expenses.

Hedgepeth had received nothing so he decided to denounce Holmes, giving details of the scheme and noting that Holmes had said 'he was an expert at it, as he had worked it before'. This had no effect on Hedgepeth's sentence;

he was still given twelve years.

Holmes had been in prison under the alias H. M. Howard, so it took a little time to work it all out. There was a natural reluctance to use a criminal's testimony as binding evidence, but details of the plot were too well known to Hedgepeth for it to be a spiteful invention. Eventually, the Fidelity Mutual Life Association realised they had been defrauded, and Frank Geyer was called in. The body was exhumed again, and found to have been killed, not in an explosion, but by chloroform poisoning.

Now began Geyer's quest for Holmes, aided by the Pinkerton Detective Agency and investigators from Fidelity Mutual. First, Holmes went to St Louis, where Carrie Pitezel patiently awaited the result of the swindle. She believed her husband was in hiding somewhere. Holmes took two of the children, eleven-year-old Nellie and nine-year-old Howard, off with him when he departed, saying he was taking them to Pitezel in Cincinnati. Alice he had left in a hotel in Indianapolis. What story he told her to keep her there is unknown. The reason for keeping Alice from her family was that Alice had seen the corpse and knew it was that of her father. She had some idea of the swindle, and her mother later confessed, 'When she left for Philadelphia, she was to say, regardless of what body she was shown, that it was her daddy.' Now she knew it was not a trick, her father had been killed.

Holmes might have thought he would be able to keep her away from a sight of the body, pleading her youthful sensitivity. To press the point would have been suspicious, however, and when she was asked to identify the teeth he could hardly have prevented her from doing so. This made her a liability. In practical terms, why he took the other children is a mystery.

After he had taken the children away, Holmes went on something of a personal odyssey. He was later found to have visited his parents in New Hampshire and even his first wife and son. He explained that he had remarried, one Georgiana Yoke, who was connected with the hospital where he had recovered after losing his memory in a train crash. Georgiana induced the surgeons 'to perform an operation that saved his mind' and he married this persuasive young woman before he realised who he was and that he already had a wife. Such a tragedy for him.

He stayed long enough to practise some casual fraud, swindling $300 from his brother, and then went back to Burlington, Vermont, where Georgiana was living with Carrie Pitezel and two remaining children: a sixteen-year-old girl called Dessie and a baby. They went to Boston together and Holmes suggested he take Dessie away, too, to join the father and three other children in Kentucky, but before this could happen they were arrested.

Pinkerton detectives had located Holmes via Mrs Pitezel. Quite when they caught up with her is not clear, and after Holmes visited her they watched Holmes for some time. Again, it is not clear why they did this instead of arresting him immediately. Carrie and her two remaining children, Dessie and baby Wharton, had gone from St Louis to her parents' home in Galva, Illinois, then to Chicago, Detroit,

Toronto, Burlington, and then Boston.

Holmes and Carrie Pitezel were arrested after Holmes was noted to be visiting booking agencies and was thought to be preparing to go abroad. Holmes was now calling himself A. L. Hayes of Chicago. He agreed to co-operate with the Philadelphia police because the detectives also carried a warrant for his arrest from the Texas authorities, for horse theft, and confided that he would rather spend five years in a Pennsylvania prison than one in a Texas prison. He and Carrie Pitezel were returned to Philadelphia by train. Holmes offered the detective who was handcuffed to him $500 if he would consent to be hypnotised but he refused.

He was first charged with embezzlement, then with murder. He said 'Murder? Nonsense. It was just an insurance swindle pure and simple. I used a cadaver I procured from a New York morgue.' He said he had conveyed it to Philadelphia in a trunk. Pitezel was 'safely in South America of course'. Throughout the interviews, he was entirely charming and plausible.

Faced with the evidence of Pitezel's death by chloroform poisoning, Holmes said his friend had committed suicide with chloroform after depression and drinking to excess. Holmes had arrived at the office one day to find a note in code on Pitezel's desk, which led to a suicide note, and he soon found the body. He had then kindly rigged the suicide to make it look like an accident, so that his widow and children would receive the insurance. The day after Holmes's arrest, more than fifty people turned up at the Chicago police station asking if there was any chance of their recovering money Holmes had swindled from them.

Holmes had one last card: he pleaded guilty. The police had an insurance fraud and here was someone putting his hand up to it. It could be another case neatly tidied up. Holmes would get two years' imprisonment and no one would bother with a complicated investigation of other possible crimes. This nearly worked: the case went to trial and Judge Hare accepted the plea but deferred sentence pending further investigations.

The most important question was: where were the children? Holmes told a nonsense story about sending the children, with $400 to defray the cost of their keep, to Niagara Falls, where they were to be in the care of Minnie Williams. This was, of course, explaining the disappearance of two people by reference to another disappeared person. He claimed they had gone to London, England, but the address he gave did not exist. He then offered to contact them by means of a secret code. He encoded a message using a code where the letters of the word 'republican' stood for the first ten letters of the alphabet if in capitals, and for the next ten if in lower-case letters; the last six letters were not encoded. An ad in this code was placed in the *New York Herald*, which it was possible to purchase in London, but to no effect.

More usefully, police found a tin box containing letters from Alice and Nellie to their mother and grandparents, which Holmes was supposed to have mailed for them, and letters from Carrie Pitezel to her children which he was supposed to have given to the children but had not. The children wrote of their homesickness and desperate boredom. Alice wrote, 'All that Nell and I can do is to draw and I get so tired sitting that I could get up and fly almost. I wish I could see you all. I am getting so homesick that I don't know what to do.' Pitifully, Nellie wrote, 'I want you to all write why don't you write mama.' These letters gave the location of the children at different times in their travels. Unfortunately, they were only exact as to the city, though some internal evidence could give clues, like one from Alice in Indianapolis where she said, 'The hotel is just a block from Washington Street and that is where all the big stores are.'

Geyer followed Holmes's trail after he had left Carrie Pitezel in St Louis, taking Howard and Nellie. They had joined up with Alice, then gone to Cincinnati. Geyer went from one hotel to another in that city, until he finally found the Atlantic House where a man (Holmes was, as usual, using an alias) had checked in with three children on the right date. But he had checked out with three children, too. He had also stayed at the Hotel Bristol, and rented a house there, in residential Poplar Street. Here he brought a large stove, but no other furniture. The next-door neighbour thought this was odd, and spoke to other neighbours about it. Holmes knocked on her door the next morning and asked if she would like the stove, since she had taken such an interest in it. He would not be occupying the house so she could have it.

He then took the children to Indianapolis, registering them at Circle House as 'three Canning children', the name of their grandparents. Discovering this was a far from straightforward piece of detection as, by the time the inquiries started, the Circle House had gone out of business. Every hotel in the city had been checked unsuccessfully before Geyer thought to check on hotels which had been in business a year previously.

The children's trail of false names at numerous hotels led north, via Detroit to Canada. Mrs Pitezel was also staying in Detroit, with two of the children, unaware that her other children were only a few blocks away from her. Holmes told her she must not venture out of the hotel as there were detectives watching them. He told the children they must not leave because they had no warm clothes, and deliberately denied them any. Holmes and Georgiana Yoke, living under the alias under which he had married her (H. H. Howard), were also close by in Detroit and he contrived that none of these three groups knew of the existence of the others.

He rented a house on East Forest Avenue, Detroit, and dug a hole in the floor of the basement four feet long by three feet wide and three feet deep. He said he wanted it for the winter storage of potatoes and other root crops but Holmes was somehow warned that insurance investigators were after him and he decamped, determined to get to another country.

Holmes and the girls but not the boy, Howard, crossed the Canadian border and went to Toronto, staying at the Albion Hotel, then the trail went cold. But Geyer now knew what happened next: Holmes rented a house. It was his style. Geyer asked at estate agents' offices and realised that it could take him a year to check them all. He contacted the press, and newspapers were prepared to publish photographs of the children. A man living in St Vincent Street recognised Alice from her picture. A man and two girls had arrived at the bungalow next door to him about three weeks before Holmes's eventual capture. Holmes had asked to borrow a spade from a neighbour. Geyer knew he had to dig. Down in the cellar, the bodies of Alice and Nellie were found under a few feet of earth.

The bodies were in a poor condition but they were recovered with the help of a local undertaker, and taken back to Philadelphia. They had been buried naked, and were identified by some charred clothes found in the chimney by the person who had the house after Holmes — she had thrown them away but Mrs Pitezel could identify them from the description the woman gave.

It was guessed that Holmes had drugged the girls with chloroform, put them in a trunk and fed a tube from the domestic gas supply into the trunk until they died. A hole of the right diameter was found in a trunk Holmes had with him when he was arrested. Mrs Pitezel was brought to Toronto to identify the remains and give evidence at the inquest. The authorities did not feel able to allow her to see the bodies in their entirety, and covered Alice's head with a piece of paper in which a hole had been cut so her teeth could be seen. Her hair, which, with the scalp, had come away from the skull, was washed and laid over the canvas which covered her body.

Carrie Pitezel immediately recognised them. Geyer wrote, 'Then turning around to me she said, "Where is Nellie?" About this time she noticed the long black plait of hair belonging to Nellie lying in the canvas. She could stand it no more, and the shrieks of that poor forlorn creature are still ringing in my ears. Tears were trickling down the cheeks of the strong men who stood around us. The sufferings of the stricken mother were beyond description.'

For Geyer there was more to do. Where was Howard? He had not even reached Toronto. Indianapolis had been the last place where three children had been seen. Assisted by an investigator for the Fidelity Mutual Insurance Association, Geyer checked hotels in Indianapolis, then in every outlying town until they had virtually reached the end of the line. They had followed almost 1000 separate lines of inquiry. They checked out every lead and every house that had been listed for rent in the appropriate month in the region surrounding Indianapolis. There was only the town of Irvington left.

Geyer wearily unwrapped his parcel of photographs in the first estate agent he came to and showed them to an old man. He immediately recognised Holmes, who had been uncivil to him — quite uncharacteristic of Holmes. The old man had given the keys of a cottage to Holmes who had gone there with a young boy, but no girls.

Geyer went straight to the basement but there was no sign that the floor had been dug up. Outside, he found some scraps from a trunk the Holmes party had with them, and in an outhouse was a large stove which had a bloodstain on top and whose bottom was filled with grease.

A neighbour remembered Holmes asking him to help erect a stove, and the little boy had watched. He asked why Holmes did not use gas, and Holmes said it was because he felt it was not healthy for children.

In the chimney were found charred bones and teeth and pieces of internal organs, baked hard. He had cut the boy up and fed the pieces through the door of the stove. Some toys owned by Howard were also found. At least the children were accounted for — some small comfort amid the mounting horror of the realisation of the extent of Holmes's crimes.

Back in Chicago, police had received permission to break into Holmes's castle. The ground floor had shops opening on to the street. The third floor housed Holmes's offices and hotel rooms. On the second floor, amid the blind hallways and secret passages they found windowless cell-like rooms with peep-holes, some of which were padded; there was also a room filled with a huge safe, into which a gas pipe had been introduced. Investigators wandered dazed as each fresh horror followed on the heels of the last and they realised what must have happened to the people who disappeared in Holmes's Castle. Some rooms were fire-proof, furnished with asbestos and steel sheeting. Some rooms had low ceilings, with trap doors in the floor which led to small rooms below. The gas in all the bedrooms was controlled by taps in Holmes's bedroom. There was a large dumb-waiter, and two chutes from the second and third floors leading to a dungeon where the real horrors began.

There were vats of acid, and two vaults of quicklime for rendering flesh and fat. There were dissecting tables and a room containing surgical equipment and instruments of torture. Parts of the skeletons of women were found, including skulls and teeth. Some burned bones were found, and a length of woman's hair. Animal bones were also found, mixed in with the human ones, presumably to confuse anyone who should find some of the bones and ask questions. Additionally there were the nails from shoes and a piece of a watch chain once owned by Minnie Williams.

Someone lit a match and a gas tank exploded while the investigators were checking the cellar, injuring four. Holmes had claimed his last victims in the sinister dungeon. Holmes once had a furnace similar to that used in a crematorium and it was the fuel for this which had exploded. He had been ordered not to use it by the buildings inspector who felt such a powerful furnace had no place in a residential and working establishment. Shortly after it was investigated, Holmes's Castle was completely destroyed by fire, presumably by accident. It was a fitting end to the chamber of horrors.

It was possible to discover what had happened to at least some of the women who had disappeared. Holmes had placed a notice in a local paper: 'Wanted: Skeleton articulator. Apply H. H. Holmes 701 63rd Street. Afternoon.'

Charles Chapman, a mechanic who had some experience with skeletons, applied and asked for $36 for stripping each body. Holmes checked his references carefully, and later he was taken to see a striking blonde laid out in the basement of the castle, who, from Chapman's description, could be identified as Amelia.

Holmes told him that the skeleton had been ordered by Hahnmann Medical School and everything was above board. When Chapman started work, Holmes went to get a dissection kit, and joined in with relish. Chapman worked with Holmes on two women and one man. Holmes sold skeletons to a dozen medical schools. The jewellery and clothes of his victims were also sold.

In fact, Holmes had no need of the services of the articulator, he had all the skill necessary himself and was used to working alone on bodies. He probably had Chapman in because it gave him a thrill to be watched taking his crime to such an ultimate conclusion. Some bodies were rendered in the cellar's lime pit.

Holmes had entered the chamber of horrors even before his trial. A Holmes Museum was opened, charging a dime admission. In the Arch Street 'Penny Arcade' the public could see a miniature replica of Holmes's castle; a pile of human bones; a skull supposedly having the exact measurements of that of Benjamin Pitezel; and photographs of Holmes, his three wives and many of his victims. After the trial the proprietors of this exhibition unsuccessfully tried to buy the trial exhibits from the District Attorney. Holmes was hardly the man to pass up the opportunity of making some money and he wrote and designed a lurid twenty-five cent booklet called *Holmes' Own Story*, which he had published via his lawyer, William A. Shoemaker.

His trial for the murder of Pitezel, in Philadelphia City Hall, started on 28 October 1895 and lasted six days. He conducted his own defence with some skill, after his lawyers walked out because the court refused to give them more time to prepare the case, but he later asked them to return and they did conduct the case.

The prosecution was able to prove that Pitezel, whose body was in a reposeful state, must have been drugged with chloroform, perhaps while he slept, and then more chloroform was pumped into his stomach. If he had drunk the fluid in a suicide attempt, as Holmes alleged, he would have suffered spasms and vomiting.

The burns to the body had to have occurred when his arm was resting on his chest, as there were no burns to the inner part of the arm.

Mrs Pitezel, in a frail condition and speaking so softly that her words had to be repeated by a court official, told of the disappearance of the children and Holmes's constant reassurances that Pitezel was alive and the children were safe.

The judge refused to hear the testimony of more than thirty witnesses on the murder of the three children. He ruled that these murders had happened in Canada and Indiana and it was there that Holmes would be tried for them. Here he was on trial only for the murder of Pitezel.

Holmes remained calm and in control almost throughout the trial. His steely demeanour when Carrie Pitezel gave her harrowing testimony counted against him. He broke into tears when Georgiana Yoke gave evidence. The prosecution alleged that he had seduced Alice. Given his track record, it would be unusual if he had not done so.

The jury found him guilty in one minute, but let a little time pass as they might be thought to have been deficient in their duty had they come out immediately with a guilty verdict which would mean death to the prisoner. Holmes was entertaining himself tossing a coin and saying 'Tails: guilty, heads: not guilty.' When the verdict was delivered Holmes swayed perceptibly and grasped the rail of the dock, then sat down.

He converted to Catholicism and sold his story to a newspaper for $7500, admitting to twenty-seven murders. He later retracted it and again protested his innocence. This confession is troublesome in that Holmes was utterly incapable of telling the truth and, while he almost certainly killed this number of people, and perhaps more, the details are lies. His first murder, he claims, was of a Doctor Robert Leacock of New Baltimore, Michigan, a friend and former schoolmate who was killed for $40,000 in life insurance. This seems suspiciously like the other story of his killing a student at Ann Arbor for insurance, though a much smaller (and therefore more realistic) sum was involved there. With no corroborative evidence Holmes's confession reads as just what it was: a salacious attempt to get into the history books as America's greatest mass murderer. Holmes was not fit to serve in heaven, he would reign in hell.

Some details have the ring of truth, however: he said Julia Conner died to some extent as a result of an abortion Holmes had performed on her, and that her daughter was killed because she was old enough to understand what was going on. Several people in the castle seem to have been killed for pleasure or because they irritated Holmes by arguing about bills. Some people he locked up and starved to death, but normally he used chloroform. One man he lured into inspecting his cremation furnace, then went outside under the pretence of getting some tools, and turned the flame on.

His description of Pitezel's death is just an attempt to out-evil other murderers. Holmes claimed he bound his friend while he lay drunk then poured benzine on his face and lit it so that Pitezel pleaded for mercy, then pleaded for death. 'I fear that it will not be believed that one could be so heartless and depraved,' he wrote, though all the evidence shows Pitezel did not suffer. Holmes was just playing out a sick fantasy of how he might have made him beg for mercy. Likewise he describes killing the girls and 'the ruthless stripping off of their clothing, and the burial without a particle of covering save the cold earth, which I heaped upon them with fiendish delight'.

In the confession was the inevitable insanity defence. Though it was not evident to anyone else, he said he was suffering from a bone disorder which affected his mind; it elongated his head and made him resemble the devil. 'I have commenced to assume the form and features of the Evil One himself,' he explained.

There were, however, still some cunning plans up Holmes's sleeve. There was the battery of appeals, all of which failed, and a plot in which a woman, induced by $20 from Holmes's lawyer William Shoemaker, swore that Pitezel had confessed to her his intention to commit suicide. The woman had contacted a detective, and he had contacted Frank Geyer. Geyer arranged for a policewoman to swear the fake affidavit in place of the woman, in order to trap Shoemaker and Holmes in their conspiracy. For this unprofessional behaviour, Shoemaker was suspended for a year, his youth and the malevolent influence of Holmes counting in his favour.

The next plot involved Carrie Pitezel. Holmes let it be known that he was distraught at the anguish he had caused her and that if he had a little time he could hand over to her the ownership of a house and lot which he owned under a false name. This might go some small way to making recompense, particularly as he now knew how poor she was with no husband to provide for her. Would she approach the governor of Pennsylvania and ask for a delay of execution? Some people, it seems, never learn, however hard the lesson was taught. Carrie Pitezel travelled from where she was living with her parents in

Galva to Philadelphia in response to the letter. At least she asked her lawyer to look into it before she signed anything. There was, of course, no house.

The last plot, and the longest shot of all, was to fool Frank Geyer himself. Holmes wrote saying he knew that in his published confession he had made errors with respect to the way the children had been killed. This was because he had not done it: 'I had a confederate and directed him to do the job. Thus, although I had given this man instructions to carry out the murders in a certain way, I did not know whether he had followed my instructions.' If Geyer would secure him a reprieve, he would help the detective to run down the real child killer who was still at large. Geyer reasoned that Holmes had planted the errors in his confession deliberately to lay the ground for just such a ruse. He refused. It was Holmes's last trick.

He was hanged at Moyamensing Prison on 7 May 1896 at the age of thirty-five. His final words from the gallows were that he was innocent of everything except killing Emmeline Cigrand and

Julia Conner, who died as a result of abortions he was carrying out on them. He liked to keep the public guessing. He left instructions that his body should be packed in cement, concerned that otherwise someone might steal it.

★ ★ ★

There were suspicions that all was not as it should be with the Pitezel insurance claim, but the inquiry was sparked by Hedgepeth's informing on Holmes after he cheated the train robber. It is interesting to question why Holmes made himself financially indebted to Hedgepeth at all. He needn't have made the offer of money to Hedgepeth — he would almost certainly have given him the name of a 'trustworthy' lawyer for nothing. Crime and the means of committing it are common topics of conversation in prisons. Conversation between professional criminals inevitably turns to the details of how they make their living. A tip of this type about another criminal need not be paid for. Holmes probably offered Hedgepeth money because he enjoyed swindling people, and swindling a celebrated robber like Hedgepeth appealed to him.

The other great error was his destruction of the Pitezel children. There was no financial gain in this, and a considerable cost in that he had to keep moving the children around hotels and rented houses. The children might talk to hotel staff, and a man with two or three children was a more conspicuous entity than a man alone. Once he had taken almost all the insurance money from Carrie Pitezel, he could simply have decamped and set up under another name. He had done this enough times before. Why kill the rest of the family? It was a safeguard to do so, because then there would be no one asking after Benjamin Pitezel, but he had murdered an ample number of other people without such safeguards, and he could have avoided the difficulty of disposing of the bodies.

Though his confession must be read with reservations, in the Pitezel case it is convincing when he confesses that all his concern for the family, throughout seven years of knowing

Pitezel, was calculatedly building up to his last, thrilling crime. He wrote of how incredible it seems

> that I could have expected to have experienced sufficient satisfaction in witnessing their deaths to repay me for even the physical exertion that I had put forth on their behalf during those seven long years, to say nothing of the amount of money I had expended for their welfare, over and above what I could have expected to receive from his comparatively small life insurance.

He wrote to Carrie Pitezel after he had been accused of killing the children, 'Knowing me as you do, can you imagine me killing little and innocent children, especially without any motive?' His motive was that he liked killing people. Best of all, he liked killing people who knew and trusted him.

The Bedroom Floorboards

CHIEF CLAUDE of the Paris Sûreté must have sighed when another anonymous letter arrived on his desk. People were always writing letters 'denouncing' their neighbours to the police. Then, if the slightest sign of an inquiry took place, the anonymous letter-writer could fuel the gossip about their enemy by asserting that they were 'under police investigation'.

This letter suggested that a certain lady, Madame Seraphine de Pauw, who had died just over a week previously, had had relations with her doctor which were more intimate than usual. It also suggested that this gentleman, Edmond de la Pommerais, had benefited rather more than a physician should by the death of his patient.

Claude had to proceed carefully. De la Pommerais probably had a connection with the aristocratic family of the same name; it might not be wise to cross

433

him for the sake of a malicious letter. Moreover, if there were an obvious crime, why had not Madame de Pauw's family complained? They would be the ones to gain or lose by her death and they had not come forward. This woman had died from cholera, hardly an unusual event.

This case was almost not investigated at all, but Claude had some discreet inquiries made about Madame de Pauw's relatives. She was the widow of an artist, and had young children. The closest adult relative who had seen her prior to her death was her sister, Madame Ritter.

Madame Ritter was only too pleased to explain that her sister had made out a will entirely in de la Pommerais's favour, just months before she died, and that she was well insured.

Chief Claude knew this was not enough for a charge. He had to have physical evidence, and the best evidence was already under six feet of earth and had been for almost two weeks. He applied to an examining magistrate to have de Pauw's body exhumed and examined for evidence of poison, thirteen days after she had been buried.

Ambrose Tardieu, professor of forensic medicine in Paris, was given the task of examining the body. He quickly determined that Madame de Pauw had not died of cholera or a hernia or, indeed, anything which could easily be established. This did not help a great deal, and he continued with his experiments.

It was time to examine Dr de la Pommerais rather more carefully. This was the Paris of Napoleon III, abounding in glamour, wealth, dreams of wealth, and confidence tricksters just one trick away from being set up for life. De la Pommerais was a homeopathic doctor who had come to Paris from Orleans. His father had been a country doctor. In 1863 he was twenty-seven years old, well dressed and well spoken and unwilling to spend the rest of his life ministering to the diseases of the poor. The 'de la' was his own invention. His assumption of the arms of Count de la Pommerais — to whom he was in no way related — did him some good in this snobbish society. He also claimed, with equal veracity, that the Pope would give him the cross of St

Sylvester and the Emperor would award him the Legion of Honour.

Madame de Pauw was a vivacious woman, if no longer in the first flush of youth. She had been married to an artist whom Dr de la Pommerais had treated until he died and now the doctor was treating her. Without her husband's income, and with three children to support, she was in some poverty.

Then the handsome young doctor came to her with a brilliant plan which was going to make them both comfortably well off for the rest of their lives. First, he would help her take out several insurance policies. Then, with the connivance of her doctor, she was going to become very ill. When they had convinced the insurance companies that she was about to die, she would propose that her insurance policies should be exchanged for annuities which would give her financial security, 500 francs a month, for the rest of her short life. Once the annuity was drawn up and signed, she could make a miracle recovery and live in luxury for the rest of her days.

De la Pommerais had a somewhat complicated personal life. In 1861 he briefly broke off his liaison with de Pauw to marry a rich young woman, Mademoiselle Duibiczy, whose money he gambled and spent freely. He had implied to the family that he was a worthy match by parading his bogus aristocratic connection and by showing them financial securities which were genuine, but were not his.

His mother-in-law, the widow of a wealthy army doctor, trusted him so little that she kept her daughter's inheritance under her own control. Two months after the wedding, however, she dined with the young couple and was later taken very ill, dying within hours, from what de la Pommerais diagnosed as Asiatic cholera. Now his wife's property came into de la Pommerais's hands, just in time to save him from bankruptcy.

By the time he returned to de Pauw's bed, in mid-1863, he was broke again, and this must have induced him to urge upon his lover the benefits of life insurance. He would pay the first premium, of 18,840 francs.

In order to make out the insurance, which would result in a total indemnity of 550,000 francs, the eight insurance companies involved each wanted to establish the lady's health. She had a thorough medical examination and was found to be in the best of health. This was not to last. Soon after the policies were taken out, neighbours heard the sound of someone falling on the de Pauw stairs. The next day Madame de Pauw was in bed with internal pains. The insurance physicians were called, including the illustrious Dr Nelaton, who could find nothing wrong with the lady. Dr de la Pommerais was also present, and he ventured the professional opinion that the patient might soon develop a severe internal illness. Nelaton thought the young doctor did not know what he was talking about, but he was wrong.

De la Pommerais had instructed his lover not to tell anyone but she was unable to keep a secret, particularly as she felt she was being so clever. She explained the plan in glee to her sister, Madame Ritter, confessing conspiratorially that the noise which had

438

been heard by neighbours was a full sack being thrown downstairs. Madame Ritter warned her against being so completely under the control of de la Pommerais, particularly as she had also made out a will which made the doctor beneficiary to her estate and guardian of her children. It was to no avail: she was completely under his spell.

De Pauw made something of a recovery, then she fell ill, just after de la Pommerais had visited her. She suffered stomach pains, vomiting and muscular weakness. She was bathed in sweat. Neighbours called two doctors, the local public health physicians. They were surprised at the erratic behaviour of the patient's heart, which raced, pounding loudly, then seemed to stop, and was almost inaudible. They were stuck for a diagnosis, though a hernia of the stomach was considered. She insisted on having her own, good Dr de la Pommerais to treat her.

Her last words to anyone other than her doctor were on 17 November 1863, to the baker's woman delivering bread. 'I have only a light case of cholera. Dr de la Pommerais has told me I will be well again in twenty-four hours.'

Within rather less time than that, the same afternoon, de la Pommerais emerged from the widow's house to tell the neighbours waiting outside that Madame de Pauw had died of cholera. He made out the death certificate and made the funeral arrangements. She was buried in the Cimitière du Sud.

There was gossip but not to any great effect until the anonymous letter which arrived at the office of Chief Claude of the Paris Sûreté. De la Pommerais was greedy, and foolish enough to advance a claim on the policies immediately after the death. Claude's inquiries quickly uncovered the insurance link, which was of some current interest to the insurance companies because de la Pommerais had just presented them with de Pauw's will making him the sole beneficiary. Claude was convinced there had been a crime but had no shred of direct evidence, not even a cause of death.

Professor Tardieu searched for poison in the tissues of Madame de Pauw's body, testing for every poison for which there was a reagent in an increasingly frustrating series of experiments.

A more creative way of looking at this was to raid de la Pommerais's house and see what poisons were there, and try to match the known effects of those poisons with Madame de Pauw's symptoms. Chief Claude authorised the search of de la Pommerais's house. His men found plenty of poison: arsenic, mercuric chloride, strychnine, aconitine, atropine, potassium cyanide, hydrocyanic acid and digitalin. They also found love letters from de Pauw to her doctor, but no direct evidence of murder.

Professor Tardieu was convinced that a vegetable poison was involved but had no idea what it was. He was given de la Pommerais' extensive collection of 900 phials of poisons but had no success in matching them up with extracts prepared from the body of the dead woman. He was beginning to doubt that he was even dealing with a poison, so in desperation he injected a dog with a preparation derived from the corpse. The dog was normal, then started vomiting and weakened considerably. The heartbeat was uneven, and sometimes stopped, slowing down to a feeble beat with shallow breathing. Finally, the dog recovered.

With the same symptoms caused in the dog and the patient, it was certain that a poison had been administered to her. The one drug it could have been was digitalin. This is an extract of foxglove (Digitalis purpurea), long used to treat heart conditions. In small doses it will stimulate the heart, in large doses there is fluctuation in the heart rhythm, then paralysis of the heart muscle, and death.

Police investigations disclosed that de la Pommerais had bought three grams of digitalin earlier in the year, a large amount for a drug which can be used only in very small quantities. Moreover, he now had only a twentieth of the amount he had purchased left. Tardieu tried it out on a dog and the animal was dead in twelve hours after vomiting, muscle weakness, heart irregularity then paralysis of the heart.

Rather late in the day, Tardieu turned to look at the love letters and found that de Pauw had several times mentioned digitalin, in letters otherwise unconcerned with health. She remarked she had taken digitalin on the advice of 'non-medical acquaintances' in order to 'stimulate herself'. Somehow, de la Pommerais had persuaded de Pauw to mention the drug in her letters to him. This would conceal the fact that he had administered it to her, and incidentally gives further evidence of her ludicrous gullibility. He may, of course, have got her to take the medicine without her realising its toxic effect. The letters would, in any case, demonstrate that she had taken the poison willingly.

Professor Tardieu and Chief Claude were stuck. De Pauw had poison in her but they could not prove that it killed her. The experiment on the dog only demonstrated the well known effects of digitalin. As her letters demonstrated, she had administered the digitalin to herself.

Claude was not prepared to allow a known criminal to escape, however. One day, when Tardieu felt his ingenuity was exhausted, a parcel arrived at his laboratory. It contained floorboards.

Tardieu had previously asked for vomit from the dead woman, with little hope of ever receiving such a sample, as it was unlikely to be available so long after the death. Claude, however, now supplied him with floorboards from the floor of de Pauw's bedroom which had been covered in vomit, and shavings from the other parts of the floor on which vomit had fallen. He later also supplied a control sample of floorboards without vomit so that defence lawyers would not be able to say it was some component of the floorboards, the paint for example, which tested positive for poison.

Tardieu expected the vomit to contain far more poison than the body did and he was right. Tests on experimental frogs demonstrated the high levels of digitalin in the vomit. Tardieu wrote down digitalin poisoning as the cause of death.

Meanwhile, there had been renewed interest in the death of de la Pommerais's mother-in-law who had become so violently ill after dining with the doctor and his young wife, eight weeks after the marriage. Two doctors had been called but their advice was not followed and the treatment was left up to de la Pommerais. A chemist made a statement that he had made up prescriptions for Madame Duibiczy, containing digitalin and hydrochlorate of morphia, which were not appropriate treatments for cholera.

Her body was exhumed, but two years had passed and it was not in such a state that poison could be obtained from it. There were enough of the vital organs left for Tardieu to say it was not a death from cholera or heart disease, and that in his opinion it was not a death by natural causes, but this was as far as he could go. The fact that de la Pommerais had made off with her money after the death did not signal his innocence, either, but when it came to trial de la Pommerais was acquitted of this murder.

He was not so fortunate in the matter of Madame de Pauw's murder, despite his exceptional skill as a poisoner. Digitalin had been a clever poison to use, because there were no tests for its presence, only animal experiments showing poisoning in animals similar to that in humans. At the trial, de la Pommerais's lawyers argued that there was no evidence even in the case of Madame de Pauw. How, the defence asked the jury, could a man's life hang on the evidence of experiments conducted on frogs? The jury was unimpressed and de la Pommerais was convicted and guillotined in 1864.

A Broken Pipe

MARY BYRNE was a servant in the house of Edinburgh language tutor Eugene Chantrelle. When, one January morning in 1878, she left her room at 6.40 a.m. to prepare the house for the Chantrelle family, she heard moans which she thought were being made by the cat. She went upstairs and realised they were coming from the bedroom of her mistress, Elizabeth Chantrelle, who had gone to bed early the previous night, feeling unwell. Entering, she found Elizabeth moaning with her eyes closed, looking pale. There was vomit on the pillow and the edge of the bed. Mary Byrne shook her but there was no response. The gas light was off, which was unusual, as normally it was on all night.

Mary went to see Eugene Chantrelle in the next room. He did not answer her first call though she had the impression he was awake. She called again, telling him Elizabeth would not speak. He raised and half-dressed himself and went in to his wife. He took her hand and put his head to her ear and said, 'Lizzie, what's wrong, can you not speak?', but she did not reply.

He seemed calm at the state of his wife. Mary said they should send for a doctor, and he told her to attend to one of the children who he said was crying. She looked in to his bedroom where all the children were in his bed, but they were all asleep, then returned to Elizabeth's room, where she observed Chantrelle coming from the direction of the window. She thought he might have been opening the window, as she saw him pushing back the dressing table which normally stood before it.

'Can't you smell gas?' he said to her. She could not, but soon the room seemed to be full of gas and she ran to turn it off at the meter.

Chantrelle dressed and called in Dr James Carmichael, who smelled the gas as soon as he entered the room. He said it might be a case of coal-gas poisoning. He had Chantrelle help him remove Elizabeth to another room and, on examining her, extracted a piece of orange pulp from her mouth. The pupils of her eyes were dilated and did not react to light. He examined the gas pipes but could find no obvious leak.

He sent a card to Dr Henry Littlejohn, Medical Officer of Health to the City of Edinburgh and a police surgeon. The card invited Littlejohn 'to see a case of coal-gas poisoning'.

When Littlejohn arrived, Carmichael took him to the back room to see where the patient had been, and told Chantrelle to keep up with the respiratory exercises on her. Chantrelle did not do this, however, but followed them into the back room, leaving his wife alone.

Neither of them were impressed with Chantrelle's seeming indifference to his wife. He showed such little interest in her condition that they ignored him and conducted the case as best they could. Carmichael sent for two of his medical students to come and help with the artificial respiration, which was one of the few treatments which could be given in poisoning cases. Besides this, the only treatment they could give her was a brandy enema. They sent out for some brandy for the procedure. After they had taken what they needed, Chantrelle polished off the bottle, which did not improve their opinion of him.

They wished to move Elizabeth to the Royal Infirmary and asked Chantrelle to fetch Margaret Dyer, her mother. He said he did not know her address, and the eldest boy was sent. When Mrs Dyer arrived, she walked past Chantrelle, going straight to her daughter's bedroom, but found it empty. Chantrelle followed her.

'Where is my daughter?' she said. He asked her to go and smell the gas.

'Never mind the gas,' she said, 'where is my daughter, where is Lizzie?' She found her daughter comatose in the next bedroom and went to speak to Dr Carmichael, but Chantrelle followed them and listened to their conversation.

Elizabeth Chantrelle was admitted to the Edinburgh Royal Infirmary at 1 – 2 p.m. Chantrelle came and sat by her bed, not speaking until the doctor attending his wife, Professor Douglas Maclagan, said it was not a case of coal-gas poisoning. Chantrelle then described the state of the gas meter in his house and explained how a part of it was broken. He showed no great anxiety about his wife.

Elizabeth died at 4 p.m. that afternoon, without regaining consciousness. Dr Henry Littlejohn told the Edinburgh Gas Supply Company to examine the state of the pipes. Peter Baillie, a gas fitter for the company, was called on the day of Elizabeth Chantrelle's death to examine her room but could not perceive any smell of gas, and the gas brackets were sound. When he turned the meter on, however, there was an escape of gas and a strong smell in Mrs Chantrelle's bedroom but nowhere else. Littlejohn now felt it was time for a police investigation and Criminal Officer William Frew of the Edinburgh police began making inquiries about Mr Chantrelle.

The attractive, debonair Eugene Marie Chantrelle was said to be the best linguist in Edinburgh. He had a colourful past, having been brought up in France where he had fought on the barricades and had been wounded in one or other of Paris's frequent uprisings.

After leaving France he had travelled in America and England and finally settled in Scotland. He was a French master at the Newington Academy in Edinburgh but also taught German and was proficient in Latin and Greek, supplementing his income with private tuition.

Chantrelle had been a student at Nantes Medical School in France for five years in his youth, and later took some medical classes in Strasbourg and Paris but did not complete medical studies. He saw some patients in Edinburgh, however, mainly shopkeepers and tradesmen.

When he was thirty-four, he had started walking home with fifteen-year-old Elizabeth Cullen Dyer, the daughter of a well-to-do commercial traveller. They went out sometimes to the sort of entertainments popular with the middle classes, like lectures on phrenology. Their relationship deepened and she became pregnant by him.

'I do not complain,' she wrote in a letter to him, 'what is the use, the thing is done and I am ruined for life. The only thing for me is to go to the street and shorten my life as much as possible.'

He wrote back, 'You are so young, I must think for you, or we might both rush into endless misery.'

Pregnancy prompted a fast growing-up process. She delayed marrying him, unsure whether he would be good to her. But there was no other opportunity, and she and her Presbyterian mother agreed that this was the best solution. They married on 11 August 1868. 'I know I shall not be happy,' she said to a friend, 'he is not a kind man and I can't trust him.'

The first child was born two months after the wedding and they settled in George Street, Edinburgh. It was, indeed, not a happy marriage: Chantrelle was given to drinking and could sometimes be violent, though the evidence seems to be that he would terrify rather than physically attack his wife.

He stayed away most of the day and came in drunk and raging. Servants said he drank about a bottle of whisky a day and used bad language to his wife, accusing her of adultery and incest.

Mary Byrne said that when he called his unconscious wife 'Lizzie' on the day of her death, it was the first time she had heard him call her by her first name.

Chantrelle told police that early in their marriage his wife was always threatening to drown herself and that when, exasperated with her constant threats, he once said that she should go and do it, she berated him with, 'You are a nice man to let me go and drown myself.' He said he often found her leaning over a full bathtub, as if to put her head under, and he had to take her in his arms to revive her. She also had a tendency to sham fainting, which he attributed to 'reproducing the scenes she had read in trashy novels'. He would find her on the floor in a swoon and would have to carry her to the bed and bring her round.

Elizabeth often wrote to her mother, saying Chantrelle had threatened to murder her and the four children, seemingly accepting this as her fate since she would not leave him. On one occasion, after he had thrown a candlestick at her, a servant ran and found a policeman but he did not want to interfere.

On another occasion, he had burst in to the room of a servant, Margaret Wood, drunk and late at night. Elizabeth Chantrelle had gone in to save the servant and he had threatened her. Both women ran to the police station, not fully dressed, and a policeman came to arrest Chantrelle. He pleaded guilty to assaulting the servant and was fined £2.

Dr Littlejohn was once seen by Mrs Chantrelle and he said, 'Her husband's conduct was such as to make her suspect his sanity. She complained of his conduct as unnatural and outrageous.' He reported that she said he had pistols about the house, 'and said she was in terror of her life.'

At one time she wrote to her mother, 'Let me hear from you soon. I am sorry to trouble you but if he murders me you might have been sorry not to have heard from me.' She once made a servant sleep on the floor in her room, presumably to offer protection from Chantrelle.

She frequently left her husband, once staying with her mother for three weeks, but usually staying for less, saying she was only going back for the sake of her children. Her mother said she did not obtain legal advice to try to arrange a separation on the grounds of his unreasonable behaviour because 'my daughter did not wish it, she was so frightened for her life', which is no reason at all. She did visit a solicitor after the incident with the servant Margaret Wood and asked about the possibility of obtaining a separation. He assured her it was possible, because of Chantrelle's obvious adultery in frequenting brothels. She asked if it would become public knowledge, and when told it could well do, she decided not to proceed.

Mrs Dyer had often heard that Chantrelle was making threats on her daughter's life. Once her daughter had written to her, 'Come and see me at once if you want to see me alive. E. has a revolver.' He did have a pistol, and kept it loaded, frequently shooting at a target board inside the house in the room he used for teaching.

His drinking meant that over the ten years of their marriage he saw a dwindling number of private students and invariably had money difficulties. He applied to become an agent for a London insurance company and learned a little about insurance.

Chantrelle investigated the possibility of insuring his wife and inquired as to what eventualities 'accidental death' might cover. On 18 October 1877, he had her insured for £1000 at a 30s premium with the Accidental Assurance Association. The insurance was for accidental death alone. He also insured himself for the same sum.

At the office of the insurance company he asked what constituted an accident, and recounted a true story about his son picking up a loaded pistol and firing it accidentally. The shot had slightly injured Chantrelle's hand. He said it was this accident which had led him to insure his wife; you could never be too careful.

Elizabeth resisted being insured but he was so insistent that she signed for the sake of peace. Just before Christmas 1877 she made one of her secret visits to her mother to thank her for presents she had sent: the visits had to be secret as Chantrelle opposed them.

'My life is insured now, Mamma,' she said, 'and you will see that my life will go soon after this insurance.'

When her mother protested, she said, 'Something within me tells me that it will be so. What's the use of insuring me against accidents? I never travel or go about. I'm always in the house. It's a waste of money unless I die soon.'

When her mother tried to reassure her, she said, 'I cannot help thinking it; something within me tells me that it will be so.'

On New Year's Eve, Elizabeth Chantrelle went out to buy New Year gifts for the children. That evening, celebrating with champagne, the family seemed as happy as it ever had been. She posted New Year cards, including one to a friend to whom she promised to write soon, which was taken as evidence that she did not intend suicide.

On 1 January 1878, Chantrelle told Mary Byrne to go away for the day and not to bother to be in before 10 p.m. When Mary arrived home just before ten,

Chantrelle was in — most surprisingly, because he normally stayed out until after midnight. Elizabeth was already in bed and had been since 6 p.m. She was weak and exhausted, saying she had not felt well but now felt better than she had. She asked Mary to bring her a piece of orange and some lemonade, which had been bought for her by her husband. Mary did so, peeling the orange for her. That night Elizabeth slept alone — again, surprisingly, because she normally had at least one of her children with her, but Chantrelle took them into his room which was very crowded as a result. He later explained that the baby had been disturbing his wife when she was unwell.

Within twenty-four hours, Elizabeth was dead. Two days after the death, Criminal Officer William Frew supervised a further examination of Elizabeth Chantrelle's bedroom. A foreman gasfitter called John Somers found that a gas pipe had been broken near the window, behind a shutter. The break appeared to be fresh and the pipe been torn apart in a manner which could not have been caused accidentally by the closing of the window or the bending of the pipe only once. It would have taken some effort to break and was probably broken by being bent backwards and forwards several times. Chantrelle was shown the pipe but denied all knowledge of it. Later he said it might have been caused by the children hanging their clothes on the shutter.

When the police were looking over the Chantrelle home, he said, 'I wish they would give me peace and let me alone. Do they wish to make out that I poisoned my wife?' though no one had said any such thing.

The post-mortem, conducted by Dr Henry Littlejohn with Professor Douglas Maclagan, revealed no cause of death — certainly not gas poisoning. There was no smell of gas from the lungs or the brain and the blood was not floridly red as it usually was in gas poisoning cases. But neither was there any other obvious cause. Their report said they 'found no poison, vegetable or mineral, in the contents of the alimentary canal or in the tissues or fluids of the body, except a dubious and at most a very minute trace of chloral in the tissues of the stomach'.

They had to look further. William Frew visited the infirmary, where the nurse in charge had taken Elizabeth Chantrelle's bedclothes, stained with vomit, and put them away in a locked cupboard. Probably these were only retained because they were the property of the patient, or her relatives, and it would not be right to destroy them until the hospital had permission to do so.

The sheets and pillow-case from the dead woman's bed were still in the clothes basket waiting to be laundered when Frew searched the Chantrelle house, three days after the death. The pieces of orange had long since gone and the tumbler Elizabeth had been drinking lemonade from had been washed. He did, however, take possession of the insurance policy.

Frew later returned to the house on George Street with Dr Littlejohn and they went to a locked cupboard, for which he had taken the key on his previous search and which contained Chantrelle's stock of drugs, which he removed.

Henry Littlejohn and Douglas Maclagan acquainted themselves with the contents of Chantrelle's drug cabinet and tested the vomit stains for drugs which would cause unconsciousness. They now reported 'That on the sheet and bedgown we found indisputable evidence of the presence of opium, apparently in the form of extracts, and that in each case this opium was accompanied by portions of grapes and orange, the substances which we recognised in the contents of the stomach.'

There was something like a poisonous dose of opium in a single spot of vomit on the sheet. The opium in the vomit had been in solid form, which is the most toxic, and had not been administered in a fluid. Presuming it had been given to her in a piece of orange, Dr Littlejohn experimented and found that it would certainly be possible to place a lethal dose of opium undetected in a small piece of orange, and that opium could be mixed with lemonade and concealed by the taste of the lemonade. After the funeral, at which he gave a display of grief for the dead woman which those present found genuinely moving, Chantrelle was arrested.

Now they knew what they were looking for, however, the doctors wanted another examination of the body. They had her exhumed from the Grange Cemetery and took out more organs for further tests. Again these were inconclusive.

When Eugene Chantrelle came to trial in 1878, Dr Carmichael said he had assumed it was a case of coal-gas poisoning because of the smell of coal gas in the room. In the absence of that, he would have assumed it was a narcotic poisoning, particularly because the pupils of the patient's eyes remained dilated and did not respond to the stimulus of light. He had sent for Dr Littlejohn because cases of gas poisoning were rare and Littlejohn had more experience than he had.

It was not contested that Chantrelle had many drugs, including chloral hydrate, a fluid extract of opium and some hard extract of opium. A chemist would testify that he had purchased opium but also a number of other drugs. He was in the habit of prescribing, as some of his patients came to court to testify.

The court heard evidence that a gas leak continuing all night would produce far more gas than was present in the George Street house: the house would be filled. Experts said there was no way that the gas pipe could be damaged except by manipulation.

Mrs Dyer said of her daughter, 'She repeatedly took refuge from his violence in my house.' Questioned as to whether her daughter had been threatened with poisoning she said, 'repeatedly ... It was not a long time after her marriage, and it was repeated again and again. She stated that he would murder her, and could poison her.' Her daughter had told her Chantrelle had said that 'He could give her poison which the Faculty of Edinburgh could not detect.'

The defence argued that the signs of gas poisoning would have been expelled from the body by the lengthy efforts at artificial respiration which would have filled the blood and brain with fresh air. There was no connection between Eugene Chantrelle and his wife's taking opium, no proof that he even knew she had done it. Why did she not just call her servant and ask for help if she felt unwell after he had administered something to her?

When his counsel approached the end of his submission, Chantrelle asked loudly, 'Is that all the evidence for the defence?' It may be that he had tried to persuade his lawyer to propose some fantasy of a conspiracy against him and the legal man refused. The jury retired for just one hour and found him guilty.

When he was invited to speak to the court, Chantrelle put up a last, weak defence, to say that the stains contained opium but they had been added to the clothes and bedclothes to implicate him. Someone had 'rubbed them in'.

He was sentenced to death. The announcement of the verdict was met by cheers from the crowds who had gathered outside in Parliament Square.

Now Chantrelle wrote his views on the case to the Home Secretary, particularly protesting that it was a case of circumstantial evidence in which no poison had even been found in the body. At this time there was no test for opium in the body after it had left the stomach, as Chantrelle well knew. It is metabolised quickly and detection techniques were not sufficiently sensitive to show up residues.

Before he was hanged, he turned to religion and told a visiting clergyman that he had 'lived a life full of wickedness, but that there had never ceased to be a working of conscience against his misdeeds,' but he never confessed to killing his wife. Those present at the execution in Calton Prison said he faced death with some courage and self-possession.

★ ★ ★

It was agreed that opium does not take long to work, and that it was surprising that Elizabeth Chantrelle lived as long as she did. She must have been dosed with it after Byrne came in, or she would have seen its effects. Her earlier illness, which took her to bed, was not caused by the opium. How did Chantrelle manage to make her feel drowsy and unwell? It could have been the power of suggestion:

he may have worked on her to make her feel tired and lethargic, or it may have been that he somehow administered to her a draught of choral hydrate which was (and is) used as a sleeping drug.

His confidence in saying that he could kill her with a poison no one could detect gives the impression that he may well have done it before. It may be for this reason that he left America after giving the impression that he was going to settle there at a time when that country offered so much. He may have been involved in an opium poisoning which was successful but which aroused suspicions.

The real mystery is why Elizabeth Chantrelle stayed with him when he was so awful to her. A separation may have created some scandal which she wished to avoid for the sake of the children, but to any rational or even half-rational mind, her death would be a far worse blow to them. Did she really believe she was going to be murdered? Written evidence from her own hand shows that she was obsessed by death even before her marriage. Every event, even taking a bath, was fraught with danger to her. Had her solicitous mother genuinely thought she was in danger for her life, she would have insisted her daughter leave Chantrelle. It seems more likely that her mother had heard it all before, and that the fuss about the insurance was treated no more seriously than the fuss about Elizabeth's mortality which had been going on for ten years previously and perhaps before.

It may be that inwardly Elizabeth relished living on a knife edge, the danger of being with a passionate, wicked man, and the constant fear for her life, which was not, in the end, a romantic fantasy.

The Man Who Would
Not Stay Down

A CROWD gathered to look at a burning cottage on the York Road, four miles out of Baltimore, in February 1873. Among those observing it was the owner of the cottage, a Mr Lowndes. After the cottage had been blazing for nearly an hour, a man approached Mr Lowndes, the owner, and said, 'I think he is in the house.'

Asked who he meant, the man said, 'Mr Goss, I think he is still in the house.' The speaker was William Udderzook, brother-in-law of Goss, to whom the cottage had been let. Lowndes was appalled that Udderzook had not raised the alarm before, but the man said he was not acquainted with anyone but Lowndes, and did not like to speak unintroduced to strangers. He also wanted to look through the crowd to ensure Goss was not among them. Lowndes is reported to have said, 'You might have alarmed the whole neighbourhood; we would rather have had a false alarm than for a human being to be burned up alive.'

It was too late now to do anything about the fire, it had to run its course. When it had died down, a body, burned beyond recognition, was found and removed while Udderzook stood by loudly expressing his anguish.

William Udderzook was a smith and toolmaker who sometimes described himself as a 'teacher of fine arts'. The charred body was supposedly that of his sister Eliza's husband, his brother-in-law Winfield Goss. Goss was an inventor by trade and had devised a ratchet screwdriver. He claimed to be trying to make an artificial substitute for rubber and had rented the cottage to work on his experiments.

It became apparent that Mr Goss had been very well insured indeed, for a struggling inventor. The first insurance was unremarkable; this was taken out four years previously, for $5000, with the Mutual Life Insurance Company of New York. But it had been followed a year before his death with another policy, again for $5000, with the Continental Life Insurance Company of New York. Four months prior to the fire he had taken out accident insurance of $10,000 with the Travelers' Insurance Company of Hartford. A week before his apparent death he had taken out another $5000 life insurance with the Knickerbocker Life Insurance Company of New York. They were all payable to Eliza Goss, his wife, and Udderzook's sister. The premiums came to between $500 and $600 a year, which was half of the annual Goss income.

Everyone was interested in how this tragedy could have come about, not least the insurance companies. How did a 37–year-old active man get trapped in a burning house of not very elaborate design? It was explained at the inquest by a reconstruction of Goss's last day. He was said to have been in the city with Campbell Goss, his brother, until noon on the day of when Winfield Goss went to his laboratory. Campbell stayed a short time, then went home to his boarding house.

471

Udderzook had then accompanied Winfield Goss to the cottage lab. They bought a gallon of kerosene and a bottle of whisky. They stayed in the cottage all afternoon, and Udderzook left shortly after dusk, when Goss filled his oil lamp. Udderzook went to return an axe to some friends, the Engels, down the road and accepted their invitation to join them for a meal. Later, he and a son of the Engel family returned to the cottage and spent some time with Goss, who was having trouble with his oil lamp. Udderzook and young Engel went back to the Engel home to borrow a more efficient lamp from them, but when they returned, the cottage was on fire. The coroner found that an explosion of kerosene, connected with the lamp, had caused the death of Winfield Goss.

The insurance companies were not happy. As well as the number of insurances, the matter of the cost of the premiums as a percentage of the Goss income was a problem, as was the fact that the day before the fire Winfield Goss had withdrawn all his money from his bank and closed the account. Some days after the fire Campbell Goss had found his brother's watch, chain and keys, undamaged at the place where the body had lain, despite the passage of time and the searching of the cottage by a junk dealer, who might be supposed to have some skill in these matters. Moreover, Campbell Goss had not stayed in on the night of the fire. Insurance agents' inquiries found he had driven into the country with a horse and carriage. They thought he must have driven to York Road and taken his brother to a railway station after one or both of them had set the fire.

The insurance companies did not pay up, and Mrs Goss sued all the companies involved. The lawyers for the insurance companies felt an exhumation and a more determined attempt to identify the body might be in order. They suggested that an examination of the teeth of the corpse might shed some light on its identity. Eliza Goss was asked to furnish a better description of her husband, to which she is reported to have been affronted. A letter from her, probably penned by Udderzook, said she had 'been shocked by the suspicions in the case, and the aspersions on the memory of her husband, and that she would say no more, but would, instead, commit the matter to the God of the widow and the afflicted.'

The insurance companies had heard protestations of injured innocence before and they pressed on. Eventually, Mrs Goss gave a description of her husband's dentition: generally good, with regular front teeth and no artificial teeth. She also gave permission for an exhumation but the Mr Goss who came out of the ground had only two teeth in his upper jaw and seven in his lower jaw.

The first case presented by Eliza Goss, in May 1873, was a test case, brought against the Mutual Life Insurance Company. The last hours of Goss were studied in detail with a thorough examination of a full cast of witnesses. A great deal of expert testimony followed, which may well have been too detailed for the jury, who were more likely to be moved by the grieving figure of Eliza Goss, who won the day.

The insurance companies moved for a

new trial and this started to worry the litigants. Having failed to prove the body was not that of Goss, their detectives might now think it expedient to attempt to find the real Goss.

About three weeks after the trial, William E. Udderzook was seen in his home town of Jennerville, Pennsylvania, with a middle-aged, heavy-set man with whiskers. They booked into a hotel under Udderzook's name and he explained that his friend was an invalid and was unable to come down to breakfast, so he took some up to him. In the evening, they drove away in a hired carriage. At midnight Udderzook returned the carriage which was later noticed to be in a poor condition: there were stains on the floor, an oilcloth and two blankets were missing. As if by compensation, a large seal ring set with a bloodstone was found between the seat cushions.

A week later, a farmer was surprised by the number of buzzards in the area of Baer's Wood and he looked to see what they were interested in. He found the body of a man partially covered in bracken. On later examination, with other helpers, it was found that only the trunk and head were here and the limbs were in a trench twenty yards away. The body was recognised as that of the stranger seen with Udderzook.

Udderzook was arrested and jailed while the body was properly identified, as was the ring, which one of the Engel family remembered as belonging to Goss. Why Udderzook disposed of the body in such an obvious way, after planning the murder apparently carefully, is not known. It is not as if he took fright and ran away; he stayed long enough to hack four limbs off a thick-set man. Why did he not hack off the head and put that somewhere else?

At the trial the case was that there had been a plot with both Goss brothers and Udderzook involved to defraud the insurance companies. Udderzook had obtained the cadaver which was found in the burning cottage from a medical college. The difficulties with the oil lamp had been faked for the benefit of the Engel boy, who had been brought along as an independent witness, to testify that the lamp had been faulty and that Udderzook was nowhere near the fire when it started. Campbell Goss had waited for their departure, then driven up to pick up Winfield Goss and take him to a railway station whence he could get far away to live in another town under an assumed name.

The major problem was the suspicions of the insurance companies. This was exacerbated by the fact that Goss would not lie low. He was not that sort of man, as many people who met someone answering his description in various bars would testify. He had lived mainly in Philadelphia but also in New Jersey. He was said by one of the lawyers to 'deal in conviviality to too great an extent with his companions'. In other words, he was a drunk. He called himself A. C. Wilson but would persist in showing people his 'patent screwdriver'. The prosecution had no difficulty in identifying Wilson as Goss, or in demonstrating that by refusing to be dead when the insurance companies were eager for any clue of his continued life, he endangered the carefully planned criminal endeavour. Udderzook therefore had a clear motive.

A brother-in-law of Udderzook called Samuel Rhodes finally finished any opportunity Udderzook might have had for convincing the court of his innocence. Udderzook had written him a letter asking for his help in some enterprise, hinting it was a crime, and had gone to him on the day of the murder asking him to help him to take a man into the woods, give him laudanum and murder him. The case for the prosecution was so strong that the lawyers who had acted for the Gosses in the insurance cases now refused to continue in the murder trial, withdrawing before the prosecution case was finished. They said they had been misled by the Gosses.

The defence was a spirited sidelong blow against the prosecution, such as one sometimes sees in people with an utterly hopeless case. They claimed the whole case was a conspiracy by the insurance companies to avoid paying out to the entirely just claim of Eliza Goss. The man found in Baer's Wood was a chance discovery which the insurance officials seized upon to pursue their vendetta against the Goss family by eliminating their best defender. This was not such a bad defence. This jury showed itself almost as willing to believe in a nebulous conspiracy as in the assembly of unassailable facts which the prosecution put forward. They were out for nearly two days and nights before the verdict went against Udderzook and he was sentenced to be hanged.

Udderzook wrote a letter shortly before his execution protesting his affection for Goss, 'a friend ever dear to me', and asking to be buried in the same lot in the graveyard, 'that our bodies may return to the mother earth, and our spirits may mingle together on the bright sunny banks of deliverance, whence pleasures never end'. He took advantage of a chance to speak from the scaffold on 12 November 1874 to give a speech warning his fellow countrymen about the pernicious insurance companies.

As one commentator noted, he did not say which Goss he wanted to be buried beside, as he had always claimed the one in the burned cottage was the real one, so presumably he was buried beside the unknown cadaver.

Lone Wolves

AS a crime of the respectable, insurance murder is committed by the most normal and unexceptional people. These are people who would not be noticed in a street. They are anyone's friends and relatives, they rarely come from identifiably criminal families.

Eric Holt was just like any other young man: having a good time drinking and joking with friends, making love with women and talking about football. It was probably his very ordinariness which led the public to be so frantically interested in his trial. It was almost as if it could have been anyone.

It is interesting to see how little has changed over the years. Warren Green bears a strong resemblance to Frederick Seddon, his predecessor by almost a century. There is the careful planning, the ice-cool demeanour, the efficient handling of the police, the arrogance and the sheer avarice of the man.

Seddon had these qualities in abundance. His word was to be trusted. If you did not believe a churchgoing insurance official who was also a Freemason, who did you believe?

The lives of the above, Green included, show how false the idea is of a criminal progression. These killers did not move from small crimes to large ones, in a build-up through theft and fraud towards murder. They led apparently blameless lives; murder may well have been the only crime they ever committed.

Fox, on the other hand, was never anything but a professional criminal. He presents a miserable picture of struggling to concoct almost hourly deceptions to keep alive. His wretched last weeks of freedom show how hard it is to live by fraud. He achieved his ends not by actual respectability but by a charade produced by a false address and good manners. In his ultimate crime the premise was the same as that of the other insurance killers: if you look sufficiently respectable you can get away with murder.

Twenty Minutes
of Insurance

THE two individuals who booked in to the Hotel Metropole at Margate in October 1929 were, in every way, the type who might be expected to stay in an elegant, seaside resort hotel. They appeared to be people of some means. Sidney Harry Fox was a man of thirty who was self-assured and handsome but for a 'lazy' left eyelid. His mother, Rosaline Fox, was a sedate woman who still retained some of her earlier good looks despite her years, and Parkinson's disease which caused her to walk slowly with a shuffling gait. Perhaps, on a second glance, they were a little down at heel, but they had been travelling.

They gave their address as 'End View', Lyndhurst, Hants. In answer to casual inquiry, it would be disclosed that Mrs Fox was the widow of William Fox, the founder of Fox's Flour Mills. They were in Margate on their way back from France where they had been visiting the graves of her three sons who were killed in the war. They had no luggage as it had already been sent on to their home.

Sidney Fox impressed everyone with his solicitous behaviour towards his old mother, always asking after her and taking her delicacies like bunches of grapes. They were to stay one night only, but she was taken ill, so they prolonged their stay. After five days, Sidney Fox asked about the bill and said he would have to go to London to cash a cheque. He returned to Margate the same day.

At 11.40 p.m. on 23 October 1929 Sidney Fox ran down the stairs of the hotel, dressed only in his shirt, and shouting that there was a fire. The first to come to his aid was a salesman, Samuel Hopkins, who alerted other guests, in the billiard room, then ran up behind Fox to Fox's room, No 67, which was full of smoke. Fox said. 'Mummy's in there,' indicating the closed door to the adjoining room, 66.

Hopkins gallantly entered the room but

was overcome by smoke. He could see a red glow in the room which was otherwise dark. He put his handkerchief round his mouth, got down and crawled into the room, groping in the darkness for Mrs Fox. He caught her bare legs, hanging over the edge of the bed, then pulled her from the smoke-filled room and down the corridor where he collapsed.

Another guest, Reginald Reed, crawled into the room to attempt to put out the fire. The site of the fire was an armchair facing the gas stove. He dragged the chair out of the room where it could be put out. Yet another guest, Frederick French, stamped out the remains of the fire on the carpet and put out the gas light.

The police and two doctors arrived and attempted to revive Mrs Fox, but she was dead. Sidney Fox was so upset when he found his mother was dead that he needed an injection of morphine. He was moaning, 'Mummy, Oh my mummy, my mummy.' After the doctor had certified her dead, Fox was allowed in to see the body of his mother. He walked up to her, looked at her and touched her, staying a few minutes before coming out of the room weeping.

He was able to give a description of his mother's last hours to the police so they could hold an inquest. She had gone into her room, which opened to his, at 9.45 p.m. and asked for the *Evening Standard* which he gave her. He lit the gas fire and asked her if she wanted him to wait to turn out the lights. She did not so he kissed her goodnight and left her, going downstairs to have a drink, then returned and went to sleep at 10.45. He woke almost an hour later and smelled smoke. He tried to enter her room but was beaten back by the smoke and he called for a porter, running downstairs where he raised the alarm.

He was very concerned about a handbag of his mother's which he said contained at least £24. The handbag was found, burnt outside but intact, though there was no money in it.

The inquest was held the next day. According to the evidence of the chief of Margate Fire Brigade, the carpet was burnt under the armchair; though not directly in front of the gas fire, between the fire and the chair. Perhaps something had formed a bridge from the gas fire to the chair, carrying the fire across. It was possible that a piece of newspaper had done this, or that Mrs Fox had undressed in front of the fire and one of her underclothes had been caught by the fire and lain smouldering on the floor. It was remarked that the fire was smouldering until the door had been opened and then it burst into flames. Medical evidence adduced the woman died from shock and suffocation: she may have woken up to find her room filled with smoke and been so overcome with shock she had been unable to raise the alarm. The verdict was death by misadventure. Sidney Fox went with the body to Norfolk where the funeral took place on 25 October. He obtained £40 on account from a local solicitor who would handle the details of claiming on the insurance policies for him, and he asked the manager of the Hotel Metropole to send on his bill.

Mrs Fox was insured for £3010 in two short-term policies. When the insurance companies came to examine Sidney Fox's claim, however, they became suspicious.

Both of her policies would have run out within twenty minutes of her death.

They were in the form of travel insurances which covered for a brief period for death and accident. Sidney Fox had taken out a number of such insurances on his mother. He had taken twelve one-day policies with the Ocean Accident and Guarantee Corporation since 11 September. The other policy, with the Cornhill Assurance Company, had been taken out on 10 August; it was renewed from time to time but had expired on 20 October. He renewed both policies on 22 October on his trip to London, the day before his mother's death. He went to the head office of the Ocean Accident and Guarantee Corporation and made sure the policy covered Mrs Fox for the full day of 23 October, up to midnight. He then did the same thing at the Cornhill, again specifying midnight on 23 October, explaining that they were going to France and his mother would not travel without insurance. In this case, the company generously extended the policy without payment of a further premium.

Considering they were now being asked to pay out on a policy which was due to run out in twenty minutes of the insured's death, they took their suspicions to the Margate police who quickly found that the Foxes were small-time confidence tricksters, living on their wits and the gullibility of others.

Everything Sidney had told the inquest and the hotel manager was a lie, though he had probably long since lost the ability to distinguish between lies and the truth. His father was not the proprietor of Fox's Flour Mills, East Dereham, he was a signalman. Fox had not been educated at Framlingham College but the local parish school; they did not live at 'End View', Lyndhurst, Hants, which did not exist. One of his brothers had been killed in France in the war (and one was killed doing munitions work after the war), but they had not just visited the Continent. They had no luggage and, in fact, no possessions except what they stood up in. Mrs Fox had only two dresses, which, in the absence of luggage, she wore one over the other when she arrived at the hotel. When she died it was in a vest she had been wearing under her dress that day. Their income was eighteen shillings a week from two pensions, one of ten shillings (50p) a week for the death of Mrs Fox's eldest son in the war, and the second for eight shillings (40p) due to Sidney Fox for an alleged war injury. He had supposedly had an epileptic seizure as a result of his experiences in the services.

Mrs Rosaline Fox, the daughter of a farm labourer, had been the 'village beauty' of East Dereham. She had three sons by her signalman husband before leaving him and going to live with a railway porter by whom she had her last son, Sidney. She was always closest to him and when she decided to leave East Dereham for London she took him with her. They always lived together.

Sidney Fox first came to the notice of the police at the age of eleven or twelve for fraudulent collection on behalf of charities in Norfolk. He did collect money for charity, and handed some of it over, but stuck two pages of his collection book together and pocketed the amounts covered by those pages. He was birched for the offence.

He then became a page boy for Sir John and Lady Constance Leslie, who were very fond of him and called him 'Cupid' because of his cherubic expression. He was dismissed when he stole some of the family silver and somehow defrauded an elderly housemaid of her life savings.

He then obtained a job in a bank and developed a career in forging cheques, joining the Royal Flying Corps when the police got too close. When he was in the services, he stole a cheque book and continued his criminal career, and on discharge he got a job in a bank, giving him ample opportunity to further exercise his talents. His fraudulent activities were conducted under the names Captain Owen James Smythe of the RAF, or The Honourable Captain S. H. Fox.

He called on a friend of Lady Constance Leslie, claiming to be his former employer's grandson. He was so convincing in this that she was prepared to endorse him in fraudulently cashing a cheque with her greengrocer. He was eventually arrested at the Royal

Automobile Club, of which he was not a member, and where he was staying under the guise of an airforce officer.

He was sent to prison, for this cheque fraud, for stealing from the bank and forging cheque books, for which he received three months' hard labour. He then did serve in the army, enjoying it and earning the respect of his senior officers.

He later served another eight months' hard labour for forgery; then six months for defrauding London shops by using the names of regular customers to obtain services. He subsequently received two further sentences of twelve months each, for larceny and fraud and for obtaining credit from a London hotel by fraud.

Fox's most recent term of imprisonment had been for obtaining money under false pretences and for stealing jewellery from a woman who was supposedly his friend. In this last case he and his mother had befriended a Mrs Morse of Southsea. Mother and son had gone to live with her, and Fox took a job with an insurance company.

Mrs Morse was unhappily married to

a captain in the merchant fleet who was in the Far East. Though Fox was a homosexual, he went against his natural instincts sufficiently to seduce her and was cited as a co-respondent in her divorce. More importantly, he induced her to make out a fresh will in which he was the main beneficiary and had her insure her life for £3000. One night she awoke to find gas in her bedroom but managed to crawl over the room and turn the gas tap off. Fox arrived on the scene and turned off a gas tap which was disused, and was located behind a chest of drawers, and was impossible to turn on accidentally. When Mrs Morse felt better, she and the Foxes parted company, Sidney taking her jewellery. He was caught and sentenced to fifteen months in prison.

Rosaline Fox had nowhere to go, and had to be admitted to a workhouse during his imprisonment, where she spent most of her time in the infirmary. As soon as Fox was released from prison he picked up his mother from St Mary's Hospital, Portsmouth, and they continued their life of fraud.

At least in the month preceding her death, and probably for a long time previously, Sidney and Rosaline Fox had been moving from one hotel to another. They either left with a promise to send the amount of the bill from their next stop, or Mrs Fox paid with a fake cheque, drawn on a bank where she did not have an account. Thus they had taken the Grand Hotel in Dover, the Royal Pavilion Hotel in Folkestone and the County Hotel in Canterbury before arriving at the Hotel Metropole, Margate.

The increasing difficulty of this mode of life is demonstrated by the way Fox obtained even the money to travel to London to extend the policies. He tried to use a cheque to pay for two bottles of medicine for his mother. The chemist would not cash a cheque, so Fox waited till he went to lunch, then saw his assistant and explained, 'It's quite all right. I saw Mr Farmer about it, and he told me to go to the bank, and they said it would be quite all right if I affixed another penny stamp and endorsed it, which I have done.' So he went off with two pounds, minus the cost of the medicines. This gave him the money to get to London.

To get back he telephoned an acquaintance of his and his mother's, a Mrs Gertrude Platt. First he called her and spoke to her office boy, pretending to leave a message for Sidney Fox. The message was that Rosaline Fox was very ill and Sidney should return to Margate at once. Fox later called Mrs Platt, ostensibly to ask if she could put him up for the night, and she relayed this message to him. 'That is funny,' he said, 'she was quite well when I left her this morning. What am I to do? I haven't money to get home. Do you think you could lend it to me?' Mrs Platt knew him well enough to say no. She suggested he pawn something but he had nothing of value left. He eventually borrowed a pound from another friend. All this labour for petty sums makes being a professional confidence trickster seem more arduous than actually working for a living.

This trail of deception started to be uncovered when accounts of the inquest were reported in the press. Mrs Maud

Staines, who owned a cottage in Margate and let rooms, read a report of the inquest and recognised in the description of the Foxes two people who had stayed in her rooms one night a few weeks earlier. The next morning, Sidney Fox said he had lost his wallet which contained several banknotes. With tears in his eyes he said he could not pay their bed-and-breakfast bill. He was desolate, nothing like this had ever happened to him before, he felt so ashamed. Mrs Staines felt so sorry for him she gave them some money to see them on their way. How odd, she thought, and explained to the police, that such penniless people should then book in to the Hotel Metropole.

The manager of the Royal Pavilion Hotel in Folkestone read about the death in the local newspaper. This was the same couple who had left without paying their bill, so he called the Metropole's manager to confer. There was no sign of the Metropole's payment either so the hotel manager contacted the police. While awaiting the result of further inquiries about the insurance matter, the police thought they had better keep Fox where they could see him, so they arrested him on six charges of obtaining money and credit by false pretences in relation to the hotel bills.

They asked for the assistance of Scotland Yard and Chief Inspector Walter Hambrook and a sergeant were sent down at the beginning of November. Hambrook already knew Fox, having arrested him once for forgery. Fox foolishly pretended not to recognise Hambrook, which implied he had more than usual to hide. Hambrook immediately ordered the recovery of the burnt material from Mrs Fox's room which had been thrown away. The refuse from the town of Margate was being used to fill the area between a new sea wall and the cliffs, so many tons of rubbish had to be sorted through to recover the burnt newspaper, handbag and clothes, but eventually they were found. Rosaline Fox was exhumed and the famous pathologist Sir Bernard Spilsbury conducted a post-mortem and found that there was no soot in the air passages of the body. She had not, therefore, died of smoke inhalation, nor had she inhaled any smoke: she was dead before there was any smoke in her room.

Under investigation, several interesting anomalies started to emerge about the behaviour of Fox in the days leading up to the death. He had been seen with some petrol in a bottle, which he used to clean a suit; two days earlier, he had claimed that his mother was subject to fainting fits and had medicine (sal volatile) from him for treatment; he had gone out to get a bottle of port on the night she died, the only night she had drunk port; he had made inquiries of the hotel manager about a local solicitor who could deal with insurance matters. Most curiously, he told a waiter he and his mother had a 'sham fight'. This is more than improbable and was presumably a device to explain innocently any bruises which might be found on her body after he had killed her.

Tests conducted at Hambrook's request showed that it was impossible to burn the underneath of an armchair using a 'bridge' from a gas fire without singeing the carpet between them. It was also impossible to burn the carpet using paper alone and no experiment produced a great deal of smoke unless petrol was used.

It was most likely that the fire had been started with petrol-soaked newspapers stuffed under that armchair. This was made more probable by the fact that one of the fragments of newspaper recovered was in French, a language neither Sidney nor Rosaline Fox could read.

Fox was charged with the murder of his mother and pleaded not guilty when the trial opened at Lewes on 12 March 1930. The prosecution case was that he had given his mother port to drink until she was drowsy. When she was asleep he had taken her by the throat and pulled the pillow from under her head, putting it over her mouth to stifle any cries. Her false teeth had been forced out of her mouth and he put these in the handbasin. Bruises on her throat and her tongue, which she had bitten, were consistent with throttling. Fox had then gone downstairs, had one or two drinks in the bar, then returned upstairs to set the fire and raise the alarm.

Sir Bernard Spilsbury had to say at

the trial that, though he believed this was a case of strangulation, he had never seen such a case with so little physical evidence. The defence demonstrated the fragility of samples of cartilages taken from different human bodies. Another eminent pathologist Professor Sydney Smith argued that it was impossible to strangle someone, particularly an elderly person, and not fracture the hyoid bone, which had not been fractured in this case. The existence of bruising was also contested. Testimony was divided at least in part because Smith examined the body three months after Spilsbury and so it was in a somewhat changed state. Spilsbury insisted he had seen a bruise the size of a large coin at the back of Mrs Fox's larynx. This had not been observed by Sydney Smith, who said it may have been a transient mark of putrefaction, but Spilsbury insisted with customary lack of modesty, 'It was a bruise and nothing else. There are no two opinions about it.'

The defence case was that there was no direct evidence to demonstrate that Fox throttled and suffocated his mother and that everyone that testified who had seen them together remarked on their very good relationship. Sidney had never been anything but a devoted son. The absence of soot in the air passage alone was not evidence that she had not been breathing in the smoke-filled room: she might have breathed through her nose for a time without the particles getting in her lungs, and the mucous membrane of the nose was not examined by prosecution experts. She had died of a heart attack.

One question Fox found difficult to answer was why he had closed his mother's door into his room when he found smoke pouring out of it, and then closed his own door when he went to raise the alarm. 'So that smoke should not spread into the hotel,' he said weakly.

Evidence from the Cornhill Assurance Company said their short-term insurances normally extended from noon to noon but on request they had extended this one till midnight. Their representative explained how he had answered questions posed by Fox about the exact meaning of the word 'accident' in the policy,

One was that if the assured, his mother, drowned in the bath, would that be an accident? Another question was that if she was poisoned by food in a restaurant, would that be an accident within the meaning of the policy. I said I presumed if she was taken ill in the bath and subsequently drowned, that would not be an accident. I said poisoning by food in a restaurant would not be regarded as an accident.

The accident which befell Mrs Fox was, of course, entirely within the meaning of the word in the policy.

Fox had filled in the forms for his mother's insurance and, as Mr Justice Rowlatt said in his summing up, they did not travel. Therefore as travelling policies they were wasted, a particularly unusual situation considering the desperate financial straits of the Foxes.

He noted how it was in Fox's favour that the murder seemed so complicated: would not a more straightforward killer have just closed the door with the gas tap turned on and gassed his mother? The answer is, of course, that he had tried that with Mrs Morse and found it was easier said than done.

The jury returned a verdict of guilty and Fox bowed his head and said, 'Amen'. He was hanged at Maidstone Gaol on 8 April 1930. He did not appeal, one of very few murderers not to have done so.

* * *

Some questions still remained: Fox had taken out a number of insurances for his mother, over a number of months. From 1 May until her death in October, he had taken out a short-term insurance policy on his mother on 167 days out of a total of 176. Why kill her now, when the insurance was £3000 instead of at an earlier time when it stood at £4000? Perhaps it was, as the judge said, just a case of murder being easier to plan than commit. His nerve failed or there was no adequate opportunity.

It could be that there was another defence, which he never used, as it would still have been murder, but which seems more acceptable with the passage of time. It was always difficult for the police, the prosecution, and writers on the case to reconcile Fox's evident and frequently demonstrated love for his mother with his murder of her. The most frequent explanation is that as he was homosexual he was 'degenerate', and capable of any loathsome act. This is name-calling in the place of analysis, and anyway is too unsophisticated for a modern understanding of human behaviour.

It is perfectly possible to reconcile Sidney's love for his mother with her death. Though he certainly intended to gain by the insurance, this may not have been the prime motive.

Sidney and his mother had reached the end of the line, and Rosaline Fox was too old and weak to keep up the only life they knew. The only place for her was the workhouse. She had been in the workhouse recently when Fox was in prison, and she did not like it. Sidney Fox could do no more for her. Killing Mrs Morse would have set them up. The insurance on her and the inheritance from her, perhaps including her flat, would have allowed Rosaline Fox to live in comfort for the rest of her days. This caper had failed and they had ended up in a worse situation than they were before, with a dwindling number of hotels available for them to defraud.

Parkinson's disease is a slowly progressive condition, also called shaking palsy and paralysis agitans. It is characterised by a tremor of resting muscles and a slowing of voluntary muscles. It is a degenerative condition for which, at this time, there was no effective treatment. Medicine can now go some way towards alleviating the condition but then it would have eventually resulted in complete paralysis: a waking death. If mother and son did not know from general knowledge how serious her condition was, she would have certainly found out from her time in the workhouse infirmary. Many parents ask their children to kill them when they become incapable of independent action. Rosaline Fox had not reached that point, but it was not far off.

It is plain also that Mrs Fox knew that

her death was imminent and that Sidney Fox would gain some money from life insurance on her. On 21 April, soon after he had taken her from the workhouse, she made a will leaving all she had to him, though of course she had almost literally nothing. The only objective could be to simplify his claiming on her insurance when she died as she surely soon would, though she doubtless did not realise quite how close the end was. It was nine days after the will was made out that Fox took out the first of the short term accident policies on his mother. She signed the policies herself.

It is probable that Sidney, knowing he could take his mother no further, killed her in part as an act of mercy so she did not have to face the future in poverty with a degenerative disease. He made sure he would gain the insurance money, but that does not mean that personal enrichment was his primary motive. Euthanasia was still murder, so this was no defence, but it is an act many have committed without guilt.

Flypaper

FEW people had a good word for Miss Eliza Mary Barrow. She was a miserly, complaining woman. She was forty-nine when she went on the lookout for rooms to occupy after she had quarrelled with the last group of relatives who were prepared to allow her to live with them.

She was poorly dressed and slovenly even though she had enough money to spend the rest of her life in comfort. She had £1600 invested in Government of India stock and owned some property in London, which gave her a total income of almost £3 a week which in the first decade of the twentieth century was a comfortable sum.

She was described as being 'suspicious, grasping, mean and bad tempered', though it was said she could be generous to her retinue, which followed her about, acting as servants and companions, and to whom she was known as 'Chickie'.

She had lived with her cousins, a family named Vonderahe, but argued with them and actually forbade them to write to her or call on her. In confirmation of her contempt, she spat in Mrs Julia Vonderahe's face. She was the wealthiest member of her family and assumed everyone else was after her money.

In summer 1910, Barrow became a lodger of Frederick Henry Seddon at 63 Tollington Park, North London, which was close to her previous address. She took the entire second floor of the four-storey house unfurnished, with a kitchen upstairs. She had a room, and there was one for an engine driver called Robert Hook, who had been with her for some years, and his wife and their nephew Ernest Grant who was nine or ten, and who had been all but adopted by Barrow. He described her as 'an affectionate and loving woman to me'. For seven shillings a week (35p) the Seddons' daughter Maggie acted as servant to Barrow.

The Seddon family consisted of his wife Margaret, who was thirty-three, five children and his father. Frederick Seddon himself was a 39–year-old insurance agent, a district superintendent for Islington employed by the London and Manchester Industrial Insurance Company, to whom he let another part of his fourteen-roomed house as an office. He was a teetotaller and had been a preacher and a significant figure in the Nonconformist community. He made the house pay, and in doing so had to confine the space available to his family. He divided one room in half and obliged six of the household to sleep there, including his aged father and the family's general servant. Contemporary reports describe him as mean and avaricious, with no redeeming features, driven forward only by the miser's acquisitive instinct. He and Barrow made a good pair.

Though Seddon usually took no interest in lodgers, leaving this work to his wife, he quickly realised the value of Eliza Barrow and began talking about investments with her. He gave the Hooks their notice on some pretext, saying it was because they had been quarrelling with Miss Barrow while all the lodgers had been drinking. They received a note from her asking them to leave but had no conversation with her about it. Seddon fixed a notice to quit on their door signed 'F. Seddon, landlord and owner'. When Hook remonstrated, Seddon said he was 'going to look after her interests' and that Barrow had put all her affairs in his hands. Ernest Grant stayed with Miss Barrow.

Like many people, as age advanced on her Barrow was terrified she would become too poor to maintain herself. Her principal concern was that the Government of India would go bankrupt and she would lose the income from her investment. Seddon played on this fear and offered her a deal: she would part with her £1600 India stock in return for an annuity of a little over £103. She consented, but drove what she thought was the hard bargain of refusing to share the solicitor's fees for transferring the stock; he must bear the total cost. Seddon put up a fierce resistance to this proposal but finally let her win, thinking herself very shrewd.

The bald landlord with the large moustache worked on his tenant's fears and played on her greed. His greed came into it too, for he was in no need of money, and presumably just enjoyed making money for the sake of it. He sold the India stock and used the proceeds to buy the freehold on fourteen houses, which entitled him to a rental income from leaseholders.

He proceeded to discuss with her the uncertainties in the property market, the bother of leasing and paying agents' fees. He would be prepared to take it all off her hands and give her a further annuity. She consented and by the beginning of 1911 she had assigned to him the lease of the Buck's Head public house and a barber's shop adjoining in return for a further annuity of £52. So she now received three pounds a week, for the rest of her life, having changed her uninteresting investments into shiny gold sovereigns.

The life annuity the insurance agent had just sold her meant she would be paid the agreed sum, no more nor less, for every week of her life, however long that life was, or however short. Mrs Seddon said she witnessed the document conferring the annuity and knew, for example, that it said Miss Barrow must be paid even in the event of anything happening to Seddon. This document was not seen again, or produced later in evidence, which was rather surprising considering Seddon's painstaking business practices.

Eliza Barrow had a fondness for gold sovereigns. A year after she started to live with Seddon, she was anxious about a bank crash which was much in the news — a concern Seddon may well have fostered in her — and drew out £216 in gold from her bank. She was also said to keep a large amount of gold and cash in a cashbox in her room, and some jewellery. All of it was now in the Seddon house. He said he disapproved of so much gold being around the house unsecured, and she was said to have given him some of it to keep for her in one of his two safes.

In August, Eliza Barrow went on holiday with the Seddons to Southend. The following month, on 1 September, Miss Barrow complained of feeling unwell and, in the absence of her own doctor, the Seddons' physician, Dr Sworn was called. She had serious diarrhoea and sickness which he diagnosed as epidemic diarrhoea, meaning he thought it had been caused by an infection rather than food poisoning, but that was as far as the diagnosis went. When she grew worse, the doctor advised her to go to a hospital but she was suspicious and surly, refusing to leave the support of the Seddon family, particularly to a hospital where she would have to pay.

The sick room was a vile place, filled with flies. The patient's vomiting and diarrhoea was exacerbated by her poor habits of personal cleanliness at the best of times. Seddon later claimed the smell kept him from entering her room.

In some misery from her illness, she insisted that Ernie Grant sleep with her. She also decided to make a will, asking Seddon to draft it for her, presumably to save the expense of a solicitor. His wife and father witnessed it. She left everything to Ernie Grant and Hilda Grant, his sister, and Seddon was named executor.

Barrow was often in the habit of saying, 'I shan't live long,' and 'I wish I were dead,' so when she called out, 'I am dying,' in the evening of 13 September 1911, Mrs Seddon thought little of it. Neither did Mr Seddon, who had just returned from a music hall and was expostulating about how he had been short-changed for a small amount. 'A sixpence is a sixpence after all,' he said.

This time, however, Barrow was true to her word, and she died early the next morning. Ernie Grant, sleeping with his old friend, had called to Mrs Seddon in the middle of the night, 'Chickie needs you,' and she had come, with her husband. Both were with her at the time of death, though Frederick Seddon was standing outside the door of the sick room. Doctor Sworn, without examining the body, certified that she had died from natural causes: epidemic diarrhoea.

There were matters to attend to so Seddon sent Ernie Grant and his children to Southend. He ordered a cheap funeral for his lodger, telling an undertaker that Miss Barrow had left only £4 and he wanted a funeral for that, with some commission due to Seddon for bringing in the business. He was paid twelve shillings and sixpence. When she was buried, at Finchley, the only mourners were Seddon and his family. She was buried in a common grave, despite having a right to a place in the family vault in Highgate Cemetery. Seddon claimed to have written to Barrow's relatives, and could even produce a carbon copy of the letter, but they said they had not received it. He also purchased some memorial cards, picking out a verse which started, 'A dear one is missing and with us no more.'

Seddon's first shock was when Frank Vonderahe, Miss Barrow's cousin, called to see her on 20 September, to find she was dead and buried and he had not been told. Seddon was out, or claimed to be, as was the case when Vonderahe came back later. The following day, Mrs Vonderahe and another relative managed to see Seddon, who produced the carbon copy of the letter he had supposedly sent to them. He also gave Mrs Vonderahe a copy of the will and told her that was an end to the matter, he had wasted too much time over his dead lodger already. He left for another holiday, perhaps a suspicious event in one not given to personal extravagance.

On Seddon's return, in October, Frank Vonderahe and a friend bearded him. He gave them surly answers, making no mention of the £400 – £500 Barrow usually had in her cashbox, supplemented by the £216 withdrawn from her bank. He said he had found only £10 in her room, and her will left all her belongings to Ernie Grant and his sister. These things were valued at £16. Vonderahe asked who was now the owner of the Buck's Head. Seddon said that he was, adding helpfully, 'I am always open to buy property at a price.'

Vonderahe and his friend insisted they be shown the original of the will. Seddon refused, saying he had already given them a copy via Mrs Vonderahe. He could certainly have shown them the will, and to some extent allayed their suspicions, for the one he gave Mrs Vonderahe was a copy of the original with no alterations.

Seddon's treatment of the Vonderahes was his undoing. They wrote to the Director of Public Prosecutions who passed the information on to Scotland

Yard. They had little to complain about, mere suspicions, but after some preliminary inquiries Chief Inspector Alfred Ward felt that the case had been made for an exhumation. The authorities were impressed by his arguments and soon Seddon was approached and given an order to attend the inquest of Eliza Barrow.

He and his wife gave evidence at the inquest about the manner of their lodger's death, and it was adjourned for the results of the post-mortem. Examination of the body revealed no apparent disease. There was arsenic, however; the body was full of it.

Dr William Willcox, senior scientific analyst to the Home Office, conducted the tests for arsenic. He cleverly adapted the commonly used Marsh Test, which tells if arsenic is present, into a test to show the quantities in which it is present. He tested a given amount of arsenic, which he had measured out. He then tested to see if arsenic was present in various weighed sections taken from the organs of Eliza Barrow. He could assess how much arsenic there was in each specimen, by comparing it with his standard measure. He could then work out how much arsenic there was in the complete organ. That is, if he knew how much arsenic there was in two per cent of the liver, multiplying it by fifty would give him the amount in the whole liver.

By this means he was able to estimate that the body of Eliza Barrow contained more than two grains, the minimum fatal dose. Some of the poison would be expelled by the body, however, and if two grains were left as a residue, it would be possible to say that the total dose administered, within two or three days of death, was five grains.

Arsenic has been called 'the fool's poison' because it preserves the body in the grave, permitting later exhumation. As the pathologist Bernard Spilsbury later told the court,

> the body was well preserved, internally and externally, apart from some post-mortem staining externally ... I think the preservation was due to the presence of arsenic in the body.
>
> My opinion is that death was the

result of acute arsenical poisoning — poisoning by one or more large doses of arsenic as distinguished from poisoning by small doses of arsenic over a long period of time. By a large dose, I mean a poisonous dose, which would be two grains, and less than that would give rise to symptoms of poisoning.

Chief Inspector Ward arrested Seddon after the postmortem report. He said, 'I am arresting you on a charge of murdering Miss Barrow by arsenic.' On his arrest, Seddon is reported to have said, 'Absurd. What a terrible charge. Wilful Murder. It is the first of our family that has ever been charged with such a crime. Are you going to arrest my wife as well? If not I'd like you to give her a message for me. Have they found arsenic in her body? She has not done this herself. It was not carbolic acid, was it, as there was some in her room? and Sanitas is not poison, is it?' Seddon afterwards vehemently denied saying all this, and it certainly does not seem like him to chatter so much or to bring his wife into it. This statement may be a conglomerate of different things the prisoner said, some prompted by the police, and coloured by the police officers' conviction that he was guilty. The crime writer Filson Young in his comments on the trial notes that these remarks, 'read much more like an extract from a policeman's notebook than the recorded speech of a human being'.

Detective Inspector Ward called on Mrs Seddon, still reeling after her husband's arrest, and leaned on her to get her to implicate Seddon or even confess herself, but she resisted. With the pressure on her having no effect, nothing was gained by leaving her free and she was arrested.

There was a ten-day trial at which Seddon was defended by Sir Edward Marshall Hall, a great defence lawyer, and prosecuted by the Attorney-General himself, Sir Rufus Isaacs. Seddon was foolish and conceited enough to think it a great compliment he was being prosecuted by the Attorney General rather than a disaster to be up against such an expert in cross-examination.

During the trial, Seddon and his wife were separately represented by counsel, as it was perceived that there was a clear conflict of interests: the innocence of one party implied the guilt of the other.

Marshall Hall conducted a defence in which he attempted to demonstrate that the diagnosis of death by epidemic diarrhoea was accurate and that the arsenic in Barrow's body came from the minute traces which were present in the medicine, bismuth and morphia, which the attending doctor had given her. During cross-examination, the doctor had to admit, however, that such a small amount of arsenic would probably not have shown up in a post-mortem.

The arsenic could have been present in her body for other reasons: arsenic was frequently used as a medicine, and with repeated small doses, a considerable tolerance could build up. Additionally, Barrow could well have been using it to improve her complexion — one of the properties of arsenic in small doses is increased red blood cell production.

In a classically great cross-examination, Marshall Hall made William Willcox admit that when he had quantified the amount of arsenic in Miss Barrow's body, he had not taken account of the loss of water which had taken place following her death, and water constituted 50 per cent of bones and 75 per cent of muscles. His account of the amount of arsenic had to be wrong.

The next point was devastating to the prosecution. It was admitted by Willcox that arsenic that was ingested would take some weeks to reach the hair nearest the scalp. It would then grow with the hair at the rate of several inches a year. Yet Willcox had found arsenic in the distal (far) ends of Eliza Barrow's hair. It was twelve inches long. It had therefore been taken even before she went to live with the Seddons. There may have been a deal of arsenic in her body, but it had built up over a long time.

Unfortunately for the defence, Willcox went off and conducted some more experiments, with some hair donated by one of his patients at St Mary's Hospital. Four days after his first testimony he was recalled to the witness box and was able to demonstrate that the arsenic in the hair of the corpse of Eliza Barrow had penetrated it from the body fluids in which it had been lying.

His means of committing the murder had always been in doubt, but Seddon himself gave some information of value to the prosecution on this point. After his arrest Seddon had mentioned that Barrow perhaps took arsenic, extracting it from flypaper by soaking it in water. Before this no one had thought of considering flypaper as the source of the poison.

Mrs Seddon certainly admitted buying flypaper, a common purchase and a very necessary one where Barrow's illness in the height of summer attracted flies. It was alleged that soon after their holiday in August, Seddon sent his eldest daughter, fifteen-year-old Maggie, to buy some flypaper, which had an arsenic base. A chemist named Thorley was able to testify to this. It became clear, however, that Thorley had been very carefully tutored by the police. At first he could only remember a fair-haired girl having bought flypaper, and he could not identify her.

Maggie Seddon was a friend of

Thorley's daughter and had been in his house twice. When he was asked to pick her out at an identity parade, it was after her picture had appeared in the newspapers and only two girls in the parade were of the right age to have been the purchaser of the flypaper. It was small wonder that Thorley eventually picked out Maggie Seddon who denied ever buying the flypaper, despite being subjected to the sort of pressure which can make even innocent adults admit to things they did not do. There was some justifiable complaint at the manner in which Maggie Seddon had been interrogated in a police cell after her parents had been arrested.

Marshall Hall further weakened the pharmacist's credibility by drawing out that though he was obliged by law to keep a record of who bought these arsenic flypapers, and though the manufacturers had provided him with a book in which to do so, he had not.

This improbable poisoning by 'Mather's Chemical Flypapers' was the prosecution's weakest link. With it, however, the prosecution had the means by which the murder was supposedly committed. Not even Dr William Willcox believed that the arsenic had actually been obtained in this clumsy manner. It may be that Seddon deliberately put the police on the track of this means of obtaining arsenic, in the belief that the jury would not be convinced, so that investigators would be diverted away from the real source of the poison.

Another great problem for the prosecution was to demonstrate that Seddon had administered the poison, for he had hardly gone anywhere near Barrow's room during her illness. It was a rare case in which opportunity was never proved. He certainly had the motive, and his wife had the opportunity, yet she was not seriously considered to be a murderess, even though she prepared all the food Barrow ate during her illness, usually in Barrow's own kitchen, on the floor above the one on which Barrow lived. Maggie had prepared her food when Miss Barrow had been well.

Sir Rufus Isaacs pointed out that Seddon was the only beneficiary of Barrow's death; that he had asked his daughter to buy flypapers containing arsenic; that he had plenty of opportunities to adulterate her food or drink in the kitchen, and that his behaviour after the death was consistent with someone covering up a murder from which he had benefited. This case was weak. It could be claimed that Seddon had behaved in a mean and truculent manner after the death, but character witnesses could certainly have been called to show that was his usual behaviour.

The prosecution case also relied upon a certain amount of improbable technical actions taking place, like boiling up flypaper in a kettle to produce a solution of arsenic, and adding it to tea, which would be drunk only by the intended victim. It would be difficult to boil it down to a residue and add it to food. Seddon does not strike one as the sort of man who spent a great deal of time doing domestic chores in the kitchen, and to start doing so would seem suspicious, as would putting flypaper in a kettle. Seddon stated, moreover, 'I have never purchased arsenic in my life in any shape of form. I have never administered arsenic. I never advised, directed, or instructed the purchase of arsenic in any shape or form. I never advised, directed or instructed the administration of arsenic.'

The speed of burial was also unremarkable. There was not much space in the house in Tollington Park and the nature of Barrow's illness made the family eager to dispose of Barrow's body and disinfect her room as fast as possible. They had put up sheets soaked in carbolic to mask the smell and presumably impede infection, while she was alive. She was only a lodger and it would be unreasonable for anyone to expect excessive mourning for her.

Marshall Hall begged his client not to testify. Like the fool he was, Seddon did not heed good advice, and went into the witness box for an ordeal lasting over a period of three days. He believed he presented such a spectacle of respectability that the mere sight of him would sway the jury to acquit.

The thing which really told against Seddon in the minds of the jury was his cold-hearted and calculating attitude to everything, including the death of

Barrow and even his own future fate. He genuinely felt that it was a valid defence to say that he did not attempt to dispose of the properties he had obtained from Barrow, but 'improved the investments and all is still intact and not depreciated, but greatly improved in value, returning double what the deceased previously received from it'. It has been suggested that any slight show of emotion or even concern might have made the jury look with scepticism on the very real gaps in the prosecution case and give him the benefit of the doubt. Their final decision had to be that very few people had access to Barrow, and only one of them had the heart and mind of a murderer, and that was Frederick Seddon.

The only time he showed emotion in the dock was when his attitude to money was criticised, when Rufus Isaacs suggested that immediately after Barrow's death Seddon brought down her hoard of gold sovereigns and counted them out. Seddon exclaimed, 'I am not a degenerate . . . the suggestion is scandalous. I would have all day to count the money.' With such slender evidence against him, it was commented that Seddon could not have been convicted without his own evidence. He cut such an objectionable figure it was as if he were a witness against himself. He was not so much found guilty of the crime, as of being a thoroughly unpleasant human being.

The case against Mrs Seddon was primarily that she had prepared Eliza Barrow's food, and was in the best position to poison her, though there was no evidence that she had done so. She also had a watch bearing Eliza Barrow's initials which she said Barrow had given her. After the death, but before the funeral, Frederick Seddon had gone to a jeweller with his wife and asked to have the initials erased from the watch. Margaret Seddon had also been involved in changing thirty-three £5 notes at shops and banks for Miss Barrow, and had given a false name when asked to supply one. She said she had cashed the notes because Miss Barrow preferred to have gold. She could give no reason why she had given a false name while cashing them but this odd event had no apparent connection with the death of the tenant anyway. She did buy flypapers, but only on Miss Barrow's request, she said. She did not use them herself.

Mrs Seddon distanced herself from Frederick Seddon's dealings by saying that her husband 'never used to take any notice when I said anything to him; he always had other things to think of', a remark which the jury found convincing. She pleaded ignorance of everything.

Observers said the judge, Mr Justice Bucknill, appeared to be against Seddon in his summing-up. When the verdict came, of guilty for Seddon and not guilty for Mrs Seddon, he turned and kissed her loudly, a display of affection it would have done him well to have practised earlier, and she was removed weeping from the dock.

When asked whether he wished to say anything before sentence was passed, Seddon went through the details of his financial transactions with Eliza Barrow, in a cold and unfaltering tone, to demonstrate he had lost money by Barrow's death: one pound one shilling and ten pence ha'penny (£1.09) to be exact, on Ernest Grant's keep and clothing. Finally, he made a Masonic sign at the judge who was also a Freemason. Seddon said, 'I declare before the Great Architect of the Universe I am not guilty.' This did the reverse of impressing the judge, who sentenced him to be hanged.

* * *

The most emotion his solicitors saw from him was on the night before his execution when he was told of the prices his household goods had fetched at auction. He exclaimed as if in pain as the price raised by each item was explained to him, 'The stingy devils!' he said, 'Well, that's done it! Disgraceful, I call it! Why, if I had been there, the things would have realised twice the prices!' He had worried incessantly in prison about the 'excessive expense' of his defence.

It may be that his concern about money at this time was a concern that his wife and family should be best provided for in his absence. He was a curious man, who could be warm only in a strangely mechanical way. Awaiting execution in prison he interrupted an affectionate letter to his wife with a list of reasons why 'THE NUMBER 13 IS UNLUCKY'. This said things like:

Attended Inquest twice. Police Court 11 times. Total 13 . . . Left Brixton Prison in van (several times) with 13 prisoners . . . Cash in hand at Pentonville belonging to me 6s 6d (Sixpences 13) . . . Sent Wife a letter, and inadvertently placed a number of crosses as kisses. Counted 13 . . . Sent Young Daughter Ada a note with 7 kisses. She replied with 6. Total 13 . . . 13 days to date fixed for execution.

He always protested his innocence, but was not excessively agitated at the thought of his own death. He went quietly to the gallows at Pentonville on 18 April 1912.

Margaret Seddon sold her story to a newspaper, the *Weekly Dispatch*, saying she had been present when Seddon poisoned Barrow, and that he had threatened her with a revolver if she told. Another newspaper, *John Bull*, discredited the tale as being entirely false and inconsistent with the facts. She remarried shortly after Seddon's execution and the whole family emigrated to California. It is difficult to feel a calm mind about Mrs Seddon, about whether she was entirely innocent of, at least complicity in the murder, even if she did not play an active part.

Eliza Barrow was to some extent the architect of her own misfortunes. Like many unpleasant people, she rejoiced in telling how unpleasant she had been to others, and found a willing ear in Seddon when she explained how she had sent her relatives on their way and what she had said to them, and their shocked reaction.

Chief Inspector Ward explained

He pestered her from that moment, and determined to get as much as he could out of her. From her point of view she made a fatal mistake in giving the fellow to understand that she did not wish to see or hear of her relatives again. Once he

535

knew that, he had her at his mercy, because if she died there would be no fussy relations to ask awkward questions. So the poor woman, who considered herself extremely clever and cautious, contributed to her own murder.

It was a real mistake for Seddon to have stolen all Barrow's loose money. He should have been happy with the life annuity deal. Leaving a wealthy woman with absolutely nothing was just too suspicious.

Seddon could so easily have dealt more sensibly with the Vonderahes and not been so evasive and truculent. Barrow had not only left a will, but a signed statement, made of her own volition, that her family were to receive nothing. Everything was to go to Ernest Grant. That Seddon did not behave with more civility is one of the mysteries of the case, but was perhaps due to his grasping, bureaucratic nature. He was simply not capable of making anything easy or pleasant; he would do the minimum and curse anyone who wanted more.

This was the way he greeted the world, and the dangerous situation in which he now found himself just exacerbated his already mean-spirited nature. The Vonderahes could so easily have been put off with regrets and apologies and full sight of all the paperwork. But Seddon could not change his habits. He could not be pleasant to save his life, and that is just what it cost him.

Footprints in the Sand

ON Blackpool sands on the windy Christmas Eve of 1919, at a spot usually devoted to lovers' meetings, a farmer out walking in the early morning idly followed some footprints in the sand. They led over the dunes and then into a dip, where lay the body of a young woman.

When the police arrived the body was undisturbed. She had clearly been shot. Her head was resting on two flat stones, which were covered with blood. Lying near the body were a fur necklet and a hat which appeared to have been trodden in the sand. A pair of man's gloves was also in the dip. Near the body was a handbag containing a wedding ring, a gold-mounted cigarette lighter, a pair of pearl earrings, something less than two pounds in change, two scent bottles, some letters and a photograph. It was possible from the handbag to make a preliminary identification of the woman as Kathleen Breaks, who was twenty-six.

Later examination found 'Mrs Breaks's underclothing had the appearance of being disarranged, but there were no indications of a struggle.' She had been beaten about the head which led her to fall, and she had been shot in that position. There was a wound on the inside of her upper left thigh; a wound on the left cheekbone; and the entry wound on the left side of the head of a bullet which had exited under the chin. This was the fatal shot. Another bullet was lodged in the sand, having missed its intended victim.

There were two sets of footprints leading to the scene, but only one set leading away, a fresh and distinct set of man's footprints going towards Blackpool. Police followed them and, 200 yards further on, found a revolver thrown aside on a dune.

Mrs Kathleen Elsie Breaks lived with her mother in a cottage at Ryecroft Farm, Dudley Hill, Bradford. Her maiden name was Fish and she had worked as a shop assistant. She had been married to a motor engineer called John Breaks but they lived together for only five months before she left to fend for herself. It was said that her entertainment needs were greater than his income could provide for. Breaks was a cultured and pleasant young woman who liked to wear expensive clothes and to live in the best hotels. Her sister attested to her beauty and to the number of men friends she had. She presumably made her living as a high-class prostitute, for she had no other means of support and she lived well.

Inquiries made of her family led police quickly to 31–year-old Frederick Rothwell Holt. Holt, who was always known familiarly as Eric, was born in Lytham, close to where the body of Kathleen Breaks was found. He came from a moderately well-off family and was educated at the local boarding school. On leaving school, he became a bank clerk and an officer in the volunteers. He was also, at some time, an accredited insurance agent.

Holt was a light-hearted individual and was very fond of women, who in turn reciprocated the attentions of this good-looking young man. He was good company and a reasonable sportsman and was also popular with male companions. His affairs with women and his social life drained his pocket but he had no serious problems.

Shortly after war was declared in summer 1914, Holt became a full Lieutenant in the 4th Loyal North Lancashire Territorial Regiment and went to the Western Front, being present at the bombardment of Festubert. He suffered from shell-shock, a condition latterly known as 'combat fatigue'. He was sent to hospital, and finally discharged from the army. He worked in Malaya but returned home in 1918.

The shell-shock did not seem to have affected his life at all. The crime writer Herbert Arthur, who talked to at least one of Holt's lifetime friends, remarked that after his discharge, 'if anything he was a more light-hearted, and a more amusing companion than he had been before the war . . . [but] . . . he appeared to be of a much more excitable nature than before. And he appeared to take offence much more easily. But in public he dined and wined, he smoked and played as gaily as he had ever done in his life.'

He resumed his life of pleasure, drinking and talking with men friends, and having amorous relationships with women. The social dislocation caused by the war allowed people like Kathleen Breaks to abandon her roots and travel the North as a classless, cultured woman moving from one hotel to another. Holt probably met her in one of these hotels, for they were the sort of place in which smart young men liked to be.

Breaks claimed to be a single woman and it was in this pretence that she met and fell in love with Eric Holt. She soon confessed to him in a contrite letter that she was not single but unhappily married and had lived apart from her husband almost since their wedding. They carried on their affair in frequent meetings in Blackpool, Manchester and Bradford over the next two years.

Theirs was a passionate affair but it was not without its frequent misunderstandings and arguments. There was

542

disagreement, for example, over Kathleen's former lover 'Tom', who wanted her to divorce her husband and marry him. In her handbag was a draft of a letter in Holt's handwriting, giving the former suitor a very definite negative. She had not copied out this letter to the suitor, nor sent him any other communication.

There is some evidence that Holt was tiring of Breaks. At the end of January 1919, she wrote letters to which he did not reply, but he was a feckless young man and his affections were up and down, as evinced by a letter he wrote a few days before her body was found.

My dear, darling Kathleen [he wrote] you have no idea how lonely I feel without you, dearest. I arrived safely tonight, but I did, and do, so want you near me, you dear, sweet thing — you are my baby at present. You love me, I love you, I feel that I must always be near you, you have no idea how I feel after I leave you, or you leave me, darling. You are the one and only to me in this world, and I think the world of you, and do want you to think the same of me. I am sorry at what happened at lunch today, but let us both forget it, and may neither of us notice such a thing again. I know we are too fond of each other for that. I know we were at fault, because now I know you love me . . .

There was much in a similar vein. Police decided they wanted to interview Holt on the morning the body was found. He was by no means inconspicuous, but went into the centre of Blackpool, passing the scene of the murder. There he bought two Christmas presents, for Kitty's sister and for another girl. He went to the lounge of the hotel where Kitty had been staying, and he asked for her. The police later found him sitting in the lounge there.

Holt said he had been with Breaks the previous day, 23 December, when they had met in Bradford and travelled to Blackpool by train. Detectives could confirm this as they were seen kissing and cuddling by other passengers. She went to have dinner in her hotel and he went to Lytham where he lived with his father. He said he was home all evening after leaving Kathleen, following their railway journey from Bradford. The police had other ideas, however, and evidence began to mount against him.

The footprints in the sand matched the clear pattern of Holt's newly soled shoes. The gloves were his. The source of the revolver which had been discarded was traced and it was registered to him.

Further investigations disclosed the matter of the insurance. Holt had spent the best part of the year attempting to have Kathleen Breaks's life insured for £10,000. No insurance company was prepared to do this: the policy was too high and Holt had no insurable interest in her life unless he married her. He then decided to accept a £5000 insurance but found this by no means an easy option either.

He negotiated with the Atlas Insurance Company for some time, and wrote to them on 30 May 1919 after she had filled in the proposal form, 'With regard to Mrs Breaks' proposal, you will notice she has entered up as being married, the reason being she is not sure whether she is a widow or not, although she has received notice from the War Office or other office that her husband is missing and supposed killed.' This was a deliberate lie. John Breaks had not even served in the war.

This proposal was rejected, as was a similar one to the Prudential Assurance Company. Finally the Royal London Insurance Company accepted the deal and the first premium was paid by Breaks, with money Holt had given her, so they received the policy on 28 November 1919, less than a month before her death.

This insurance was supposed to be part of a reciprocal lovers' arrangement, where Holt was to be insured in Breaks's favour but his side of the bargain was never delivered. What he did do was to ensure that Breaks's husband would not receive the insurance money by having her make a will in his favour. This was executed on 23 December, the day she was killed, with Holt and one of Breaks's sisters as witnesses. Some small personal items and £200 from the policy were to go to her family, and £4800 to Holt.

Police were also able to discover that Holt was overdrawn at his bank, the London City and Midland, in the sum of £1245. The insurance premiums were high for two people with so little evidence of income, but Holt must have reasoned that it did not matter, he would not be paying them for long.

The police reasoned that Kathleen and Holt had arranged to meet in Bradford on 23 December. They travelled to Blackpool by train and parted to dine separately. They then met again near the Sandhills and were seen walking off towards the dunes. They went through the soft sand to the desolate area of coastline between Blackpool and Lytham, where the only landscape was low sand dunes and rough, tussocky grass. Presumably the object was to lie down and have sex there, something they had probably done in that spot many times before.

Whatever transpired there is not known, except that it ended with Holt beating Kathleen Breaks about the head, knocking her unconscious, then shooting at her four times. He then took a tram back to Blackpool where he visited various hotel lounges, acting in his usual cheerful manner, discussing his plans for Christmas and the prospects of a football team whose fortunes he followed. He then went home to bed.

Holt had a scratch on the inside of his right wrist and four scratches on his left cheek, which it was deduced were made by Breaks in her desperate attempt to fend off the first blows which felled her and left her in the position in which she was shot. He was charged on 26 December, at which he said, 'What can I say? I have already given a statement. How long will the job be on?'

The trial, starting on 23 February 1920 at Manchester Assize Court, was one of the most celebrated murder trials of the first quarter of the century. Hundreds queued outside to gain admittance to the public gallery. It was as if this trial of a former soldier, his lover dead and his young life ruined, meant something to the public far in excess of its importance as a commonplace murder.

The question at the trial was never

really one of Holt's guilt or innocence — he certainly killed Kathleen Breaks. The question was whether he was insane, or so insane that he could not be considered responsible for his actions, for no one would deny he was eccentric to the point of dementia.

Holt's behaviour was indeed odd for someone on trial for his life. He had not acted towards his solicitor as if he recognised the seriousness of his condition. He was apparently light-hearted and would talk, but would not give any information as to his movements on the day of the murder. At the committal proceedings (in a magistrates' court, prior to the trial, to establish whether there was evidence for a trial) Holt slipped as he entered the dock and said, 'I didn't see that one,' and then giggled for minutes afterwards as if it were the funniest joke.

While he would not talk about the crime, he made wild claims about alleged ill-treatment by the police, saying that they set dogs on him in his cell and had also introduced malaria- and typhoid-carrying mosquitoes which had been trained to bite him.

The first thing the jury had to decide was whether Holt was fit to stand trial. If he were insane, to the extent that he could take no part in court proceedings, the trial could not proceed. The Attorney-General, Sir Gordon Hewart, prosecuting, argued that Holt's apparent delusions were simulated in order to evade justice. Far from being mad, he was 'a man of no little ingenuity, resource and boldness'. His letters written from prison seemed to be quite sane.

The services of Sir Edward Marshall Hall, the best defence lawyer alive, had been secured and he called medical witnesses to show his client was insane and stated that two of Holt's relatives had gone insane, a grandfather and a cousin. He was 'unfit to plead' and even to instruct his lawyers.

It was no use. The jury decided that if he were sane enough to insure the life of Kathleen Breaks, he was sane enough to stand trial for her murder. They took just ten minutes to decide he was fit to plead.

Marshall Hall, now denied an efficient defence of insanity, stressed the tender relationship between Holt and Breaks, as evinced by the letters which had passed between them, which certainly showed a very close relationship when read selectively, but a rather more turbulent one when read in their entirety. Many people in court were visibly moved by the emotion of the letters, but these could just as easily be seen as evidence of Holt's callousness, calculated to ensure that Breaks was malleable enough to go through with business connected with the insurance and will.

Holt had written, 'you know I love you so much, darling — I do so long for you. I don't know how I shall manage without you — you are so sweet and tender. I long for Christmas and some long days; I feel you will never leave me after Christmas. I long for some good Christmases with you in times to come, and feel that some time there will be no parting us.'

In her letters, Kitty called him 'Mr Dreamer' and wrote:

I never thought any man would make me love him the way I do you.

Forgive me, Eric darling, you are the one person in the whole world to me, and I want to appear nice. Today I felt hurt when you reproached me, and miserable. I know you will forgive me very soon . . . Eric dear, somehow I cannot thank you nearly so much as I want for your extreme goodness to me. In my opinion, darling, you are just the biggest and whitest man I know. I want you, dearest, to try and get over as soon as you are able. No Bradford, and no friends, just we two.

It was claimed on Holt's behalf that the crime had perhaps been committed on a mad impulse of jealousy, because Holt feared that Breaks's lover would take her away from him. 'Tom' had written to Kathleen pledging his love and Kathleen had not yet replied, either in her own terms or in the terms of the rejection letter Holt had drafted for her. Perhaps they had argued about this, and Holt was seized with an uncontrollable violent passion.

Yet his behaviour after the killing

when he went drinking and talking about football showed no evidence of a mind which had recently been gripped in a paroxysm of violent insanity.

Holt took an interest in the early days of the trial, as if he were observing the trial of someone else. He took an almost childish interest in the exhibits and photographs, once remarking of one of the latter, 'That is a good picture, that is!' He then lost interest, and sat with his arms folded, giving the impression of brutal indifference.

'I do not suppose,' said Marshall Hall to the jury, 'that there could be a worse crime than that of a man who, under the guise of making love to a lovely woman, was really keeping her quiet until the moment came when he could murder her and put the proceeds of her insurance in his pocket.' This was not, he claimed, the action of a sane man who showed such evidence of loving Kitty Breaks as he did in his letters. Marshall Hall hoped that a defence of sudden insanity, seizing a mind to commit a murder on an 'uncontrollable impulse' might be accepted by the jury.

The emotionally charged atmosphere of the court was fuelled by feelings of guilt and betrayal about the 1914 – 18 war. Judge and jury were still pathetically lachrymose about the sacrifices of a pointless conflict which had benefited no one. Here was a handsome young man full of promise who had served his country as everyone expected him to do and it had come to this: a stupid, brutal action towards someone he loved, a mind in tatters. The destruction of the life of this blithe young man was in some way symbolic of the wholesale slaughter on the Western Front about which the nation, though victorious, was already feeling very uneasy.

The only sign of emotion Holt showed was when Marshall Hall referred to the love Kitty Breaks had for him, at which, on each of four occasions, his eyes filled with tears which he quickly wiped away. After less than an hour, the guilty verdict came through. In the customary request of the prisoner, whether he wished to give any reason why a sentence of death should not be passed on him, he shrugged. Several people were deeply moved, including the judge, Mr Justice Greer, who actually wept when Holt was sentenced.

Holt's solicitor, Max Woosnam, was perhaps the most affected. He petitioned the Home Secretary on Holt's behalf after the verdict and was at the Home Office pleading for his client the day before he was hanged. Marshall Hall wrote in a letter to be presented to the Home Secretary, 'I have never yet, after a case in which I was professionally involved, taken any steps to influence the result, but in the case of Holt, I feel so strongly that he is now mad, and as a man, I contemplate with horror the idea of executing a madman . . . '

Marshall Hall thought that Holt was 'under the influence of some sudden uncontrollable passion acting on a mind enfeebled by shell-shock and disease'. He could not say that Holt was mad in the time leading up to the crime, though he had been in a very strange condition of mind. The 'real madness supervened on the act, I am certain. Whether within twenty-four or forty-eight hours, I cannot say, but it did supervene, and since then, and at the present time, the man is mad.'

Marshall Hall had a particular interest in the insanity plea, having sat on Lord Atkin's committee on insanity and crime (reporting in 1923) and he had decided views on the matter.

The guidance for the courts was the McNaghten Rules. These were based on the judgement in the case of a man who, in 1843, had an imaginary grudge against the Prime Minister, Sir Robert Peel, and went to kill him. He failed but instead killed Peel's private secretary and stood trial for murder. The judges stopped the trial because of his obvious insanity, and sent him to Bethlem hospital, an asylum. There was an outcry and the verdict was challenged by the House of Lords which called upon the judges to justify themselves, and give certain answers to questions about criminal responsibility and madness. These form the basis of the McNaghten Rules which basically state that anyone who is so insane as to be incapable of responsibility for his actions, shall be convicted not of murder but manslaughter. Marshall Hall had long thought the McNaghten Rules were outmoded and inadequate to deal with insanity of a less gross but still all-encompassing kind.

So what was Holt's insanity? Shell-shock was a clearly defined conclusion caused by spending too long in the battle line with physical hardship, incessant bombardment, low morale and emotional conflicts. It was defined as consisting of hypersensitivity to such stimuli as loud noises; easy irritability progressing even to acts of violence; and sleep disturbances. Holt's precise diagnosis, for which he was invalided out of the army, was neuraesthenia. This was a syndrome of chronic mental and physical weakness and fatigue, supposedly caused by exhaustion of the nervous system.

He was said to have suffered from depression and loss of confidence after leaving the army. At the trial his father said that he was irritable and excitable and would be moody, sometimes sitting in front of the fire, saying nothing and taking no notice of anyone. If everyone who exhibited such symptoms were a murderer, there would be a great many more murders.

In defence of the insanity argument, it should be said that Holt kept it up long after it would be much use to him. On being sentenced to death, he showed no concern, but put his hands into his pockets and walked away. When he returned to his cell at Manchester Prison he said to the governor, 'Well, and that's that! I hope they won't be late with my tea!' He lived in prison as if he did not have a care in the world. He did not engage himself with his relatives and friends who came to visit him, greeting them cordially, then resuming his conversations with the prison officers. This may, of course, have been done to spare his relatives and friends pain, and to galvanise them into working harder for a successful appeal, or a pardon by the Home Secretary.

At the appeal, Marshall Hall succeeded in persuading the court to allow him to present new evidence — the first time ever that this was permitted. He brought forward the evidence of a doctor who had treated Holt for syphilis in Malaysia. One of the eventual complications of untreated syphilis is insanity, but in the second stage of the condition, syphilis can show itself as temporary dementia. More information was given of the form the madness Holt's grandfather and cousin took. The appeal failed, as did the attempts to persuade the Home Secretary to ask the King to exercise his prerogative of pardon. The Home Secretary asked doctors to give Holt a further examination to establish his state of mind but still found himself unable to advise the exercise of the prerogative of mercy. Holt was hanged on 14 April 1920, showing his usual sang froid right to the gallows.

Holt's insuring Breaks and killing her on the very day the will was made out in his favour is so suspicious as to be ridiculous. You would have to be crazy to commit such an obvious crime. This killing certainly looks more like a crime of passion than a methodically planned insurance murder. As is often the case when there are two conflicting theories, the truth is probably a combination of both. Holt had insured Breaks with the intention of killing her. Much of his affection for her was feigned but his emotions were not straightforward and he still felt possessive about her. He also needed her to stay devoted to him for the insurance plan to come off. She may have teased him, refused to send 'Tom' on his way or done something else on that December night, but, for whatever immediate cause, he struck and killed her in a fit of passion. It was easier to kill, because he already had the idea in his mind, but to kill her on that day in that place in that way cannot have been his intention.

Holt was highly strung, but on the question of insanity a sceptical mind would point to the apparent lack of change in his behaviour before the war and after, when he had been invalided out with an apparently crippling mental illness. His behaviour after Kathleen Breaks's murder looks crazy, but it could easily be feigned insanity. Perhaps he had fooled the military authorities with his apparent insanity, and now he would fool the civil authorities. Leaving so many clues to his lover's death also looks suspicious: the sort of thing a person might do to lead others to think, 'Only a madman would leave all this evidence.' His behaviour seems absurd, but it is not characteristic of any of the major patterns of mental illness and could well be a case of Ganser Syndrome: showing inappropriate responses in a way which would feign insanity to escape punishment. Perhaps it all started as an act but it became easier (and certainly less emotionally painful) to coast along with the glib persona he had created, keeping his real personality 'on hold'.

Really, it was all too much for him. Holt was a feckless young chap whose life was bounded by drinking with friends and football matches. The war had thrust him into a world of wholesale slaughter with which he was unable to cope. Back in England, he had been unable to settle down and earn a living, yet he still wanted to spend money and enjoy life. His complicated relationship with Kathleen Breaks put a strain on his unsophisticated personality and she died because of his ill-conceived attempts to raise money from insurance and his frustration at his inability to cope with his relationship with her. After he had killed her he simply dropped all pretence at dealing with the world as an adult and became the foolish character who was sent to the gallows.

Bibliography

GENERAL
J. H. H. Gaute and Robin Odell, *The New Murderer's Who's Who* (London 1989), is the best source, particularly as it is so well referenced.

Colin Wilson and Patricia Pitman, *Encyclopedia of Murder* (London 1961), and Colin Wilson and Donald Seaman *Encyclopedia of Modern Murder* (London 1983) are also valuable but unfortunately are not referenced.

J. M. Parrish and J. R. Crossland, *The Fifty Most Amazing Crimes of the Last Hundred Years* (London 1936). It is amazing that, despite its age, this classic work is still the best source for many cases. The narrative strength and attention to detail are unsurpassed.

ELABORATE DECEPTIONS
On the Warren Green case: information

came from court reports in the national and local press, particularly the *Wigan Observer*, whose staff were particularly helpful. Information also from the *Wigan Evening Post*, and from an interview with Julie Warburton in the *Mail on Sunday*. Personal interviews with members of Wigan CID.

Information on the Sheila Stroud case came from the *Cheltenham News*, whose staff were generous with information and time, and from the *Gloucestershire Citizen* and *Daily Telegraph*. Personal interviews with Detective Inspector Gladding of Cheltenham CID.

TEAM EFFORTS
The story of Cromwell and Perveler is told in Vincent Bugliosi and Ken Hurwitz, *Till Death Us Do Part* (New York 1978), where the names Stockton and Palliko are used. The correct names have been used in this account, where known. Information also from the *Los Angeles Times* and *New York Times*.

The McGinnis case is covered in detail in David Heilbroner's *Death Benefit* (New York 1993). Information also from *Los Angeles Times*.

Kallinger: Flora Rheta Schreiber, *The Shoemaker* (London 1983); *New York Times*, New Jersey editions, 1975 – 79.

Smith and Bradfield: Joseph Wambaugh, *Echoes in the Darkness* (New York 1987); Loretta Schwartz-Nobel, *Engaged to Murder* (New York 1987). *New York Times*.

THE AEROPLANE BOMBERS

The Graham case is best covered in an article by James A. V. Galvin and John M. Macdonald in Macdonald's *The Murderer and His Victim* (Chicago 1961). This also covers some other aeroplane murderers.

Margaret Larkin, *Seven Shares in a Gold Mine* (London 1959), is the principal source for the Arellano-Sierra bombing. It also carries a useful appendix on aeroplane bombings, including those for motives other than insurance.

Other relevant books are: Leonard Gribble, *When Killers Err* (London 1962) and *Murder Most Strange* (London 1959); Bruce Sanders, *Murder in Lonely Places* (London 1960).

STEALING BODIES
The best source for Rouse is Helena Normanton, *Trial of Alfred Arthur Rouse* (Glasgow 1931).

Other relevant books: F. A. Beaumont, 'The German Rouse Cases', in J. M. Parrish and J. R. Crossland, *The Fifty Most Amazing Crimes of the Last Hundred Years* (London 1936); Jorgen Thorwald, *The Century of the Detective* (London 1965, 1966, 3 vols); Douglas G. Browne and Tom Tullett, *Bernard Spilsbury* (London 1980); Leslie Randall, *The Famous Cases of Sir Bernard Spilsbury* (London 1936).

WILLING VICTIMS
The de la Pommerais story is told in Jorgen Thorwald's *The Century of the Detective* (London 1965, 1966, 3 vols), and in Arthur Griffiths' *Mysteries of*

Police and Crime, vol. 2 (London 1898).

Other relevant books: A. Duncan Smith, *The Trial of Eugene Marie Chantrelle* (Edinburgh 1906); John Glaister, *The Power of Poison* (London 1954); Edmund Pearson, *Murder at Smutty Nose* (New York 1926).

Holmes and Geyer: Holmes is in Charles Boswell and Lewis Thompson, *The Girls in Nightmare House* (Manchester 1955) which starts with the quaint line, 'In America, the mass murderer crops up only rarely . . . '; and in David Franke, *The Torture Doctor* (New York 1976). Holmes' account is in *Holmes' Own Story* (Philadelphia 1895) and Geyer's in Frank P. Geyer, *The Holmes-Pitezel Case* (Philadelphia 1896).

LONE WOLVES
The Fox case is best covered in F. Tennyson Jesse's *Trial of Sidney Harry Fox* (Glasgow 1934).

Other relevant books: Frank R. Betts, 'The Fox Case' in W. Teignmouth Shore,

Crime & Its Detection, vol. 2 (London 1931); Walter Hambrook, *Hambrook of the Yard* (London 1937).

Seddon: Filson Young, *The Trial of the Seddons* (London 1952); Charles Kingston, *Enemies of Society* (London 1927). Fox and Seddon are both mentioned, with prominence given to Spilsbury's evidence, in: Douglas G. Browne and Tom Tullett, *Bernard Spilsbury* (London 1980), and Leslie Randall, *The Famous Cases of Sir Bernard Spilsbury* (London 1936).

Holt: Herbert Arthur, *All the Sinners* (London 1931); E. Marjoribanks, *The Life of Sir Edward Marshall Hall* (London 1929); Nina Warner Hooke, *Marshall Hall* (London 1966); *The Times* and *Daily News* accounts of the trial.

THE SONG OF THE PINES
Christina Green

Taken to a Greek island as substitute for David Nicholas's secretary, Annie quickly falls prey to the island's charms and to the charms of both Marcus, the Greek, and David himself.

GOODBYE DOCTOR GARLAND
Marjorie Harte

The story of a woman doctor who gave too much to her profession and almost lost her personal happiness.

DIGBY
Pamela Hill

Welcomed at courts throughout Europe, Kenelm Digby was the particular favourite of the Queen of France, who wanted him to be her lover, but the beautiful Venetia was the mainspring of his life.

SKINWALKERS
Tony Hillerman

The peace of the land between the sacred mountains is shattered by three murders. Is a 'skinwalker', one who has rejected the harmony of the Navajo way, the murderer?

A PARTICULAR PLACE
Mary Hocking

How is Michael Hoath, newly arrived vicar of St. Hilary's, to meet the demands of his flock and his strained marriage? Further complications follow when he falls hopelessly in love with a married parishioner.

A MATTER OF MISCHIEF
Evelyn Hood

A saga of the weaving folk in 18th century Scotland. Physician Gavin Knox was desperately seeking a cure for the pox that ravaged the slums of Glasgow and Paisley, but his adored wife, Margaret, stood in the way.

SEASONS OF MY LIFE
Hannah Hauxwell
and Barry Cockcroft

The story of Hannah Hauxwell's struggle to survive on a desolate farm in the Yorkshire Dales with little money, no electricity and no running water.

TAKING OVER
Shirley Lowe and Angela Ince

A witty insight into what happens when women take over in the boardroom and their husbands take over chores, children and chickenpox.

AFTER MIDNIGHT STORIES,
The Fourth Book Of

A collection of sixteen of the best of today's ghost stories, all different in style and approach but all combining to give the reader that special midnight shiver.

THE PLEASURES OF AGE
Robert Morley

The author, British stage and screen star, now eighty, is enjoying the pleasures of age. He has drawn on his experiences to write this witty, entertaining and informative book.

THE VINEGAR SEED
Maureen Peters

The first book in a trilogy which follows the exploits of two sisters who leave Ireland in 1861 to seek their fortune in England.

A VERY PAROCHIAL MURDER
John Wainwright

A mugging in the genteel seaside town turned to murder when the victim died. Then the body of a young tearaway is washed ashore and Detective Inspector Lyle is determined that a second killing will not go unpunished.

DEAD SPIT
Janet Edmonds

Government vet Linus Rintoul attempts to solve a mystery which plunges him into the esoteric world of pedigree dogs, murder and terrorism, and Crufts Dog Show proves to be far more exciting than he had bargained for . . .

A BARROW IN THE BROADWAY
Pamela Evans

Adopted by the Gordillo family, Rosie Goodson watched their business grow from a street barrow to a chain of supermarkets. But passion, bitterness and her unhappy marriage aliented her from them.

THE GOLD AND THE DROSS
Eleanor Farnes

Lorna found it hard to make ends meet for herself and her mother and then by chance she met two men — one a famous author and one a rich banker. But could she really expect to be happy with either man?

DEATH TRAIN
Robert Byrne

The tale of a freight train out of control and leaking a paralytic nerve gas that turns America's West into a scene of chemical catastrophe in which whole towns are rendered helpless.

THE ADVENTURE OF THE CHRISTMAS PUDDING
Agatha Christie

In the introduction to this short story collection the author wrote "This book of Christmas fare may be described as 'The Chef's Selection'. I am the Chef!"

RETURN TO BALANDRA
Grace Driver

Returning to her Caribbean island home, Suzanne looks forward to being with her parents again, but most of all she longs to see Wim van Branden, a coffee planter she has known all her life.

DEATH ON A HOT SUMMER NIGHT
Anne Infante

Micky Douglas is either accident-prone or someone is trying to kill him. He finds himself caught in a desperate race to save his ex-wife and others from a ruthless gang.

HOLD DOWN A SHADOW
Geoffrey Jenkins

Maluti Rider, with the help of four of the world's most wanted men, is determined to destroy the Katse Dam and release a killer flood.

THAT NICE MISS SMITH
Nigel Morland

A reconstruction and reassessment of the trial in 1857 of Madeleine Smith, who was acquitted by a verdict of Not Proven of poisoning her lover, Emile L'Angelier.

A GREAT DELIVERANCE
Elizabeth George

Into the web of old houses and secrets of Keldale Valley comes Scotland Yard Inspector Thomas Lynley and his assistant to solve a particularly savage murder.

'E' IS FOR EVIDENCE
Sue Grafton

Kinsey Millhone was bogged down on a warehouse fire claim. It came as something of a shock when she was accused of being on the take. She'd been set up. Now she had a new client — herself.

A FAMILY OUTING IN AFRICA
Charles Hampton and Janie Hampton

A tale of a young family's journey through Central Africa by bus, train, river boat, lorry, wooden bicycle and foot.

THE TWILIGHT MAN
Frank Gruber

Jim Rand lives alone in the California desert awaiting death. Into his hermit existence comes a teenage girl who blows both his past and his brief future wide open.

DOG IN THE DARK
Gerald Hammond

Jim Cunningham breeds and trains gun dogs, and his antagonism towards the devotees of show spaniels earns him many enemies. So when one of them is found murdered, the police are on his doorstep within hours.

THE RED KNIGHT
Geoffrey Moxon

When he finds himself a pawn on the chessboard of international espionage with his family in constant danger, Guy Trent becomes embroiled in moves and countermoves which may mean life or death for Western scientists.

THE LISTERDALE MYSTERY
Agatha Christie

Twelve short stories ranging from the light-hearted to the macabre, diverse mysteries ingeniously and plausibly contrived and convincingly unravelled.

TO BE LOVED
Lynne Collins

Andrew married the woman he had always loved despite the knowledge that Sarah married him for reasons of her own. So much heartache could have been avoided if only he had known how vital it was to be loved.

ACCUSED NURSE
Jane Converse

Paula found herself accused of a crime which could cost her her job, her nurse's reputation, and even the man she loved, unless the truth came to light.

CLOUD OVER MALVERTON
Nancy Buckingham

Dulcie soon realises that something is seriously wrong at Malverton, and when violence strikes she is horrified to find herself under suspicion of murder.

AFTER THOUGHTS
Max Bygraves

The Cockney entertainer tells stories of his East End childhood, of his RAF days, and his post-war showbusiness successes and friendships with fellow comedians.

MOONLIGHT
AND MARCH ROSES
D. Y. Cameron

Lynn's search to trace a missing girl takes her to Spain, where she meets Clive Hendon. While untangling the situation, she untangles her emotions and decides on her own future.

TIGER TIGER
Frank Ryan

A young man involved in drugs is found murdered. This is the first event which will draw Detective Inspector Sandy Woodings into a whirlpool of murder and deceit.

CAROLINE MINUSCULE
Andrew Taylor

Caroline Minuscule, a medieval script, is the first clue to the whereabouts of a cache of diamonds. The search becomes a deadly kind of fairy story in which several murders have an other-worldly quality.

LONG CHAIN OF DEATH
Sarah Wolf

During the Second World War four American teenagers from the same town join the Army together. Forty-two years later, the son of one of the soldiers realises that someone is systematically wiping out the families of the four men.

NURSE ALICE IN LOVE
Theresa Charles

Accepting the post of nurse to little Fernie Sherrod, Alice Everton could not guess at the romance, suspense and danger which lay ahead at the Sherrod's isolated estate.

POIROT INVESTIGATES
Agatha Christie

Two things bind these eleven stories together — the brilliance and uncanny skill of the diminutive Belgian detective, and the stupidity of his Watson-like partner, Captain Hastings.

LET LOOSE THE TIGERS
Josephine Cox

Queenie promised to find the long-lost son of the frail, elderly murderess, Hannah Jason. But her enquiries threatened to unlock the cage where crucial secrets had long been held captive.